HELL IN BARBADOS

THE TRUE STORY OF A MAN IMPRISONED IN PARADISE

TERRY DONALDSON

Every effort has been made to contact the copyright holders of material reproduced in this text. In cases where these efforts have been unsuccessful, the copyright holders are asked to contact the publishers directly.
Some people named in this book have been given pseudonyms to protect their privacy.

Published by Maverick House Publishers.

Maverick House, Main Street, Dunshaughlin, Co. Meath, Ireland.
Maverick House SE Asia, 440 Sukhumvit Road, Washington Square, Klongton, Klongtoey, Bangkok 10110, Thailand.

info@maverickhouse.com
http://www.maverickhouse.com

ISBN: 978-1-905379-27-9

Copyright for text © 2006 Terry Donaldson.
Copyright for typesetting, editing, layout, design © Maverick House.

5 4 3 2 1

Printed by Nørhaven Paperback.

The paper used in this book comes from wood pulp of managed forests. For every tree felled, at least one tree is planted, thereby renewing natural resources.

The moral rights of the author have been asserted.

All rights reserved.
No part of this book may be reproduced or transmitted in any form or by any means without written permission from the publisher, except by a reviewer who wishes to quote brief passages in connection with a review written for insertion in a newspaper, magazine or broadcast.

A CIP catalogue record for this book is available from the British Library.

Hell in Barbados

The True Story of a Man Imprisoned in Paradise

DEDICATION

Dedicated to all of the inmates of Glendairy Prison; past, present, and future.

ACKNOWLEDGEMENTS

I would like to thank Carson Cadogan, of Eagle Hall, Barbados, Roxanne Gibbs of the Barbadian newspaper *Nation*, and *The Barbados Advocate*, for permission to use their photographs in this book.

I would also like to thank Kay Danes of www. foreignprisoners.com for her invaluable help in bringing the focus of international attention to the condition of those suffering in Glendairy Prison, Barbados.

PROLOGUE

What springs to mind when you think of Barbados? Is it the warm tropical climate, the golden sands, or the clear blue ocean? Or is it the cool, laid back attitude and friendliness of the people? If you were asked to think of a single word to describe the island, most people would say the same thing: Paradise.

Over 500,000 people visit Barbados every year, and almost half of those are from the UK and Ireland. Most come back having enjoyed the holiday of a lifetime. Few, thankfully, get to see the truth behind the postcard image of this place; fewer still get to tell the tale. But those unlucky enough to fall foul of the law as I did are left in no doubt–this is far from heaven.

Corruption, squalor, poverty, crime; they all raise their ugly heads in this place, and though I deserved to be sent to prison for a crime I should not have committed, nobody deserves to have their human rights taken away, and nobody should be forced to endure the horrors of that place where I spent more than three years of my life.

Yes, I have made mistakes, and I have paid for them, but I very nearly paid for them with my life, as I struggled to overcome disease, violence, and a full-blown riot in a place where there is one rule for the haves and another for the have-nots, where conditions are horrendous, and where there is no distinction between a murderer and a pickpocket.

I have looked back over my life in an effort to understand where and why I went wrong, and I have come to realise many things about myself. Some things will remain unanswered for me—there are some things I will never know—but one thing I do know is that I never want to go back to prison, and I never want to go back to Barbados.

You might consider it Paradise, but I consider it Hell.

CHAPTER ONE

EARLY DAZE

'Here, hold onto this for us for a bit, can you?' this guy asked me, as he held out a bottle of orange fluid. I was 13. I didn't know what it was.

'It's phy,' he said, as if that explained something. Like an idiot I took it off him, gaining a sense of importance at entering this secret circle. I wasn't sure what I was supposed to do with it, and something of this uncertainty must have registered in the dim dark recesses of his mind.

'Phy' I repeated, rhyming it with the Greek letter *phi*, like I was in a trance. The full version of that word, I would later learn, is Physeptone, a brand name for methadone, a heroin substitute prescribed to addicts. In theory, it helps them come off the stuff. In reality, it compounds the problem even further. Withdrawing from heroin takes about two to three weeks, all in. Whenever I've withdrawn from methadone, it has always taken much longer. Following my arrest years later in Barbados, it took all of six months to run that stuff out of my system.

He had handed me the bottle, and then deep in his pinpoint eyes a kind of cunning had appeared; like when you are outside, banging on the front door, and eventually a little light comes on at the end of the passage: *Heaven's name, the dealer is in after all! Liberation Day! Let's hope all is well and he has got something to serve up!*

'Ok,' he said, 'you can take a sip out of it, but not too much.'

I hadn't even thought of taking a sip of it. But there it was. He ended up giving me the bottle; my first experience of drugs. Looking back, all he was trying to do was get me started. Junkies are like that. They are almost all deeply angry deep down, and want to strike out at others. They like nothing better than to see others falter.

It would be a long journey from the streets of north London to a hellish prison in Barbados, and an even longer one back to where I am now. But each journey starts with a single step, and my story started that day. From there, there was no turning back.

***

It has always been in my nature to look at different realities, to turn away from this one. It is a form of escapism, and it has been a trait of mine since I was very young. I have always been drawn to stories from mythology, for example. They removed me from the place where I actually was, in an 'anywhere but here' way, and made me feel better.

That guy left me with something more than just the bottle of methadone that day; he left me with my first taste of an escape route out of my own existence, and I didn't even have to go anywhere. He also left me a stash of syringes he wanted me to hide but which my father found. I'd agreed to hide them because doing so made me feel like I had entered his world, and more importantly, escaped from mine.

A few days later I knocked back the methadone. I think I drank it all, starting with a small sip, then finding I could handle it, I downed the lot. I nearly passed out. Somehow

I stayed put in my room and managed to avoid too much contact with anyone. How I managed that I don't know, but it never came to light.

After that, it all started, but I was never really out of control as a kid. I just wanted to belong to this other world I knew was going on. I continued to get occasional bottles of meth from the same guy, from time to time. I'd been let in, and I didn't want to get out of this exciting new world just yet. The high was strange; a feeling of weightlessness, of entering a kingdom where suddenly I had not a care in the world. I have looked back and tried to work out why I started with methadone. I think it just turned out that way really. I was just a curious kid, 13 years of age, with nothing better to do, and a tendency to run away from reality. Methadone just happened to be the first thing that came my way. If speed had been available at the time I would probably have started with that. I had no idea where it would all lead, and not in my wildest dreams did I ever think I would end up in a completely different world, thousands of miles from home, fearing for my life. But that is how it worked out.

Back then, I just wanted to get out of where I was. It was a natural desire that ran in my family. My dad was brought up in the East End and in those days it wasn't easy. The communities were very tight, unwelcoming to 'outsiders', not at all like they are today. The working class was a very closed club, and movement out of it or into it was a rare and difficult thing. My old man had two brothers and a sister. At the end of the day they had to go scavenging and collect vegetables that had fallen or been thrown on the side of the road after the markets closed down. My Mum was from an Irish family.

Together, my parents got their place in a London flat complex where a number of well known villains used to reside. The Richardson family, second only to the Krays in

London's gangland, were local, their scrap metal merchant yard just a few streets away from the Guernsey Street flats where we lived.

When I was 11 my mum and dad first started having their big rows. I remember being really scared. My sister and I would hear their voices coming up through the floor, and wait for it to blow over. Sometimes, my dad would hit Mum. On one occasion he knocked out one of her front teeth. Drink, in particular whisky, seemed to fuel the violence. It made me hate him. Years later, when I was bigger, I was able to stand up to him. I sent him flying with a right hook, leaving him in shock and blood all over the banister.

The rows got worse. Maybe that was why I began teaming up with a couple of lads from the local school, hanging around the streets instead of at home. We would go out on Saturdays to go thieving, but this was short-lived, and ended one night when I was coming out from swimming. It must have been a Monday evening. My old school was right next door to the swimming pool. As I looked at it, I became filled with anger at all the old injustices my former headmaster used to heap upon me; how he used to make me bend over and slipper me, for the flimsiest reasons or sometimes for no reason at. Even at that age you can tell when someone is taking the piss. So, I made my way into the schoolyard. Surprisingly, the doors were unlocked. I crept along the dark corridors until I found his study. Amazing! It was actually open. Creeping inside, I threw all his stuff around and smashed everything up. I took my dick out and pissed all over his desk. Unfortunately for me, the cleaner spotted me as I left the building. I didn't care. Something in me, some kind of blockage or anger, had been freed, in that stupid, wasteful and yet liberating act of vandalism.

It was to come back to haunt me a couple of days later though. I got home from school to find a man sitting in the kitchen with my mum. He introduced himself as a policeman, and said he was investigating something that had happened on Monday evening at my old school. I immediately started to deny everything, but my mum, being a nutty old cow, chimed in and told me to tell the truth.

'I did it,' was all I said.

The next thing I knew I was being nicked, and my mum was crying her eyes out over the sink. The dashing young copper was doing his best to comfort her, putting his arms around her, as I recall. My mum was like that. Never miss a trick. Things died down a bit after that, and after getting probation, I decided to give crime a miss.

Around this time I also started smoking with one of my new-found friends, Biss. We would get together enough for a packet of Park Lane cigarettes. At first I found it difficult to inhale, but with practice I got used to it. All my life I had seen my parents smoking, so it didn't seem that weird a thing for me to be doing. I thought it made me look grown up, to have a fag dangling out of the end of my mouth. Images on TV, advertising and films supported this image, the Marlon Brando look, you might say.

I got on with my schoolwork, but come weekends I would team up with the lads to turn into my new alter ego, The Skinhead. We would put our scarves on and bowl down to White Hart Lane, Tottenham Hotspur's football ground to pile in through the back doors. Up along the stand, we would reassemble; ready to start piling into the fans of whoever Spurs happened to be playing against. With my big, cherry red bovver boots on, and with the steel toe caps they were fitted out with, I would make short work of the standing capacity of whoever I could get to. Many a big tough geezer went down like a sack of shit when my steelcapper collided with one of his shinbones. I developed something of a reputation for it.

One evening when I was going out for a walk, my mum asked for a kiss, which I duly provided her with. She felt something inside the lining of my overcoat nudge against her. When she insisted I take it out, she discovered the rounders bat I had secreted in the lining there. In the ensuing search, she found the flick knife, meat hook, and cutthroat razor that I used to load up with prior to my evening stroll around the town.

'Terry, what's all this for?' she asked me.

'Insurance, mum,' was all I said.

In hindsight, I have come to the conclusion that I may well have been more troubled as a youngster than I realised at the time.

Eventually, I got bored with the skinhead thing, and the phy, and at 16 became a weekend hippy. This meant plenty of dope smoking, playing Jimi Hendrix and the soundtrack to Easy Rider. I just fell into it because it was easier than stealing or fighting, and it suited my escapist mentality.

I teamed up with a lad called Vic and we would have a right good smoke of hash. My mind would switch off from everything and only after several hours would I return to Planet Earth. That was just the way I wanted it. The less time I spent conscious of where I actually was, the better.

My exams at school came and went. I applied to go to the London School of Economics, and imagine my surprise when I managed to get sufficiently high grades to be admitted! They had asked for two Bs, which I actually surpassed in my A-level exams. This obviously meant a lot of interesting experiences were about to come my way, as the doors of the hallowed London School of Economics were opening to me.

***

Starting at the LSE was a big thing, for me. But I couldn't get over the reaction of my parents! My mum would spend hours on the phone, telling all her mates how brainy her son was. The amount of satisfaction women seem to get from making each other sick with jealousy has never ceased to amaze me. Even my old man seemed to be walking about ten inches taller, and had taken up smoking cigars.

Like most young people, my eyes were opened for the first time when I started college. I started to take an interest in politics and joined up with all sorts of societies campaigning for social justice, from Labour to the International Marxists and the Communists, but to be honest, what attracted me at first to these groups were the model-like young women they unfairly put on display to lure you towards them.

I was pretty clueless when it came to women at this time. In fact, much of my sexual experience had been gained with my faithful rubber dolly. It would take me 30 minutes to blow it up and about ten to shag it senseless. One day, though, my mum found it when she was clearing out my room. I came home that night to find my dolly all blown up and sitting at the kitchen table, like a guest coming in for tea.

Needless to say, it wasn't long before I found my fellow dope smokers at college. They were holed up in one of the little side rooms next to the student union office. From there, great clouds of hash smoke would billow out and down the corridor, like frankincense in a temple. Whenever I entered, I could see a motley collection of long-haired individuals, of indeterminate sex, sitting in a circle. The glowing embers from a joint-end would glow more brightly for a second, as someone toked at its other end, held their breath, and then breathed out what was left of the fumes.

It was as if I'd joined some secret society. I realise now that this is one of the underlying delusions/illusions of those that engage in drug-taking; that they are part of an elite unit or order, or have been chosen by something, or for something. As far as I was concerned, this was just something I was supposed to do—experience life and all it had to offer, and become a part of a world outside of that I had grown up in. It wasn't harmful, I thought; it was good for me.

With my newfound social awareness I found myself involved in many demonstrations, against US involvement in Vietnam, the 17 November, 1967 military coup in Greece, the apartheid regime in South Africa and the military junta in Chile. Immediately prior to Freshers' Week, the military had taken over in Chile, killing President Salvador Allende and many others. General Pinochet established a military junta, and proceeded to imprison and torture all those who opposed his power. We all knew that the overt or at the very least covert support of the western governments was felt by all these regimes. So, for someone such as myself, with an interest in politics and a naïve, but deep belief that the world could be changed for the better, there was a lot to do apart from studying, and getting through the exams.

Around this time, I picked up two tarot decks in London. They really appealed to me for some reason, even though I didn't know how to read them. When I looked through the meanings and interpretations of the various signs and symbols, it all seemed to make perfect sense, and I started to get interested. I eventually got the hang of them and would later use them to great effect, taking them with me wherever I went. In those days tarot decks were much rarer and people would flock to me to have a reading.

1973 saw the Miners' Strike, which highlighted to us students that the system simply was not working anymore. The lights in all the houses and offices were shut off, factories, entire industries, were coming to a halt. Half the nation was on a three-day week. The newspapers ran lurid tales of a possible take-over here in Britain. It really did seem as though we had been born in a very interesting time, sufficiently so to see the dawn of the British revolution, and the collapse of the old capitalist regime. For me, like many others, capitalism was a bad word.

At the LSE, the organisations of the revolutionary left went into overdrive, and so did my outlook. Meetings were held; rallies took place left and right. There was scarcely a spare moment to read course material, but somehow I plodded through that. Some of us wondered if our subjects were ever going to be useful in the New Britain that seemed to be emerging around us. Delegations of Welsh miners came up to sleep in the college and we as the Student Union voted overwhelmingly to accommodate them.

Meanwhile, my social awakening was not limited to the rights of the worker, or the occasional dope smoking get-together. I found myself being invited to an 'acid party', and I was intrigued. What would happen there? If I took this stuff, what might I see? Would I experience one of the visionary states that we used to hear about from others that had already tried it out? It was definitely considered to be very senior to have dropped acid—far more so than just being an ordinary dope smoker. So, I put my name down for it. My first experience was not one to be remembered, and after a night being chased by imaginary serpents and seeing my college mates kiss each other, I decided that all I wanted to do was go home and have a cup of tea. That was not the end of my tripping days, though. Far from it.

Life wasn't all trips. Somehow I managed to make it through the course. At the end of it, I sat through three weeks of exams. The temperature outside soared into the nineties. It was the sweltering summer of 1976. All summer long, there was hardly a breath of wind in the air. People were passing out in the street and in their homes. There was a water shortage, and the use of hose pipes to water gardens was strictly banned.

I staggered through the Finals and just about passed, not particularly distinguishing myself with a Third. It could have been worse, but I still felt like a total failure. When Admin stuck the pass list up on the notice board, there was my name, just above the thin red line, below which were listed all the real failures. I was filled with a feeling I would become familiar with over the years; disappointment. I knew I could have done more, that I could have done better, but there I was, scraping by, and I just wanted to get out of there.

This feeling was to come back and haunt me throughout my life, sending me all over the world in search of something but never knowing what that something was. All I knew was that I didn't want to lead a normal 9 to 5 existence. In the end, that meant dropping out, and I was to do that spectacularly.

CHAPTER TWO

SQUATLAND

I managed to get a position as trainee in an accountancy firm in the City of London. But I couldn't get into it. It was like wearing a pair of shoes that just didn't fit. Each and every little thing would rub me up the wrong way. My very left wing beliefs probably didn't help matters. One of the turning points came after I had been working a couple of months. A senior accountant asked me what I would do with my accountancy qualifications, should I actually make it through the three years' worth of exams. I answered that I would join the Inland Revenue, and spend the rest of my days persecuting all these capitalist bastards.

'If I had my way, I would put them all on a big cross and hang them out to dry,' I said. His face was thunderstruck!

When I wasn't day-dreaming about the revolution to come, I was finding work difficult. I could never get sets of figures to tally. I could add them up horizontally, and then in their individual rows vertically, but getting them to tally was virtually impossible. I became quite famous for displaying this unique gift. The qualified accountants would give me sets of figures, and by the end of the day I would still have rows of random numbers. It was almost as if people were taking bets on it. Then, after I had been struggling for most of the day, my manager would take the sheet from me, and give it to one of the young temps in the office. Hey presto, a set of beautifully tallying figures within half an hour!

Once a week we would be taken out to some remote building somewhere, for audit practice. This is when the accountants go out and test the accounting procedures of a company or organisation. But I could rarely find the place I was supposed to get to. It was always some off-the-map hellhole you needed a car to reach, usually miles from any underground station. I remember going out on one audit, and being told that I was being let into a big secret. In the small team of five directors, four of them were on about £50,000 each, and the poor bugger doing all the running around was on about £4,000. The cheeky bastards at the top of the firm had set it up so that he couldn't actually find out how much they were earning. They were so smug—all little looks to each other, little smirks. I waited until the audit was over and then sent an anonymous note to the fifth member with all the proof from his own company records. I don't know what happened, but hopefully he went in there and killed the shits.

I just didn't want to be there either, and it became obvious. So, sooner, rather than later, I was presented with the Royal Order of the Boot.

'About fucking time too,' was all I said, when they confronted me with the fact that my services were no longer required. The senior manager had a bad heart condition, so on my way out I barged into his office to give him a piece of my mind.

I was unceremoniously escorted downstairs and past the lobby. I was back on the street. Even though I hated the job, I felt the same old disappointment creeping in. Looking back, maybe I didn't like facing the fact that I wasn't up to this job, so I refused to acknowledge it as a viable way of living.

I sat myself down and had a good think about what I wanted to do, and where I wanted to be, and while I didn't exactly know the answers, I could feel my need for escapism rising to the surface again. I didn't want to be part of the society I saw around me anymore, didn't feel like I could be part of it, and in a way, I just decided to drop out. I wanted an alternative to 'consumer society'. As with many in those days, I had become disenchanted with capitalism and what was happening in countries such as Chile and Vietnam, and desired to create something other than just a wage-slave existence. But underlying all this, in my case, was a deep sense of failure, and a complete absence of any abilities. I didn't have any knowledge, or even capacity to keep a job—when I tried I invariably came across someone whom I would eventually tell to put his job where the sun didn't shine. People in working situations invariably annoyed me; these little suits kow-towing to the bosses, all on paltry sums per week, running like rats in traps around their little wheels. I would sooner tell these people where to get off and walk out the door with my middle finger proudly raised in mid air. In hindsight, I suppose it might have been helpful to have had some kind of guidance at that point, but there was none in those days, and I really felt like my views were right, no matter how confused they may have been.

Shortly after this, I said my cheerios to Mum and Dad, and set off with some new-found friends into the world of squatting. You didn't need a job. You could just walk in, take over an empty place and make it yours. I ended up in Chalk Farm with a couple of experienced squatters. We had to be careful where we stepped. There were discarded syringes all over the place. Junkies had discarded their old 'works' on the ground just in case the local kids found themselves with nothing else to play with. When I first arrived, one of the guys asked me for some dosh, so he could go out and score, and suddenly I realised that this was the way my life was going to go—a series of squats and drugs and living by the day.

'What's available?' I asked him, cheerfully.

His demeanour changed, as if someone had clicked their fingers and a glass of brandy suddenly appeared in his hand.

'Well,' he began, a man obviously unused to being speechless: 'There's speed, downers, uppers, whites, browns, greens, benzies, Charlie, dots, pyramids and nembies.'

I was unfamiliar with many of these, but I thought: In for a penny, in for a pound.

'What's the speed like?' I asked, as if I knew anything about it.

'Not bad,' he said, rubbing his chin, looking at me as if I was 100 yards away.

'Ok,' I said, pulling out a tenner. 'Let's try out some of that, then!'

I slipped the money into his hand. I had never done speed before. This would be a new experience. He headed towards the door, slowly at first until he gathered some momentum.

'I'll be back,' I heard him holler from halfway down the staircase as a cold breeze blew in. The bastard went and left the door open. I got up and went to close it myself. 'Bollox,' I thought, 'there is no door!'

He returned a few days later, which wasn't bad for him, apparently. When I asked him what happened he launched into an energetic tale that involved being stopped by police, and throwing away all that good stuff. I had learned my first, but not my last lesson.

***

We were very near Camden Lock market, which was just starting up, and it was amazing to walk past all the colourful stalls with their displays. People were making their own jewellery, clothes, and crockery. Others were bringing rugs back from India or leather goods from South America. There were all manner of things from almost every place in the world. It was a teeming, hubbub, bee-hive-like place, crammed with young people from all over the world. Just walking through the narrow alleyways crammed with stalls and people was an experience. Exotic smells and incense were thick in the air. People were walking around in all manner of strange fashions. The atmosphere plainly said that something was going on here. Along the adjacent Camden High Street, huge chairs and giant boots were affixed to the front of the shops. It was like a scene from Alice in Wonderland.

I found myself in horrible squat after horrible squat, meeting strange, shifty people who trusted you as much as you trusted them, which was not at all, handing over cash for whatever drugs were on offer. But I didn't mind, because I saw it differently. This was pure escapism from reality. One place in particular I recall seeing as if it was some sort of Aladdin's Cave. It was a squalid, horrible place, but for me at that moment it was the innermost chamber of a palace in another world, and it was exactly the type of place I had always wanted to be.

I sat in that place transfixed by the sight of people preparing and smoking or shooting up their drugs, like a tiny mouse in the presence of a cobra, or a sheep caught in the middle of a road by the headlamps of an oncoming car. There was no rush. No one was going anywhere. I was in a timeless zone, with no past and no future. Syringes were prepared and carefully laid beside me on the floor.

What am I getting into? The thought flashed across my mind, moments before a thin black cord was tied around my arm. There was a sudden pressure at the end of my arm. Then, a flash of sharpness, as the needle sliced into the flesh and hit a vein. I saw a thin red tree branch out in the barrel of the gun, then fill it, turning all the water to red. They knew how to go in deep to get the big juicy vein, the mainline where all the traffic was coming home from work. Something hit my lungs. I felt love flooding through my body, sweeping away all my thoughts in its ecstasy, filling my head with devotion. I could actually feel the presence of God. I had found love! I had entered through the heavenly gates of my Lord's kingdom. I felt all this wonderful knowledge out there waiting for me to reach out and pick it from the tree. I saw then that I had been living my life in ignorance rather than stretching forth to know the mind of God. I was a missionary. Maybe the great mystical being behind all altered states of consciousness had a path marked out for me. Finally, a purpose to my existence!

Then my thoughts were interrupted. Someone was saying something to me. It was not so much what he was saying as the way that he was saying it to me, as if we are sharing a huge secret. The trip was over. We were all coming down. Everyone was edgy, tense, irritable. The atmosphere was terrible. Something really bad was about to happen. The money was finished, the trip was over. Somehow, each worshipper had to pick themselves up off the floor and make their own way home. See you at the next one. Yeah, yeah. Go an' fuck ya'self were the unspoken words as I donned my clothes and headed out the door. And no, I haven't got the price of a cuppa tea. As I walked away into the cold night air, some faceless nameless drone of the underworld was at work, securing the door behind me with its thousand and one locks.

A while later; a day, a week, I didn't know, I ran into one of the guys from that squat. His face was almost transparent.

He told me he had some speed for sale. I slipped him the required tenner, and he slipped the packet into my hand. Within the blinking of an eye he had vanished, leaving me wondering if he was ever really there. God, it was so easy to get nice and high.

I met a guy I knew who liked a bit of whiz, and told him I'd just picked up. His eyes lit up with a green flame. We scuttled back to what he referred to as 'his place'. It was a tiny room at the top of an old squat. It was freezing cold in there. For some reason it was colder in there than outside. Maybe it was haunted. We crouched down, and from nowhere he produced a couple of syringes. I showed him the stuff. His face frowned. He tipped his tongue to the end of his right forefinger, and gingerly dabbed the powder. He tasted it.

'Fuck me!' he cried out, 'It's Vim!'

Vim was a scouring powder. That would have killed us if we'd banged it up. When I told him who I bought it off, a look of understanding dawned across his face.

'He is one fucking rip off,' he said, eventually. His breathing was heavy. I thought of how I might have died if I had just gone straight in and shot this shit up. It would have been a nasty death. The shock of that stuff, running quickly through the system, the pain from the burning, the sense of despair and failure as realisation hits, moments before falling down in absolute agony. And all so one man could get a quick tenner together.

That guy was probably handing that same tenner over to a dealer for a bag of the real thing. In a minute or so he would be feeling the rush of amphetamine, blossoming out throughout his blood like a great flower, like the kind you see in those nature programmes when they speed up the camera, and you see in seconds what has taken days or hours to happen. I felt shock, anger, rage, helplessness wash over me, but strangely not relief. My life had been spared. If we all have nine lives to start out with then I had only eight left. Something in me felt as though it had died. A part of me was older now, or had just gone. For the first time I wondered whether it was such a good idea, running around with these people, shooting up drugs I knew fuck all about, thinking that nothing could happen to me.

But it didn't stop me. The situation in squatland was so constantly changing—this near-miss was something you more or less got used to, in the same way that if you were a soldier in some far away battlefield you would rapidly acclimatise to the occasional bullet whizzing past you. It wasn't going to make you quit and go running back to barracks. I decided to keep my wits about me and tried to watch out a bit more carefully to avoid anything like that getting close to me, but basically I was hoping for the best. Now and again I would see the results of someone who had been less lucky. People would get robbed—by fellow drug-users—set up, grassed up, spiked, left right and centre. For fun there were those who like to go around and deliberately infect others with HIV and Hep C. I had even seen them, offering other junkies their syringes, which had already been opened and used (by them), but which they then tried to rewrap and make it seem as though these syringes had never been opened. Other times they wait until someone was really clucking, or suffering withdrawal, then offer them a shot from the same spoon, knowing full well that they were infected, and that by letting someone take a hit from the same spoon they would be spreading the disease. There are some really evil bastards out there.

I got in deep. Within a week, I had a set of yellow and purple bruises running up and down the length of my arms. I looked like a pin cushion. The wounds didn't heal and I started to think I had gangrene, which I didn't. I had gone into a bad way very quickly, but I knew I wasn't as bad as some of the people I saw around me, rotting away like zombies, waiting for their next fix. Still, I knew things could go either way for me, and after getting into a bit of trouble more than once, I decided that maybe a bit of actual travelling might not be a bad idea.

I had been thinking about this for a while when something happened to finally make up my mind. I met a couple of fellas down in Notting Hill who told me they could get acid at a bargain rate. The usual price for a thousand trips was £200. They are talking about £140, so I thought it looked good. We met up at the local hall and took a stroll.

'Where's the money?' one of them asked me.

I immediately knew something was wrong.

'Where's the fuckin' stuff?' I said back to him. In my right pocket my hand had already slipped to the knife I always carried.

He started shouting, 'He's gotta gun, he's gotta gun!'

Then his mate jumped me. He made a grab for my right arm and clamped himself to me, to stop me pulling the knife. The first guy recovered enough to start brandishing a thin wooden stick. It was far too light to do any real damage. I shook off my attacker and my right arm was out, only it was the wad of money in my hand, not the knife. Blows were raining down on my head as they both realised what had happened. I felt something warm and wet trickle down the back of my neck. I heard a scream. It took me a while to realise that it was my own voice. I was on the ground with blood everywhere. My blood. My attackers ran off as I drifted into unconsciousness. It took the ambulance crew half an hour to pry the money from my grip. The last thing I remembered was a kind face and voice.

'This is something to help the pain,' said the voice as I felt the familiar pinprick of a needle seeking a vein.

That was it; I needed to get out of that place for a while.

I felt the strong need to get out and 'hit the road' to get away from what looked to me like a lifetime of slavery and misery. I wanted to move on to new experiences, and new places, where things would somehow be different. It was a naïve attitude, but what was then a very deeply felt one amongst my generation. It was almost migratory, such as you see periodically when the reindeer or one of the many species of birds goes on the move.

'Why not go to India?' my mate Bald Head said.

India? Ok, then. I started to think about it. I got a travel guide and itinerary for an extensive, psychedelic bus journey from London, through to Istanbul, and from there to India and Kathmandu. The timing was perfect—some local heavies were also squeezing me for money I'd made forging student cards, and in the heat of the moment I'd made promises I couldn't keep. It was just as well, I thought to myself, that my Magic Bus ticket was already paid for, and I was heading out of London the following day, heading to Afghanistan, where, I thought, the laws were lax and the dope was for free. This was to be the start of a wonderful adventure I would never regret. I couldn't have been more wrong.

CHAPTER THREE

ON THE ROAD

The Magic Bus left from Trafalgar Square on a cold February day. It was a converted prison bus with bars across the windows, and held about 30 people. It was cramped and uncomfortable, and it was in these conditions that we would be rolling virtually non-stop through Europe, night and day, to Istanbul.

I brought my tarot decks, and a few hundred acid tabs, which I was going to bring out in stages as the trip opened up. Smelling the hash smoke heavy in the air, the driver reminded us that as we approached Greece and Turkey all dope was to be smoked up. No dope or drug of any kind could be taken into either of those countries by anyone on board the bus. He didn't mind people smoking, but if anyone was caught at either of those two countries' borders the bus would be confiscated and the driver would go to prison.

Europe rolled by. Istanbul was an amazing place to arrive into. Turkey's beautiful mosques inspired me, and gave me my first taste of Muslim culture, which I was to return to later. We hurtled through Turkey, not stopping until we hit the Iranian border. Rumours of trouble in Iran followed us to the Iranian-Turkish border. At our crossing point there was a great hall. On one side of the hall there was a huge picture of Ataturk, the moustachioed leader of the 1920 Turkish revolution. On the other side was a photograph of the Shah of Iran. The sun seemed to be shining from behind the Shah, his right arm was raised, his palm upturned.

'It looks like he's askin' God for a handout,' said one of my fellow travellers.

'Shut it,' said a more seasoned traveller, 'In Iran they'll nick you as soon as look at you for taking the piss out of their leader. And there are informants in every nook and cranny, so watch what you say.'

In Iran I had a close call when a young local lad wearing dark glasses boarded the bus and asked to buy some LSD. Like a twat I nearly went for it. I'll never know if he was an undercover policeman or not, because I decided to give the guy a miss. But as we pulled out I felt yet another one of my nine lives leaving me.

We were almost there. Our initiation was nearly over. Sometimes we felt like pilgrims on a great journey of enlightenment. Other times it was just another laugh, rolling through all these far-out places, blowing off clouds of dope and watching the stars and moon go by at night. Afghanistan was where the trip really began.

At the Iran-Afghan border things suddenly became much more subdued. On the Iranian side, the boarder post consisted of huge complexes of wire and electric fences There were pillboxes, guard boxes on stilts, rolling off across the countryside into the distance. On the Afghan side was a small sign, saying 'Welcome to Afghanistan.' A single guard stood there, his face betraying his Mongol ancestry. He was young and spoke no English. Over his shoulder he had slung an ancient rifle. In the muzzle he had stuck a single flower. Now I knew where the hippies got their ideas.

To get into Afghan passport control, in a scene that would foretell my destiny, we had to pass through a mini-museum devoted to the methods smugglers had used to try to get their merchandise out of Afghanistan: a pair of platform boots, ripped back to reveal a hollowed-out compartment, where two kilos of hashish had been secreted. A handwritten sign next to the boots read 'Sentence: three years'. Next to this was a suitcase, cut back to reveal a false bottom. 'Five kilos of hashish, Three kilos of opium' read the sign. 'Sentence: five years' And so it went on, dozens of these things all placed on display, with appropriate warnings against anyone trying their luck.

It really had no effect on me. In Herat, a few of us went into a clothes shop and had a look round. Instantly, there was the owner, offering us all manner of hashish slabs. Some of them looked really succulent; soft and tender, and they were the size of dinner plates! Some were embossed with the brand names of the local crops. The real action started when we got down to prices. We had been bargaining away for about an hour when I suddenly remembered that I had acid tabs with me. I mentioned it to the guy, not even sure that he would know what it was. His eyes lit up. He wanted some. Add a bit of acid to the deal and the prices dropped even further. Out we went, and straight back to the hotel with our goodies. On the way I swallowed a big lump of opium that the shopkeeper had given me. Straight down the hatch. Lovely. The hash was powerful, too, really giving you that lift but without the tiredness and dizziness I'd felt so often smoking the stuff back home. All the colours seemed to brighten. The night became enchanting and magical. What an amazing trip we were on.

Along the road to Kabul, I discovered the joys, and horrors, of smoking opium. With a new-found friend *Carl*, I would lie down on the floor, with a wooden block under my head, and smoke through proper opium pipes from Iran. The feel of the smoke was a thousand times smoother than tobacco, or hash. This was like silk compared to sandpaper. When I breathed out, the smoke would form a swirling dragon curling round and round itself in the air, infinitely fluid and enervating. The smoke was thick and white, cool and smooth. At first it felt great. The trouble comes when, after a few months of regularly smoking it, you try to stop. It began to take up more and more of my day. I had originally wanted to learn the language, but now that didn't seem so interesting. I could get by with what I knew, and, sod it, they would have to speak English.

My interest in Islam had been growing all along the road to Afghanistan. I became a student of the faith and received the Kalima, the statement that, 'There is no God save Allah, and that Mohammed is His messenger.' I went on to learn portions of the *Koran* by heart. I performed the prayers, five times a day. But increasingly, as I slipped further and further into the world of opium, everything else seemed second-rate, or just not as appealing as it had done before. I only said my prayers now and again, and I raced through them instead of doing them properly. Before the opium took hold, I would savour the Arabic words, inwardly experiencing and absorbing their meaning. The light of the Koran is a wonderful thing, but a person's heart must be clean for that light to properly shine forth.

Carl was a morphine freak. The morphine would come back along the hippy trail from India and freaks would buy, on average, 200 or 300 grams of the stuff, at around $2 per gram. They would carry their goodies inside their bodies, across the borders on their way back to their home countries. Along the way, they would stop off, pull out the goodies, and do a little hit for themselves, and, if they needed a bit of extra cash, sell a few grams here and there. The morphine powder was brown, and shooting this stuff gave you what was known as a morphine burn. It was rough at first, especially if you had been spoiled with loads of heroin first. But we got used to it. Heroin was always a much smoother high, less physical than the others, more ethereal. If opium was silk, then H was more like velvet. I started banging it up in the usual way. I'd get a small packet—a gram was £20—and at first this would do me for quite a while. But as things spiralled downwards, the little packets were running out faster and faster, and needed replacing more and more often. In the end I got pretty desperate, because the fucking things were running out virtually as soon as I'd bought them, and I still couldn't stop.

When the money ran out, my real problems began. I needed that fucking stuff. Like I needed to drink water. Or breathe air. I wasn't getting a kick out of it. No high whatsoever. I looked like a skeleton. *But that didn't really matter, did it?* I thought to myself. *I mean, it's not like you're in any fashion parade, you're not exactly male model material, are you now, Terry?*

All up and down my arms were pinpricks, some of them looking very angry underneath all that punishment. I didn't give a fuck. My body was just a way to get that chemical into my blood stream. There were times when I spent the entire day getting £20, and when I banged it up, I still didn't feel it. I was on a treadmill. *Now that you've done that one, run rabbit run. You've got to get back on the case and get another one together. Enjoying the ride?* There were times when I would think back. Something or someone I saw or heard would start me dreaming me about the past. Wait. You never used to be this way. You've got to get back. You've got to get off this stuff. You know you have to. But it was always too hard to find the right time, the right place.

No one wanted to know, anyway. Everyone was far too busy planning their own trips.

Then I got really sick. It wasn't just the morphine, creeping up on me. I had hepatitis. In the Kabul Hospital, they put me in the Dying Person's Unit. My skin turned deep yellow. On my way in, I passed a mirror and saw a skull looking back. A second look revealed my own face, the yellow jaundiced skin hung in folds. My eyes had turned deep orange. My piss was a deep, deep brown. I was so weak I could hardly make it to the stinking piss hole they called toilets anyway.

It took me six weeks to recover from the hepatitis. No one knew where I was. I hadn't given a thought to anyone from the past, or had time to think about anything other than my infernal habit while I had been using. Now that the drugs were out of my system, those memories came flooding back. I realised I wanted to do a lot more with my life than remain a walking pin cushion. What a fucking idiot I had been. I resolved to give drugs a wide berth next time. It had been a close call and I was pretty sure that yet another one of my nine lives was gone. I thanked my lucky stars, Jah, Krishna, Allah, all of them, for my life. There was no way that I was going to waste another chance.

But within hours of leaving the hospital, I was back on the needle. It's hard to say why. As a junkie, which by now I was, you live most of your life on automatic pilot. You are not your own master. There's always someone else in the cockpit, and though you might think it's you, it's not. It's somebody else. Much later, when I started moving in rehab and recovery circles, I kept coming across this idea of addiction as a disease. I don't think that is totally true. There are elements that make it tempting to think of addiction in this light, especially when a relapse occurs and the addict is swept back along into their former pattern of behaviour. But addiction is a form of behaviour. It is something that has to be learnt, originally. In the same way a pattern of addiction can be unlearnt. To think of your addiction as a disease, to me, is so disempowering.

***

Carl hit upon the idea of doing a drug run, and as an out and out junkie now, not knowing what I was thinking, I thought it was a great idea. He had done this before, and said there were no problems. But our funds were pretty limited. Pooling our money together, we could just about finance a run, from Thailand back to India. At first glance this might seem like taking coals to Newcastle, but Christmas was coming up, when all the rich freaks from around the world made their way to Goa. Out of the teeming thousands that turn up, some were bound to be interested in getting their hands on some nice Thai White, extremely high-grade heroin. Far superior to the brown powder produced locally, the high was way beyond your ordinary basic smack. It was also far more addictive, and, handy for us, far more expensive. We got our exit visas from the central police station in downtown Kabul, and booked our tickets for the next day. We crawled by train across the great sub-continent, along the way being offered everything from morphine to fake dollars to rocket launchers, but we kept to ourselves.

Arriving in Thailand was like suddenly waking up in New York: Big, wide roads, massive hotels. It was like stepping out of the 1900s into the future! We had to go easy on our money now. It was starting to slip through our fingers. The first thing was to get some stuff. The taxi driver who picked us up at the airport was an obvious first choice.

'Two bics, two bics,' he kept saying.

'What he means is that he's got two grams in there,' said *Carl*. In his hand the driver was holding a small cylindrical container. It was clear plastic, with a yellow screw cap as a lid. Inside was a massive amount of what I presumed was heroin. Pure, white H. Like the kind you hear about, but rarely get to see, unless you come to Thailand to do your Christmas shopping. We paid him the money for the gear and the lift, and vanished into a beautiful, spacious hotel. This was a change! Up in our room, *Carl* took out the bic, and we weighed it. Exactly one gram. The driver had diddled us. He had bought two of these containers for what we had paid him. That way he was going to have another one in stock when we called him back the next morning.

I put a dab of the white stuff into a spoon. It looked big and fluffy, almost like soap powder. Looking at it, I wasn't so sure it was real. *Carl* took one look at how much I was putting in the spoon and gave a start.

'That's far too much. Half of that.'

I took out half and filled the barrel of the syringe with water. I dropped it carefully into the spoon. Instantly the powder disappeared. Just like that. I was astonished. I had only ever seen smack that you had to boil up, with a candle underneath, and a drop of lemon juice added in for good measure. When I took a hit of this stuff, it was like being blown away by a soft wind. It was so smooth. And so strong. It was like trying to stand up in the sea when there is a really big wave coming towards you. At first you get pulled towards it by the suction power of the water, moving outwards as it gathers its strength. Then you are just whooshed forwards. By the time we had both regained consciousness it was morning, or evening, I couldn't say for sure. But it was definitely time for another hit. I was in cold turkey already.

The H—this white stuff—was really strong. I was getting totally blasted each time I had a hit, even though I was putting less in the spoon than I usually would. I was out of it. Just zapped completely out, lying on the bed, watching the fan spinning round above me. And when I came to, I would find myself back in cold turkey land. I was trapped between the devil and the deep blue sea. When I was clucking, I could hardly find the strength to stand up. The cluck was a really strong one, disabling me the moment I found myself in it. This was much stronger than anything I had ever encountered before or since, for that matter. Getting off that stuff is really difficult. It's like when you start sliding down a hill, and there's nothing to hold onto. You reach out instinctively for something to grab and steady yourself, but there's just nothing there. So, down and down you go, until something happens or you just reach the bottom. As you are going down, you try to minimise any damage that you might be in for. You don't want to get hurt more than you actually have to.

On this stuff, I became really naïve. My capacity for doubt, or even just using my own faculties became minimal. If someone told me something, I would just believe it. Heroin seems to put a certain part of the brain to sleep and makes the addict really easy to manipulate.

***

Carl and I went off up to the Golden Triangle, the extreme north of Thailand where the stuff actually comes from. It was up there that we would get the best deal. The goods were just too expensive in Bangkok. We took a bus up there. It took all night to get into Chang Mai. The countryside was absolutely beautiful, with rolling hills extending in every direction. The pace of life was gentle here, the people, charming.

We rented out a motorbike, and using that made our own way to Chang Rai, which was even further north and was the place for it, so *Carl* said. It was like a scene out of Easy Rider, with *Carl* doing the driving and me sitting on the back. As we made our way along a little country road, we went past some really beautiful houses, all set back from the road and walled, little cloisters of absolute luxury. Many of the houses had 'ghost houses' in their front gardens. These are small, doll-house like structures that are placed outside the actual house and are for the spirits to live in. It gives them an alternative to having to live in the same house as mortals.

As we came into Chang Rai, we were approached by a local man, also on a motorbike.

'Did you want any stuff?' he asked us, in excellent English.

We told him that we did, and he told us to follow him back to his place. We drove right behind him for about half an hour, and he led us into the deserted courtyard of a great house. There was a massive wall around it, and he secured the powerful gate behind us, scanning the road to ensure that we hadn't been followed. He led us past a fountain, and up into the house itself. There wasn't a sign of anyone else around, only the singing of the birds from the surrounding countryside. It was a completely peaceful haven. Our new best friend went into a back room, and came back with a massive plastic bag. As he sat down next to us, he opened the bag, and I could see it was full of Thai White. There must have been several kilos in there. No doubt, if we had had the money, he could have brought us even more.

'You would like to try?'

We brought out our spoons and did a hit. The stuff was excellent. Yes, we wanted 100 grams. That was about our budget for the drugs and our plane fares back to Bombay. He weighed it out on a set of scales, and, as it measured the amount we wanted, he dug the little shovel deep into the powder and threw on a bit extra for good will. The scales tipped nicely in our direction, and we bagged up and moved out.

I don't know how we made it back to Bangkok. We were getting so blasted from this stuff. It was wiping us out. It was so strong, we would do a hit, and then we couldn't even make it out of the room for the day. So we stayed in. If there is one thing that tips off the Bangkok hotel staff that they have western junkies staying in their places, it is this. The junkies don't get out and about like any normal tourist does.

I managed to head out one night to sample the night-life, while *Carl* stayed behind.

When I got back to the hotel, I knew something was wrong immediately. No *Carl*. And all our things had been turned upside down. Then someone from the hotel came rushing round and said that the police had called by. They'd found *Carl* with some stuff and had arrested him. This was bad news, indeed. I made my way over to Patoomwun Police Station and walked up the steps. It was early morning, and all the prisoners were being kept in a single large cell. People were just beginning to wake up on the concrete floor. There must have been 40 men in the single cell in the station. At the back I could see *Carl*, looking fucked. I was starting to cluck already myself.

'Where's the gear?' I asked him, starting to get frantic. 'Did those bastards get it all?' I wanted to know if there was any stashed, anything I could get my hands on right then and there.

'They found only one gram,' he said, wearily.

'Where's the rest?' I asked.

'I was bagging it up, into little plastic packets ready for the flight back. I've got it all stashed inside the lining of my jacket,' he said. 'When they came they found only one gram. They say this means one year. They have just brought a new law in here, Terry. For every gram you are caught with, you get an extra year. Up to ten grams. Then, you get the death sentence.'

This came as a shock to me. Together we had 100 grams, which when we bought it didn't seem like an awful lot. But now it did. That was well into the range of getting a death sentence. I only hoped that the stuff remained out of sight. There was no way *Carl* could get any to me, anyway. A guard sat at the row of bars as we talked, and he was watching us like a hawk. If we'd had money we could have slipped him $50 and he would have looked the other way, but at that exact point we had no spare cash.

Around me, the scene was starting to come to life. Drug dealers were lining up now, and after receiving crumpled up banknotes from their friends inside, they would take out their little packets and flick them across. The guard watched it all as if it wasn't happening.

'Terry, can you please get me a syringe?' *Carl* asked me. 'At the moment I'm having to use the one that is in here, and that's being used by about ten other men.'

It wasn't the health risk *Carl* was worried about. It was the fact that when you borrow somebody's syringe in a situation like that, you've got to give them some of your stuff.

I was getting desperate. *Where would the drugs be?* I looked around for the captain's office. I walked round the back of the police station and saw his window open. Climbing up through it, I was able to get into his office, where I knew the stuff would be stashed. Sitting right on top of his desk was a nice big metal box. I opened it, and there inside were all the little bic phials and small bags of Buddha sticks that the cops had confiscated that night. I grabbed hold of everything I could find, and stashed it inside the lining of my Afghani waistcoat. Then I was back out the window, and away. I could feel the cluck getting closer as I made my way back to the hotel.

I found a dozen policemen waiting for me at the top of the stairs. They searched me, but didn't expect to find anything. They probably thought I would have had the sense to stash it, which is what I should have done. But as they searched me, one of them found the stuff hidden in the deepest recess of my waistcoat. I felt my world collapse. I had been so cock-a-hoop on turning over the captain's cabin, but now I was going to be double-fucked. They ordered me to take off my trousers so they could search them. A passing Thai maid came along just as they ordered me to take off my underwear. Thai people have this idea that white men are big, in much the same way that white people think the same about black men. They have something of a complex about it, actually. It makes them feel inferior. But the fact that my equipment is quite small actually acted to salve the inflamed minds of the Thai police present. Particularly when the maid commented on it, and made them laugh. So, instead of arresting me, they all just walked away, leaving me holding up my trousers with one hand.

The cluck was growing inside me, and there would be no way I was going to be able to get together the necessary monies to get hold of any drugs, even if I knew where to go. I could hardly walk, but I managed to do up my trousers and staggered into the street and right into an American tourist.

'Please help me,' I said, 'I must get to a hospital.'

This guy, a complete stranger, helped me into a cab and paid the driver to take me to the Bangkok Police Hospital. As soon as I arrived, they put me in a wheel chair. The orderly pushing me was absolutely insistent that I remain in the chair, as he slammed straight into the plastic doors that separated each section of the hospital. They laid me out on a bed and left me there for the best part of the day. I drifted in and out of consciousness, only occasionally coming to, to cry out for some pain killers. Aspirin was all they could give me.

A nurse woke me up. I was bathed in sweat. Even the bed was a damp mess. The stink that was coming out of my body was awful. The chemicals were breaking down and seeping out my pores. The nurse held a small bottle of a very red liquid. I downed it quickly, and after a very short while, felt really elated. I even managed to get up and walk about. I was in euphoria, walking about, singing, and even doing a little jig to the amusement of the nurse, who was watching me all along. I was amazed at the transformation. I knew what this stuff was: my old friend, methadone.

They kept me in hospital for one more day and then released me as an outpatient. Each day I presented myself at the methadone clinic, along with 100 or so others, all locals. Child addiction to heroin had reached epidemic proportions in Thailand. As a result the King had decreed the return of the death sentence for those found guilty of dealing or smuggling. Being there every day, you get to recognise some of the faces. One young lad, in particular, spoke good English and we hit it off. We would shoot up together whenever we could get enough money for some heroin. There were times I came to on the floor of the toilet with the needle still in my arm, sticking straight out. On another occasion, the syringe blocked up and as I pressed down on the plunger, the whole thing back-sprayed into my face. There was blood, my blood, everywhere, all over me. I went into hysterics of laughter. My young friend didn't find anything at all to laugh about and went off in a huff. Just then I broke down, and in floods of tears begged him not to leave me. He was shocked that I was crying so much. Even I didn't understand why. I think it's safe to say, though, that during this time, I wasn't in my right mind.

Looking back, I am horrified by my actions, but I don't think I was even aware of what I was doing back then. Smuggling drugs was not my plan when I set out. I just wanted a good time. Basically, I was content just to coast along in India and thereabouts, not necessarily having a lot of money but at least heaving a lot of certainty. From my experience there, I knew how to move and stay afloat, how to get around the police, if need be, and how to look after myself. I had more or less assumed that Thailand would be similar. But it was a real shock, just how ruthless and vicious everything there was.

Whereas in India, and Afghanistan, if things got really difficult you could get around with very little money; in Thailand if you didn't have money you soon saw the harsher side of things and the contempt they showed to all junkies.

Basically, as *Carl* seemed to know what he was doing, I had just left all the thinking to him, and did whatever I was told. You can go brain dead when you are on hard drugs, even so-called 'soft' ones, which makes it very easy for someone controlling you to involve you in the most serious imaginable crimes. At the time, you don't even have the capacity to stop and think about what you are doing, or how things might turn out if everything 'comes on top'. You are in a delusional world where everything is ok and nothing is wrong. People planning serious crimes often try to get drug users to do their really dirty work, even up to murdering others for them, because they know that their minions can be easily controlled and are generally unable to say no. This is the reason the King of Thailand brought in the death sentence for drug dealers—and enforces it. Drug dealers are the most ruthless band of people planet earth has been able to produce, happy to ensnare children, mothers, anyone that is vulnerable into all manner of terrible crimes against humanity.

Eventually other countries in the world will probably have to resort to this same approach if they wish to even begin to slow down the massive expansion of drugs which is taking place, regardless of how people may feel about capital punishment. It will probably be an unavoidable option, unfortunately.

Eventually the British Embassy flew me out because I had received word that my mother was dying. Just before I left Thailand, a guy staying in the same guest house dumped a huge pile of Buddha sticks in my lap. This was some of the best herb in the world and I just didn't want to know. I left them in the bin as I boarded the plane back to England, carrying a small plastic attaché case that had somehow stayed with me all the way from India, and somehow, my tarot deck, which had survived it all too.

CHAPTER FOUR

THERE AND BACK AGAIN

Even though I had recovered somewhat, my mind was clearly still not right. On the plane back to England I gave some thought to what had happened. I had had a very close scrape with the law, in a place where they had just brought in the death sentence for drug dealers and bolstered up the legal penalties in general. I had gone through a very serious cold turkey, in which the sheer severity had actually crippled me, rendering me incapable of even standing in the street, and having to be carried away in an ambulance. Luckily I had been able to get to a place where they provided treatment for my condition, and weaned me off with methadone. You would have thought that that might have taught me a lesson.

In a way it did. But what I came away from that experience with was the fact that I was one lucky bastard, and couldn't be stopped! Somehow, the gods had smiled upon me, as they always did in the end, and I had leapt out of all that potential destruction like a hero out of mythology, and was now heading off to be home in time for cornflakes. I looked at my reflection in the mirror of the toilet on the plane. What a guy! I thought. I had faced off the toughest of the Thai cops, and shown them what the time was. Small matter that *Carl* was sitting inside one of Bangkok's notorious prisons for God-knew how many years ahead and that I had nearly died.

Coming through Heathrow was a buzz. It was great to be back in England. All around me were English-speaking people, and for a change I could understand what was being said. The weather was cold but very bright, and I was happy to see the quaint old houses beside the railway line as I travelled along the Piccadilly Line, up along towards Wood Green. I noticed every little thing, my senses were really sharp.

I went back to my parents' house. In some ways things had stayed exactly the same, but in others they were radically altered. I had been away for three years. During that time my Mum had to have a lung removed when she developed lung cancer but it had returned, and she was trying to get around on only one lung. She would struggle for breath every now and again, and have to reach for the big oxygen cylinder that the health service had provided her with. She would put the mask over her mouth and from over the top of it, I could see her frightened eyes looking at me. I did what I could to comfort her. I held her hand and told her some watered down versions of my travelling tales. I was clean from drugs and looked the picture of good health. But my Mum was grey and thin. She looked as if she had aged about 40 years since I had last seen her.

All we could do was make sure that Mum was as comfortable as possible, and on a cold and bleak February day, we took her to Brompton Hospital, where she passed away peacefully. She had gone. My Dad reached out and closed her eyes, and from somewhere inside me I remembered a prayer from the Koran, which I recited in Arabic. It was the prayer from the very beginning of the Koran, called El Fatah, or the Opening. My Dad and my sister were sitting there with me, not consciously understanding the words, but silently joining in the sentiments that this powerful prayer invoked. I then started to repeat the Lord's Prayer, which they knew, and after the words 'Our Father' they joined in.

In one of the conversations we had shared before she went, my Mum had suggested that I get a job as a home help. I wanted to try again at the honest, clean life, so, I made my way to the local social services building, and asked to speak with the lady in charge. I was shown in and a stout, dark-haired lady behind a desk listened while I told her my story. She agreed to let me make a start as home help, and I was given an itinerary, listing the elderly people I was to visit each day. I would go round and do the chores for them that they were unable to do for themselves, such as cleaning, dusting, or the washing up.

It was not meant to be though. A woman who knew my mother asked me to call in on her daughter who had just gone through a divorce and was feeling very lonely. She put emphasis on the word 'lonely'. This young woman was one of those girls who had absolutely no personality at all. It was an effort just to sit there. I always breathed a sigh of relief whenever these sessions came to an end and I could get the fuck out and back home. She would try to show me all her wedding pictures, but this marriage hadn't lasted as the guy had turned out to be 'a wanker'. Then, one night, she brought up the subject of heroin, and said she knew where to score. *Oho*, I thought, *where might that be?* My interest was immediately ignited again, though I thought I had put it behind me.

'Over in Paddington way, in a pub there,' she said by way of explanation.

The next thing we were heading off down there, two or three times a week, to pick up our little ten quid deals off a

Turkish guy from this place. There were several other dealers in this pub, all vying for what seemed to be a burgeoning trade, and the one we were consistently scoring off gave us his address. It was, when we went there, on the fifth floor of a block of flats in South Kensington.

Soon afterwards we got busted while trying to score round at his place. I was charged with conspiracy, and she was let off on condition that she be a prosecution witness against me. When it came to court, most of the other defendants went down for a few years apiece, and I got a fine. I saw her sitting in the foyer, giving me a really cold look as I went in to the court and 'up the steps' to get weighed off. Chicks like that will always turn against you, I realised. Better it happen sooner rather than later. *At least it gets that bitch out of the way*, I thought to myself. But by then she had done enough damage; I was back on the stuff, and registered as an addict on a methadone script. And once you are back on that infernal treadmill, it is as hard as hell to even think about coming off. What made it worse was that I had also gotten involved with this woman I really cared about. She hooked up with me when her partner was sent to prison, and I felt like we were getting close, but as soon as he got out, she went back to him. I felt like my heart would break, and in my hour of need, I turned to drugs to ease the pain.

I was lucky to get away with a fine after my arrest, because I had also started to get into fraud, in order to pay for my unexpectedly regained interest in drugs. But, not in my right mind, I was sloppy, and inevitably, the police came calling. I was woken up one morning by the sound of someone knocking. Not really expecting a visit, I opened the door, and lo and behold, it was the Old Bill. I was arrested and taken down to the police station. They confronted me with the evidence of the thousands of pounds of cheque fraud I had committed.

'You're going away for this lot, matey,' one copper said to me, like something out of an old television programme.

'You'll be getting about three to four years, my old cocker,' a second cop merrily chipped in, as they put me in a cell, shut the door, and closed up the little hatch. I sat there in the cell, looking down at the obligatory piss puddle on the floor and trying to breathe through my mouth. How was I going to get away with this?

My only chance was in getting bail. Once out, I could head back to India. Let them look for me there! India is one hell of a big place to hide in. When the duty solicitor came round, I had to do some fast thinking. To be eligible for bail, I had to protest my innocence, so I told him that I was denying the charges, but would fill him in on the details at a later time. To get bail in those days, you had to own a property. When the solicitor asked me if I owned my own house I said that the house I was living in was mine; I had inherited it off my old Gran. He nodded, writing everything down on his yellow writing pad. Bail was awarded. I walked out of the courtroom with all my possessions in a big plastic bag in one hand. The Old Bill were gutted to see me walking away. I gave them a little wave, blew them a kiss and walked off with a spring in my step.

As the day of my court case got closer and closer, I got nervous. My ticket was booked for the day before it. I was still nervous getting on the plane, expecting the cops to turn up at any minute to drag me away, even as the hostess closed the door, and locked it. Only as I felt the engines roar into take-off, did I know I had made it. Once more the disappointments of reality had had a crippling effect on me, and I just wanted to forget it all and escape. My mother's death, my inevitable decline back into heroin addiction, my broken heart—they all combined to make me wish I had never returned to England, and to the real world. I was looking forward to walking into a different world again, where I didn't have to worry about anybody or anything, where I could just drop out.

***

Getting back to India was great. Everything had stayed more or less the same. Guys would simply approach the westerners with offers of heroin. I made a purchase from the first one who found me and went back to my little room. I sat up all night, chasing the little lines of dark-brown liquid up and down the silver foil, and listened to the sounds of the trains from the nearby Old Delhi railway station. It was a return to what I knew, and I was happy to be back in it, no longer worrying about earning a wage, helping others, getting along in society. All that mattered now was me and my next fix. But I was to be reminded of the horrible downside very soon.

One morning I bumped into a really pretty French girl who introduced herself as Celine. She was staying with two guys, and had just come back from Benares, the holy city of the Hindus. They invited me to their room and we got on very well, so I was looking forward to seeing her again. But a few days later I realized that something was wrong. I hadn't seen Celine for several days. Then clouds of flies started to appear all over the place. There were hundreds of them, crawling underneath the door to her room. I called the manager over. He looked really nervous, sweating and gulping a lot. We opened the door with his key. The guys had already paid in advance, he said. It looked as though they had also moved out, because only the girl was still here. She was on the bed, dead and rotting in the heat. The sight of her swollen body hit me like a ton of bricks. I immediately emptied my stomach straight onto the floor; I couldn't help it. Then, the stench hit us and we fell back out into the corridor. There must have been hundreds of flies, crawling in and out of her mouth, and nostrils, swarming all over her like a hideous black shroud. Sticking out of her arm was the syringe that had killed her, the flies trying to burrow their way into the spot where the needle had penetrated. They were swarming furiously in their desire to get to their food.

The police, when they came, wanted to put all of us into jail. This is always their reaction when a dead body turns up, especially when it involves a foreigner. It has something to do with the foreign embassies that are inevitably involved in cases like this. Eventually we convinced them that none of us had anything to do with her death and they let us all go. It was some time before I could close my eyes without seeing Celine's body.

I moved on, and met a guy called Lal Babu, a notorious heroin manufacturer. Over the months I was with him, we got to know each other quite well. I would stay in his shop, and even help him out in the laboratory. It was frightening how simple it was to make heroin from raw opium. There is no rocket-science about it. The lab consisted of a suction pump, a few basins, a gas burner, and the bags of chemicals, virtually all of which were quite easy to get hold off. I used to go down to the chemical suppliers in his Toyota and pick them up. If I had been paying more attention and not been so stoned, I would probably be able to remember the formula. But then again, it's probably just as well that I don't!

After a while, the inevitable guilt set in and I felt really ashamed that I was back on the heroin, and got out as fast as I could, before they could catch up with me. I could see the look of shock on their faces as they took in my condition. I weighed about eight stone those days, far under my proper weight, and must have looked really ill.

★★★

I was smoking about a quarter ounce of the stuff a day, probably about the equivalent of 20 or 30 addicts' worth in Britain. Even though heroin was cheap there, I still had to find money. I found myself drifting back towards Islam again. The giving of alms to the needy is a traditional part of Islam. I must have looked very needy because soon people started giving me money, for food, in theory, but it mostly went up in smoke.

I started doing tarot readings for anyone who seemed interested, and fairly soon I was making a bomb out of the money people were giving me. I had a map listing all the streets where I'd already been and which ones I'd yet to hit. I worked my way through the cities of Peshawar, Islamabad, Rawalpindi, Karachi, to mention but a few. I could have done well for myself but I was just a skag head taking all the money they gave me straight to the local dealer. Whenever I was lucid enough to think about what I was doing, I felt guilty. But I needed the money. I was smoking piles of heroin by now and couldn't stop, so I knew I had to leave. I needed to get away from heroin.

Travelling by local buses, appearing as a Muslim, I was given free seats by the Muslim bus owners as I journeyed from city to city, passing through vast deserts. My body shook with pain as I moved further and further away from the heroin I had become so addicted to, but I gave myself no choice; I was going cold turkey, and as the days turned into weeks I began to feel better.

In Istanbul I managed to get a job teaching English. Unfortunately, though, as I was still coming off heroin, I was discovering the pleasures of drink. I was putting on weight, ferociously eating the bedazzling food that Turkey offers. Coming off heroin was unpleasant, but I had to do it. I knew that if I had stayed in Pakistan for that approaching summer

I would have been a dead man. I liked the irony of going through cold turkey during a freezing winter in Turkey.

By now going cold turkey was getting to become second nature. You have to take things as easy as you can arrange for yourself; keeping enough money for when your appetite kicks in again. You try to stay fairly close to your room, from which you are going to base your activities. I would set up a little routine every day, going out for a little stroll, to take in some fresh air, and see the sights. Coming off heroin, all your senses come rushing back—even the intensity of the colours you see. You smell the thousand and one odours from the food being cooked down the street, your hearing seems accentuated, your world seems fresh and renewed. But while all this is going on your body is moving slowly, like an old person. Your joints and muscles ache, and it is as much as you can do to get up to the toilet when you need to. Somehow you manage, though. I found it helpful to go out to a western –style pub where they played tapes of the current top hits. Here I could sit down with a large frothing lager and just hum along to the sounds of Duran Duran, and other groups that I had never even heard before, but which had a good rhythm.

The food I was shovelling down my throat was coming straight out the other end, but eventually this, too, faded away and was replaced by a steady stream of semi-solid waste. Breathing was something I had to work on. What had previously taken about three breaths now seemed to take 23. I felt I had done my lungs in, with all that 'dragon chasing'. Hopefully these would come back, but it would take a lot of patience and a lot of dedication. From deep inside my system a heavy stink of ammonia began to emanate, too. Sometimes it was a damp musty smell, like old urine, other times more like a heavy chemical or bonding agent, such as is actually used in the crude manufacturing process. Now and again it would even smell like vomit, even though I hadn't actually been sick. It began to dawn on me how heavy those chemicals which go into the drugs we users were willy nilly banging into our bodies really are. I could barely imagine the damage I had done to myself. Mentally I didn't feel too bad, although I wondered at times if I would ever be able to concentrate on anything for longer than a few seconds, let alone be able to take up some gainful employment. It hit me then—the extent of the devastation I had wreaked upon myself. I felt shocked. What kind of a freak was I that had tried to cripple myself like this? It was almost as bad as if I had tried to kill myself, which, in a roundabout way, I suppose I had. I began to understand that drug-taking is something that people do when are desperate to escape from their own internal pain, and from painful, even shattering experiences and memories. This goes for the drink, too.

As the days passed I found myself remembering people, friends, situations, and women that I had loved. Many of the memories were filled with regrets, of things that might have been, should have been, could have been. I felt as if I had failed everyone, and at times longed for the peace-bringing qualities of heroin to come and lay that cool hand on my brow.

What helped to hold me back was the almost certain knowledge that out there in Istanbul I would get either ripped off, or busted, if I tried to score again. Floating around Istanbul—as in any major cities, really—is a brown powdery substance that looks like heroin, tastes like heroin, even runs on the silver foil the same way as heroin when a flame is put underneath it. But it is not heroin, and when subjected to any proper chemical test will show up as negative. But Istanbul had always been well known in hippy circles as a place of great danger, especially from Turkish guys who would sell you some drugs and then get you busted. So, I just banned myself from having anything to do with drugs while there. The penalties for getting caught—especially with heroin on you—could be as severe as ten or 20 years inside. This was a great deterrent, and helped keep me away from that evil stuff.

Before I knew it three months had passed and I had been working in the English language schools for most of that time. But then a piece of bad news came to me—a friend of mine had just been arrested by the police, and had been tortured by them. The word was that he had confessed to being involved in something, and worse yet, had put my name into the bag to stave off the heavy beatings they were probably giving him. This was bad news. I decided not to hang around and see what happened. As well as that, my tarot deck had been stolen, which really pissed me off. After I bought a replacement deck, though of ordinary playing cards, I checked my money, but didn't even have enough for a train ticket out of there. Getting out by train was known to be tougher than by truck, if the police were looking for you. Apparently it was two different wanted lists that they ran, and the latter was a bit slower to get updated than the former. So, I made my way to the huge 'autostop' trucking centre on the west of the city, where there were literally thousand of trucks rolling into and out of Istanbul constantly.

So, having precious little money I headed for the big lorry park where I hoped to get a free lift to the Greek border. I was there for days. I couldn't convince any of the drivers to take me with them. I suspect that this was because I had come from Pakistan and they were afraid I was a smuggler. If I were to get caught with anything, they would get nicked as well. Most of them just shook their heads as I went round the tables and asked. Eventually one of them took pity on me and took me along with him. We rolled through the countryside, and over the border. The Greek official on the other side looked though my passport and, noticing all the Afghan and Pakistani stamps, asked me if I was smuggling any drugs. I laughed and told him no. Just then I looked down at my feet and noticed that I was wearing two odd shoes. I don't know how that happened.

Then we were through into Greece, and the countryside became very beautiful. Turkey is, too, but it is a more forbidding kind of beauty. Greece was warmer, almost summery, compared to the winter we had left behind on the Turkish side. The driver was a good man. He got me out of a tight spot back there and I thanked him for it. He asked me if I wanted to go with him up to Germany. I said no, I wanted to go down to have a look around Athens and see if I could get a job. I had heard that, in return for getting customers in, the cheap hotels would give you free accommodation, food and a commission. It sounded like easy work to me! He dropped me off on the road outside Thessaloniki, in northern Greece.

It was just outside Athens that I discovered another talent. There had been a party on the beach where I had enjoyed free wine, and I woke up the next morning, stretched out in the sand, hungry and hung-over. Staring at my hand while wondering what to do next, I remembered having read a book on palmistry a few years before, and suddenly it all came back to me. I got the idea to trace my hand on a piece of paper I got from the bag I had been using as a pillow, and drew in the planetary symbols where appropriate. Early morning swimmers were coming onto the beach, so I started asking if any of them would like their palm read. To my surprise, and delight, many of them did, and soon I had enough money to buy breakfast.

For the next few weeks I patrolled this beach looking for punters and made enough to get by and buy a proper deck again, as well as a few books on astrology, which I studied whenever I got the chance. I learned how to read a person's chart and by looking at the position of the planets, tell some aspect of what their future held for them. It was a skill I was glad to acquire, and it helped me get on quite well in life.

I made my way to Athens, where I met a guy called Benny, who looked quite like me. He had a plan to make us both some money. I would go down to the bank and pretend I was him and cash all his traveller's cheques. Then, he would report their 'theft' to the police, collect his refund and we would split the cash. Easy. To ensure that I wouldn't run off with all the cash Benny asked me for my passport. Fair enough, I thought, and handed it over.

I went in and cashed the cheques in, my heart beating fast. The girl on the other side of the screen didn't even look at the picture on the passport. I came out with the money and a big smile on my face and look around for Benny. He'd gone. I eventually tracked him down, and asked for my passport back. He told me that he thought I'd been nicked, and he threw my passport down the drain.

'Benny,' I said, meaning every word of it, 'I was playing this straight with you, but you have fucked up. I was going to give you half this money, and your passport back, but now I am just going to walk away, with the lot!' and with that I got up and walked away.

The next day I left, and headed to Amsterdam, where I hooked up with some friends I had met on the Indian hippy trail. The money was running through my fingers, and I had to do something, so I decided on an ambitious plan. Looking back, I obviously hadn't regained my senses. I figured I could buy a whole big pile of drugs, and smuggle them all back to Greece for the summer. There, I could hang out and sell them to the many tourists who would be on their way down for the remains of the summer. It all made perfect sense to me, and in my state of mind, there was nothing wrong with what I was doing. I may as well have been selling t-shirts, as far as I was concerned. So, from a pub in the centre of A'dam I bought 100 grams of pure white speed and 1,000 acid trips. This would keep me going all summer long, so that by the end of it I'd be set money-wise for the coming winter. Maybe I'd head back to India afterwards.

The trouble was, I ended up shooting this stuff rather than selling it. I think deep down I knew this would happen, and my addiction had been whispering in my ear, encouraging me to surround myself with all of these drugs. The speed was 'fuckin' blinding,' as they say. Shooting it would make you gasp. It would kick you right in the heart, then the lungs, then seconds later it would light up the inside of your head like a Christmas tree.

I bagged up all my gear in anticipation for my trip back south. It would be nice being able to really go through all the Greek islands, I thought to myself. As the Greek border drew inexorably closer, I started to get worried. What if Benny's passport came up on the alert lists on the Greek side? I had managed to get out of the country ok, but that had been immediately after pulling off the bank job. I got to the border almost too quickly.

'Bollox,' I thought, 'let's go through with it.'

To my amazement, I got through, but I started to get paranoid.

Was that someone following me? No, I was just getting a bit edgy. But imagine how I felt one morning, when I went back to where I had stashed all my gear and the whole lot had vanished. Someone had been stalking me, and had seen where I'd hidden all my stuff. By a strange coincidence, later that day I was arrested; Benny had reported me for stealing his travellers' cheques. It was just as well that the stuff had disappeared. If the Greek police had caught me with all of that I'd probably still be out there in jail. I didn't feel any bitterness towards Benny. He had to report the cheques stolen to get a reimbursement from American Express.

The next day I was in Koridalos Prison.

'Fuckin' beautiful,' I thought to myself, as I dragged on my last cigarette, its embers momentarily lit up the darkness of my cell.

I had to wait a fair while until my trial day. I had no money for a lawyer. Without one, I would get slaughtered when my trial did eventually come up. There was no legal aid. I wrote to my family, but all of a sudden no-one had any money, at least for a lawyer.

When my case went to court they gave me seven and a half years. Just before going in the lawyer said to me, 'Deny everything, then beg for mercy,' and disappeared. When the judge gave me that verdict, the pain was unbearable. I was so ashamed of how badly things had gone that, at first, I tried to pretend I had only got three years. It felt like I'd been raped.

I got transferred to a smaller prison, outside Corinth, near Argos, called Tyrinthos. It was here that I began an even more serious study of astrology. I managed to get hold of some astrology books inside; the kind that teach you how to 'do it yourself'. Again I was able to start drawing up peoples' charts, and look at who they were, using their horoscopes.

I also made up a deck of tarot cards from empty cigarette boxes. Drawing simple pictures on each of the 78 cards was easy, and with this deck I was able to do basic readings for my fellow inmates. Imagine my astonishment when some of the lads started giving me cartons of cigarettes for my work. Somehow the predictions that I made for them actually started coming true! I was happy just to be able to do it. I felt that I had utilized my time there as best I could and had done fairly well.

After serving my time, I was taken back to Athens in a van, and put on a plane back to England. Getting off again at Heathrow, on the tube back to Wood Green I yet again felt that I had just come full circle, but there were plenty more twists and turns before I was to settle down.

CHAPTER FIVE

CRACKING UP

When I got back to England after my spell in Greek prison, I decided to try to use my skills to make a better life for myself. I was clean again, having come off drugs while inside, and I wanted to put that life well and truly behind me. I was sick of wasting my life away, and I was determined to make something of myself.

A friend offered me the chance to do some tarot readings by his stall down at Brick Lane Market. Somehow it seemed to work, and I would regularly walk out with £30 or even £40. A small fortune!

'Get yourself down to Camden Lock, Tel,' he suggested to me one evening, over a can of lager.

I vaguely remembered Camden Lock Market from my squatting days.

'Just like that! Just turn up?' I said

'Sure, why not? My old man can make you up a pair of signs, Tel. Hand-painted signs that will make you look like the business.' This fella was a diamond.

A few days later, his dad presented me with a couple of rather lurid but certainly noticeable signs. The first said, 'It Pays to Know Your Future', and carried the design of the

Wheel of Fortune card. It showed a married couple on the top of the Wheel, toasting each other, then, on the downside, a man falling off. The second showed an owl and had the words, 'It is Wise to Know Your Future'. Armed with these two signs and a pack of tarot cards I set off to Camden Lock, in search of my own fortune.

I was given a small space in a garden area next to a disused houseboat that lay moored to the quay. Underneath a tree, I put up the portable card table and two fold-up chairs. Even when it started raining, there was a steady flow of people turning up for readings. By the time my first day was done, I felt as though I had been given quite a baptism, and was amazed that I had earned £60! After paying the rent I was left with £50. Enough to buy a large umbrella; the kind they use to go fishing with.

Day after day I would sit under this umbrella, in all weathers. I was earning enough to live on. I was able to come off the dole and get enough together to put down a deposit on a small place of my own in Crouch End, north London, a bright, cheerful place which overlooked a wooded area from the back.

I also had a stall at Covent Garden Market going, and in this time I was starting to develop a reputation as one of London's top readers, especially since I offered my clients the opportunity to have their astrological charts drawn up, using the traditional methods of hand drawing and personalised interpretation. I had many budding, would-be students of tarot and astrology coming to me, and within a short space of time this steady inflow became a deluge.

It was there I first met Evelyne, who was to become my wife. She was with a friend and jumped back when I offered to read the cards for her. Something must have clicked though, because a few days later she came to my stall in Camden Lock and asked me to read her cards. I predicted a new romance on the horizon for her, but knew that to really get a look at what was in store for her, I would have to draw up her astrological chart. This would show her inner strengths and hidden potential.

Over the eight years I was at the markets, it grew into the London Tarot Training Centre. I loved being able to put what I had learned to good use and I found my own knowledge deepening each day. With Evelyne, we delivered courses to classes that were ever-expanding, and things were really starting to take off. I was becoming a huge success.

It was round about this time that I started to get calls from the *Big Breakfast* programme, asking me to come down to their studio. I had an interview with Chris Evans the host, and got to meet Gabby Roslyn. On one occasion I got to read the soles of Zoe Ball's feet, in an act of on-the-spot channelling. I also got to interact with Zig and Zag, which was great fun. Most of it was great fun actually, but I never trivialised the tarot or made light of it.

I continued to do readings for some famous people; singers, musicians and even members of the House of Lords! Evelyne was there the whole way through, doing all the admin and general back-up. She helped out with the teaching too.

Then, out of the blue, I was contacted by a new television channel called LiveTV, a cable channel operating out of Canary Wharf. I was given an audition, in which we filmed a make believe version of a future show. I did a sample reading and was interviewed by a pretty co-presenter.

'Terry, how did you get into all of this?' she asked.

I replied that I had woken up on a beach in Greece one day and basically started doing it so that I could get enough money to buy something to eat.

They started cracking up, because they had been expecting some tall tale about healing people from the crib, which they had already heard too many times.

'Terry, what happens when you see something really, really bad in someone's cards?' she asked me then.

'I lie,' I answered, cracking everybody up again.

They found my honesty a refreshing change to the style of many of the other readers they had interviewed, so they offered me the job. I couldn't believe it.

It took off from there. I had to do three live shows a week, and was also commissioned to do outdoor events, such as at Glastonbury, where I had to cast a spell live on air.

My reputation was increasing, and I was asked to write a series of books on tarot and mythology, folklore and magic spells for a number of British and American publishers, including, much to my delight, a *Lord of the Rings* tarot deck.

Eventually, the *Daily Mirror* was carrying full-page adverts of my show, with the statement: 'Who knows the future? Terry Tarot!' and a picture of Princess Diana on a balcony. In a previous show, I had been asked to do an absent reading for her. This is when as a reader you do a reading as if the person is there, when they are not. I proclaimed that Diana's marriage would soon be over, and that she would become pregnant with a non-white child. The presenter had looked at me shocked—what the hell was I coming out with?

'Terry, I suppose you are saying she will get back with the Palace and harmony will prevail?' she nervously offered.

But I was having none of it.

'No,' I answered. 'There will be a breach with the Palace.'

I also suggested that there would be an attempt on her life. Of course, nobody knows if that is true or not.

***

Things were really looking up, but at the same time I was feeling under immense pressure due to my many commitments. As well as the stall, I had the TV show, several publishing deadlines, the tarot school, and then a tarot phone line. It was too much to handle at once—too much reality— and it was only a matter of time before I started to take drugs again as a means of escape. I had been off them for years at this stage, but it was just too easy to go back to the comfort of some speed, to lift me out of the chaos that was my new life, and to give me the energy to meet my many demands. It worked, in that I lost touch with reality, but it began the downward spiral that destroyed all that I had.

When Evelyne announced she was pregnant I knew it was time to sell up the little flat and move us into a proper house, which by now I could afford. It also meant that she was unable to assist me as much as she used to and so I sank deeper and deeper into my habit in an attempt to deal with the pressure.

My daughter was born in the hot summer of 1996, up at North Middlesex hospital. I was there all the time with Evelyne, looking after her, giving her water, chasing after the nurses whenever they disappeared. When the baby was delivered, I cut the gristly cord, with a pair of snippers the doctor placed in my hand. As I cut, I had a sudden image of snipping a big fruit from a tree. My daughter arrived with her own name. We had no idea what to call her before she was born, but when she arrived her name appeared in great red letters on the wall of the delivery suite: Claudia. Neither my wife nor I had any prior idea what to call her when she came along, but it just seemed right when I saw it.

The pressure was building up. I now had deadlines to fulfil, a timetable to adhere to, and I wasn't handling it at all well. My drug consumption was starting to go through the roof, and I started to live a double life. In an attempt to escape once more from reality, I created an alternative one in which I was above all moral questioning, and could act as I pleased. My thinking was addled, and my health went out the window. I dropped from 15 to 8 stone, but in my state, I thought I looked great, while everybody around me was wondering what the hell was going on.

Each day I would receive dozens of phone calls, and Evelyne was unable to cope with a new baby and work full time. We brought in a nanny and a secretary. In the front room of our new house was a huge marble fireplace, and a great chandelier, just like the ones I used to look at in shop windows when I was squatting, hung overhead. A white Mercedes stood outside the front door. But around the corner were three mistresses, each one unaware of the others. They started out as students in the Tarot school. I fathered a child, a boy, with one of them, a New Zealander who went back home when she found out she was pregnant.

I started living a double life, like a Jekyll and Hyde type, doing my show, running my businesses and rearing a family by day, then heading out to London's dark and seedy underbelly at night. After my hectic day I would shoot up some speed and go out looking for female company. I wasn't always after sex; it was never that simple. I wanted to escape, to become a part of another world not connected to the one I had fallen into, of deadlines and pressures and having to look after people. I wanted to opt out of it all because it was becoming too much, and by living this double life I felt I was managing to do just that.

I was of course systematically destroying all that I had worked hard to obtain, and hurting the ones closest to me. I think I knew that deep down, but my addiction was urging me on, as if telling me to leave all of that behind and concentrate on getting more drugs into myself. I would share a smoke with some of the girls I picked up, and became a familiar and welcome face around King's Cross.

I soon became known by most of the girls on the streets, and I became very useful to them, which also suited me when my own money started running out and I could no longer afford to share my own supply. I'd give them lifts to different areas, for which they would usually reward me with something to smoke. Sometimes they would ask me to watch their backs. I was happy to do whatever I was asked, because once more I felt like I had been let into their secret world. I just switched off, and let the world sail by. This is what happens with drug addicts. It can take years for them to rise to the surface again; sometimes they never do.

All I can say is that if I had been in my right mind I would not have acted as I did. I was becoming delusional, and really thought there was no problem with what I was doing to others. I became quite blatant with my flings and, understandably, it really got to Evelyne. I just couldn't help myself.

I started to hallucinate. I was seeing voodoo spirits everywhere. I thought they had come to live in my house. I could hear them moving around upstairs, even whispering to each other. I kept finding back windows open, and finding my wife hiding in empty rooms, from where I could hear her having discussions with people I couldn't see. It reminded me of the scene in Psycho where you overhear Norman Bates talking with what you at first assume is his mother in the room upstairs. I was really losing it, and it was all down to the huge amount of speed I had started to take. But at the time I thought I was handling everything really well. I know now that the extent of the damage which drug taking can bring about, in everyone's life, is like a tornado sweeping away everything in its path. The short term high is cancelled out a thousand times by the massive devastation caused to mind, body and spirit.

To top it all, I had also somehow been invited to become a Freemason. Getting in isn't easy. You have to know just the right people and these people must be willing to propose and second you for membership. Evelyne had worked around the corner from the Freemason's Hall and introduced me to some fellas, who eventually showed me around their lodge rooms. I was amazed by the astrological symbolism all around. It took me over a year to get nominated. I wasn't supposed to know anything about the initiation ceremony, but my mind was boggling at all the jokes about goats and donkeys that seemed to follow me around.

I arrived wearing the plain black suit that is the 'uniform' of Freemasons the world over. I was divested of metal and blindfolded. Then, my jacket was removed, and my shirt opened up to expose my heart. My right heel was slipshod, and a cord was placed around my neck. Feeling like the Hanged Man card in the tarot, I was led, completely blind, into the Lodge Room, and initiated into Abercorn Lodge Number 1549. My initiation was a beautiful ceremony. It meant something on a deep level to me.

I am not supposed to say too much about it, it was part of the oath I took not to. Much of Freemasonry involved extensive learning of ritual and the Bible. A great deal of mystery surrounds the Freemasons in the public mind, and this is compounded by the strange and esoteric symbolism that is to be found within their rituals. I always enjoyed the sense of belonging, especially to something with such a mystique. I met a wonderful variety of people while a member of the Freemasons, from many levels of society, and experienced a sense of equality and acceptance that is difficult to find anywhere else.

At the end of each lodge meeting was the banquet. There would be speeches, a toasting to the Queen, and a chance to meet other fellows 'on the square'. I went along to the research lodge of Quator Coronati, and used to sit next to a very scholarly Freemason and author. As I had by now, written some half a dozen books on the tarot, for both British and American publishers, the person in charge of the seating probably thought I'd be a good conversational companion for him.

Another interesting man I met around this time was a titled man, now Grand Master of the Order. After commissioning me to draw up his astrological chart, Evelyne, Claudia and I were invited up to his castle for his 50th birthday bash. It was 2 April, 1997.

The party took place over a full weekend. We were taken clay pigeon shooting, and driven around the extensive grounds in horse-drawn carriages. In the evenings we were treated to the most lavish food and drink imaginable, all served impeccably by the staff in a massive banqueting hall. In the drawing room was the most magnificent fireplace with carvings of goddesses along the sides. An African team of drummers were brought in, and I took a turn on the voodoo drums.

The welcome he gave us was unparalleled. But by then I was completely out of touch with what was right and what was wrong behaviour, and, like a clown, I had brought some speed along with me to his party. I was playing pool with an Iranian princess and made the mistake of offering her some.

'What is it?' she asked me.

'Coke,' I said, lying, too embarrassed to be thought of as offering anything so proletarian as 'speed'.

But she backed off. Oh dear, I thought, that's blown that.

The next thing I knew, the host was coming for me, his face a mask of outrage.

'Get the fuck out!' he was beside himself with rage.

I knew I had blown it.

***

My weekend hit rock bottom when the police called to my house telling me I had been accused of rape. I couldn't believe it. I had done some bad things in my life, and would do more in later years, but there was no way I was a rapist. I'd had a fling with a woman who came to me to have her chart drawn up. We saw each other for a few weeks, but she wasn't happy when things didn't work out and I decided to stop seeing her. That was it. I was arrested and charged.

I began to feel like Frodo going up the side of Mount Doom with the weight around his neck getting heavier and heavier. It felt as though everything I had accomplished— my business, my house, marriage, my daughter coming along—was all going to be stripped from me and I was going to be branded as a sex offender. I had flashbacks of what it must have been like for all those women who had been accused of witchcraft, to have been dragged away from their homes and families and burnt alive, to the great delight of all the people in their village who they thought they could trust. Similarly, in my case, a lot of the people I had thought of as friends were rubbing their hands together in delight at the prospect of me getting weighed off, especially on a crime like rape. I certainly came to know what it was like to be accused of something you hadn't done. To add to my trouble, a police informant leaked the story of my arrest to one of the tabloids.

My so-called brothers in the Lodge were only too quick to throw me out as soon as this case started. They were shitting themselves in case they got any of the fallout;

Negative publicity which you used to hear more of, when it came to the subject of corruption and freemasons. After this case I fucked off my stupid apron and sash. It was all a load of bollox, I realised. These were not my 'brothers'.

My solicitor found out that the woman concerned had used a spermicidal cream immediately prior to coming around to my house for sex. An application was made for the woman's psychiatric reports to be made available to the court, which the judge granted. Apparently this woman had a history of pulling this stunt in the UK and abroad. She withdrew the case, but I still had to go to court to hear this, and was so far gone on speed that I didn't really know what was happening, and as I walked out of that austere old building, I felt like there was no turning back. I was finished.

I was on a downward spiral now. The more depressed I became about my situation, the more I hit the speed. Evelyne divorced me and took Claudia with her. I lost my job with LiveTV. I became very paranoid, thinking that people were following me. In hindsight, they might well have been. Eventually I thought I was seeing spaceships. I kept thinking I was in a circle, with attendant deities and spirits ministering to me. Outside the house I could see commandos hidden in bushes, radioing each other to keep themselves posted on my movements.

'He's in the bog now, over,' one of them said.

'Is it a number one or number two, over,' came back the reply.

I seemed to be locked into some program from which I couldn't easily withdraw. I had my lines assigned to me, my role was pre-ordained. Everyone I knew assumed some role of significance in this unfolding drama.

There were people 'out there' trying to capture me, so one day, completely out of touch with all reality, I got into my car and drove off. Somehow, I would be guided to where I was 'supposed' to be. I remember seeing the red dragon on the way into Wales. At the time I thought it was a good omen. Red is my lucky colour.

I was as high as a kite walking around the Butetown area of Cardiff. On the side of the quay was a ship, and I tried to get into it, thinking that it was going to transport me to some mythical island where I would meet dear friends from long ago. I wept with grief as I realised I was coming down again. On my way back to the car I found two burly Welsh policemen waiting for me.

'Is this your car, sir?' one of them asked me.

When they searched the car they found a big bag of speed, and some syringes. At Butetown police station, they brought in a doctor to examine me. He tut-tutted as he looked up and down the long lines of pin-pricks all along my arms and legs.

'You are hallucinating,' he said, and then went away.

Denied bail, I was off to Cardiff nick.

It took me quite a while to come down and get my head together, but prison is a great place to do just that.

Some of the lads recognised me from my spot on the telly, and we would have a get-together in my cell where I would do readings using an ordinary pack of cards. It seemed to work, too. For some reason, coming down off speed seemed to enhance my psychic abilities. I found that I could really see into their lives. As I talked about their situations, I could actually see their family members, and describe them in incredible detail. I wish I could do it at will, but the gift is not always ours to use as we wish. It is only ever lent to us for a certain time or a certain purpose. When I eventually got to Cardiff Crown Court, some four months later, I was found guilty of possession, but not intent to supply, and they let me go.

In the meantime, Evelyne had sold the house while I was inside. I wanted to go somewhere to get my head back together. Even though we were now divorced, Evelyne decided to come with me when I left for Ireland. I wanted to try and make things right with her. We bought a cottage together, overlooking Galway Bay from the top of Sky Road in Clifden. The view was tremendous, but it didn't help. Evelyne and I didn't get along any better.

I tried doing some writing, and got another book published, my second on the subject of The Lord of the Rings. The frustration at not being able to fix the problems Evelyne and I were having got too much for me. One day I just got back behind the driving wheel and headed off down the road. I was beyond help. When Evelyne contacted me some time later, it was to tell me that she had sold the house. We split the money. My portion of it went to the gods of heroin and crack.

***

I returned to London and the needle. I would spend hours trying to get that old high back, opening up dozens of mining operations along my arms and legs trying to find a connection. Very often, I would find a vein, but the blood would clot inside the syringe before I could shoot. I'd end up with scores of pin-pricks all along my arms and legs. Sometimes the puncture wounds would swell if I missed the vein and started pushing down on the plunger before I'd really got inside.

I had brief spells where I tried to get back on track and do something with my life, but they were short-lived. I studied hypnotherapy at the London College of Clinical Hypnotherapy and managed to get a Distinction grade, and even practised for a short time, but soon enough I was lured back to my habit.

When the money from the sale of the cottage in Ireland came through, the first thing I did was go out and buy a BMW. I started kerb crawling again, now out of extreme loneliness and a desire to meet 'interesting' women. It was a real thrill to set off into the mysterious night and go on the prowl, like I was some sort of wild or mythological beast. I met *Lucy* the day after Friday the 13th, on the night of the full moon. She was a young woman in her 20s with elfin features, who was also looking for someone to be close to. It was a case of fatal attraction.

The night before I met her for the first time, I cast a spell that would lead me to my one true karmic love. So, for a long time I was convinced that she was this love. People who knew me thought I'd lost my mind; teaming up with a girl I had met at King's Cross who also enjoyed doing Class A drugs. It saddened me that she also liked to go out and pick up other men. I was so disappointed when I realised that nothing I could say or do would ever change her. She actually loved the life style. Anonymous sex is a real turn on for a lot of people, and when you smoke crack for as long as *Lucy* had, your mind stops functioning properly. Crack cocaine quickly gets its claws into you, rendering normal thinking obsolete. You lose touch with reality, and slide into a fantasy realm of wishful thinking, all the time needing more and more of the drug to stay there. It's like living in an apartment where the rent doubles every week. Crack is an aphrodisiac. This is one reason so many addicts relapse and go back to it. They think that the relationships they form with people who are also on that stuff are deeper and more meaningful. The sex is usually infinitely superior, which for the female addicts is usually a big deal. Each moment of a sexual encounter whilst on crack is a thousand times more colourful, more intense, more pleasurable than any sex ever experienced whilst not under the influence.

Bit by bit, my money got wasted away and I ended up losing my small flat. *Lucy* and I just moved around, but I don't know where. In the world of crack cocaine, everything became a grey area. Eventually my money ran out, so we started borrowing off my dad. I only had sex with *Lucy* once, and apart from that single blip on the screen, nothing sexual ever took place between us.

Then *Lucy* started bringing punters back to wherever we were crashing. She would pop out only for a few minutes, and return with someone she had just met, taking him by the hand into the front room. I didn't care. When you are in desperate need, when you are an addict, all that matters is getting another fucking hit. So as soon as we had the money, we would be out the door again to our friendly local dealer.

We went at this hectic pace for months. I was on a methadone script too. Sometimes, when there was no money, even for brown, it was all we had. I'd get up early in the morning and head down to the local chemist in Wood Green to collect my fix. There were always dozens of other junkies there too, queuing up from nine on the dot. Sometimes I would sell my script for a tenner. With that tenner I could get an actual hit of brown, and the methadone would go to support somebody else's habit. Thus the addiction circle would slowly but inexorably spread its tentacles out into society. After all, it was methadone that got me started.

When my car was stolen by a fellow junkie, I loaded up a small canvas bag with three big blades. I had been smoking crack earlier that day, but the short-lived effects had long since worn-off, leaving me in a low, that sense of extreme anger and depression that all-too inevitably accompanies the high. I picked up a bottle of wine from an off-licence, and knocked this back as I made my way through the streets to his door. I rang the bell, and he opened, looking a bit confused at first. He wasn't sure how much I knew. I went in to his front room, and opened the bag, showing him the blades. The next thing I knew I was on the street, walking down Tottenham High Road. A police van pulled up alongside me and half a dozen policemen jumped out and knocked me to the ground.

One of them shouted out, 'This one's injured too!' and handcuffed my hands behind my back. The last thing I remember before I passed out, was the sound of the siren and seeing the flashing light from the top of the van coming through the windows.

It was just beginning to rain when I came to. I was on a medical table. A doctor and a couple of nurses were cutting my clothes off. A policeman put them into an evidence bag along with my shoes. Then they administered a painkiller and I started to get groggy. When I woke, I was handcuffed to a hospital bed with two policemen standing at the end, looking at me.

My mind was a complete blank.

'What happened?' I asked one of them, genuinely unable to remember.

'If you are going to be ok, I can unlock you and you can relax yourself,' he said.

I assured him that I wasn't going to be any trouble. He reached over to unlock the handcuffs so I could sit up.

Rubbing my hands where the cuffs had been biting into them, I tried to work out what had happened. I could remember going into my 'mate's' front room, but after that … nothing. It turned out that I had cut his hand off. They were still trying to sew it back on in another hospital.

I was charged with GBH; grievous bodily harm, and given bail from the court. I walked out of the courtroom carrying all my possessions in a plastic bag. I had 20 stitches where one blade had, during the fighting, bounced back onto my head. The police had very kindly returned my crack pipe to me. Obviously it wouldn't be needed for evidence like my clothes.

My first thought was to get my methadone. As I held the little bottle up to my mouth, the sunlight struck it, illuminating the bright green liquid just before the sweetness came to life in my mouth. Then it passed down my throat to my belly, where it brought warmth and relaxation. My next objective was to get a tenner together for some brown heroin. However nice a dash of methadone might be, there's nothing like the real thing to get you truly back on your feet.

When I start to cluck, the first things that go are my legs. They collapse under me, leaving me crippled and helpless. But with the methadone kicking in I could use my legs again. I was striding as I made my way over to the derelict house by Duckett's Common. It was a half-burned out hovel that served as a squat and general shooting gallery. I walked through into the long corridor that ran the length of the house to the back. There the bonzos and drongos that I associated with would be waiting for someone with gear to walk in. If they expected me to sort them out, though, they were in for a surprise. I had just about enough to sort myself out.

I ended up hanging around with shoplifters and petty criminals to help finance my next score, and saw the worst of society, the seedy underbelly of London. King's Cross was wild in those days. There were dozens, maybe hundreds, of crack dens, dotted all over the place. These places made massive amounts of money, every night; even the smallest of them would make thousands of pounds. The girls would start coming to from the previous night's revels about sunset. No money, no crack, it was time to find a few punters. The girls turned tricks in the side streets, in the backs of cars, anywhere. If they had enough crack to keep them going, they wouldn't sleep for days at a time. They would do dozens of punters, one after the other, only stopping to pull into the crack house for a blast of crack or a shot of heroin.

This was the part of London that never slept. Hundreds of cars containing punters hovered about the area all night long, ferrying a fresh supply of males from all over London. The crack dens were almost all run by Jamaicans. They would sit inside the door with the crack and heroin wrapped up in tiny little plastic packets inside their mouths. If the police steamed in they could swallow the evidence.

With a tempting mix of drugs, money and lawlessness it was hardly surprising that robberies, or attempted robberies, were common. These were hard men and they fought fire with fire. I heard stories of dealers losing ears to the thieves' blades rather than hand over their gear. It wasn't just the money; a man's honour and prestige were at stake. The loss of an ear was a small price to pay for being known as a hard man to do business with.

The working girls set up a lot of the robberies. They knew who was carrying the stuff as they made up the majority of the business in the dens. The girls would strike up an alliance with professional or wannabe robbers, and guide them in to a particular place or person. Punters were, of course, another favourite target for a con. The girl would pick up a fella on the main road and then direct him to a little back alley, making out she was too paranoid to go any further. Then, one or two of her male friends would leap on the guy and beat him senseless; take everything he had and drive off in his car, taking the girl with them.

Where were the police in all this? I guess they had bigger fish to catch. The same girls who set up the punters were often recruited by the dealers to do a run abroad. They would know when the big shipments were coming in. So the police left them alone in return for any information they had.

Millie was really good at pulling one of the oldest scams in whoredom. She would wait out on the street for a likely punter. When he propositioned her she would point to a door and tell him a big long story about how she needed £100 deposit, completely refundable of course, before she could let him into the whorehouse. I used to play the role of the satisfied customer and pretend to be leaving the place. The guys would take me to one side and ask me about this deposit business, and I would tell them it was perfectly normal. Millie and I would split the takings and leave these sad plonkers banging on some stranger's door

'Well, where's the fucking girls, then?' I heard one irate punter shout, as the woman inside threatened to call the police.

But there was no honour amongst thieves. Back at the crack house Millie would always try to con me out of my half of the money or the gear. She would give me some romantic bullshit about how she had been waiting for me for so long, or she would try steal my car keys off me while we were smoking. When you hit on a big stone, the high can be so intense you completely lose awareness of what is happening right around you, and I had no idea I had signed my life away.

CHAPTER SIX

BARBADOS

It was one of our local dealers who suggested I do a run to the West Indies.

'A sweet little run, Tel,' he said. 'Just got back from the West Indies myself. A doddle.'

I was offered £5,000 for the trip, plus spending money. As things stood at that point, there was no other way I was going to make it. I really think this was the lowest point I reached in my entire life.

I felt I didn't really have a choice. I was fed up sitting around while *Lucy* went out and dragged guys in off the street, bonked them on our bed, and then smoked up the proceeds with me. She was a good girl, in some ways, and had no problem in sharing with me, but I had spent about £60,000 in the space of about four or five months.

I had a guy offer me £1,000 to run his ex-wife over in a car right in front of her children. I didn't trust him, though, for obvious reasons. Right after the 'hit' I was to drive the car to a car crusher place, where all the evidence would be made to disappear. Yeah, I thought, I'd probably be disappearing along with it. For the sake of a grand, I could see him putting me into the fucking crusher along with the motor. It's amazing what shit some people will pull if they think they can get a broken-down old junkie to do some of their dirty work for them. I began meeting other junkies who would 'take punishment' such as cigarette burns all over their balls, for money, and was asked if I wanted to join them in this business. That seemed really close to the edge. What would happen, I wondered, if they tied you up and then wanted to kill you? Apparently most of the punters in this category were sadistic women who wanted to torture men.

I also met junkies who started blazes in exchange for piss-take amounts of money; normally just a couple of smokes, even if people died in those fires, which was, from what I could make out, often the plan. It was all heading up to something grim. I felt trapped inside a Frank Miller Sin City storyline which wasn't going to have a very happy ending. I didn't want to end up being tortured so that I could earn the money for my next fix. The prospect of doing a run to somewhere—I was told Guyana—seemed a soft option.

I agreed to do the trip, and the dealer, Dean, gave me £100 worth of gear on tick. I didn't want to do this; I had to. My drug addled reasoning was that if everything worked out and I got through, I would be £5,000 better off. If it didn't, and I got busted, then at least I'd have a chance to get off the gear and maybe start afresh. Things could not go on as they had been. Something had to change, or one day I'd be found dead in a shop doorway.

Next thing I knew, Dean wanted my passport. 'Just so we can get you a ticket for the trip, Tel. You know, if you had a girl you could bring with ya it would be great. Know anyone?'

I told him I didn't. So, the dealer made off with my passport, and for the next day I heard nothing. Just when I started to think it was all a wind-up, a scam to get my passport so someone could open up a bank account in my name for some fraudulent purpose, he was back. There was a young woman called Mons with him. She was short and attractive, and took me by the hand as she came in through the door. She was very flirtatious, with a bandana in her beautiful black hair and a sweet woman's body underneath her skirt and blouse.

'We'll be here Monday at 6am to pick you up,' she said. 'Dean's going to take you out to get some new clothes and stuff first.' Dean sorted me out with gear on tick too.

In addition, all my expenses would be paid for, they said, and I would get £500 spending money to last me for my week-long stay. The first thing to cross my mind was that I was going to lose my methadone script as a result. Shit. That script was hard to get. It wasn't much but it was all I had.

'Bollox!' said another part of my mind. 'If you get back you can buy what you want. And if you don't, then you won't be needing it anyway.' It made perfect sense to me back then.

On the Monday morning, at 6am, they came knocking at my door. Not gentle knocking, but a hard, 'Come on you old bastard, let's be having you,' kind of knock. I jumped up and opened the front door. Mons was there with a suitcase in one hand. She walked straight into the back room where *Lucy* and I were staying. Mons opened the suitcase, and inside were piles of underwear, vests, shirts, trousers, and shoes.

'Some of these things are for you, the rest is for you to hand over to the man that will come and see you. You are to stay at the Hotel Ocean Spray when you get there. Get a cab from the airport straight there, and pay for the whole week in advance, ok?'

It seemed fair enough to me, although I noted that the detail about all my expenses being paid had already been changed.

I slipped out of my old clothes and into the touristy ones she showed me. The trainers were a size or two too big. But it didn't matter. They were to last for as long as the trip took. After that I'd be able to get my own clothes, wouldn't I? I looked down at the cheap trainers they had bought me. They looked ridiculous, like Charlie Chaplin shoes.

Lucy gave me a cuddle, throwing her arms around me. Just then I regretted being such a drug addict, and not being able to have a normal life. Now, it felt like it was all over. Game over. Try again.

Like a lamb to the slaughter, I went outside, dragging the suitcase with me. The shoes felt like two boats on the end of my legs. I put the case in the back of a very smart BMW. Inside was an elderly, distinguished-looking man. I had to do a double-take. Fuck. The guy looked exactly like Trevor MacDonald. Mons got in, and handed my passport back, along with a travel agent's envelope with a pair of tickets inside. The accompanying letter made reference to two tickets that had been purchased.

'Oh, so I am going with someone, after all?' I asked. At that she got nervous.

'Er, no. That's a mistake. No, you're going alone,' she said, taking the letter back briefly to check it. Then she gave it back to me, looking sideways to the Trevor MacDonald clone.

I looked at the destination: BARBADOS. That song from the 70s came ringing back into my mind: 'Hey, we're going to Barbados, flying with Coconut Airways.' We pulled out onto the street and headed towards the airport. I was numbed to everything, so I didn't feel nervous, excited or scared. I was just letting this happen to me.

The distance flew by, and we drew up to the entrance to Gatwick Airport. Mons told me to go inside and get a photo of myself from one of the machines, and then to come back.

She handed me the suitcase, and told me to check it in. Then she would let me have the spending money. I got the photo done. This was so her man at the other end would know my face. Mons said she was going to fax it through to him.

Going into the hubbub of Gatwick terminal was a nightmare. I was still coming down off the stuff *Lucy* and I had smoked up the night before. But there was no going back now. I checked the suitcase in, and then tried to find the car. I couldn't. Where had she gone? I started to panic. I went back into the building to see if I could find her. Just as panic threatened to overwhelm me, I saw her cheeky little face come waltzing along.

She indicated that I was to follow her at a discreet distance. Alright, now we were getting places! This was exciting now, like we were kids at school playing secret agents. We seemed to walk a loop around the airport, up the stairs and down again. Then out the door to the car, which was exactly where it had been when I left it earlier. When you have been smoking crack, it can make you very disorientated. I felt relieved to be back in the back of the car. She handed me an envelope. Inside was £500.

'Your best bet is to change it into dollars,' she said. 'Out there people will accept Sterling, but dollars are easier to change. It's two local dollars to one US.'

I took the envelope and nodded dumbly.

'And be careful who you talk to. The locals out there are very nosey, and if you talk too much they might suss. Don't tell them anything about bringing anything back.'

With that, I got out of the car and, with the money in my pocket, walked to the bureau de change to change the money into US dollars, as she had suggested.

★★★

Going through onto the plane was the worst bit. Standing there, in this ultra-clean and smart uniform, was some customs robot. He gave each person who passed by to get onto the plane a sticker on the cover of their passport. You either got a red one or a green one.

'How long are you going for?' he asked me.

'A week,' I said, and at that he stuck a green one on the front of mine.

Jesus, I thought, what does that mean? Maybe green meant that I was 'alright' and could be allowed to go through. After all, green was for 'go' wasn't it? A red one would have been a lot worse, because that meant 'stop' didn't it?

On the plane I asked for a drink, indicating that I had money to pay for it. But no-one ever brought me a drink. After a while I began to feel the cramps of heroin withdrawal creeping in, and felt the overwhelming need to stretch out on the floor. One of the hostesses came up to me and asked me what was wrong. I said that I was alright, that I just wanted to stretch out my back as I found the long flight taxing. The hostess didn't look too convinced at that, but eventually she went away.

The flight was long and boring. I tried to interest myself in the free flight magazines and look at the films that were on. Eventually, the huge blue sheet of water underneath the plane turned into land, and outside through the window I could see palm trees rushing up to greet us as we came into land. Then the palm trees were whizzing past at a terrific speed, and we were taxi-ing to a stop. Before we all got off the plane, two hostesses waltzed along the aisles spraying us with some kind of bug spray. I didn't like the look of it. It was like something from a futuristic film where they do an experiment on people. I wondered if I was going to start having breathing problems. Isn't it amazing how a crack smoker can smoke 100 grand's worth of charlie and heroin, and not worry about how it might affect him, but the thought of inhaling some insecticide scares the crap out of him?

I got off the plane, and immediately the warmth of the day hit me. On the tarmac were rolling jeeps containing big burly members of the Royal Barbadian Police Force. Were they looking at me? Had they been warned I was coming? I was grateful for the shade when I got to the terminal building, which was more of a warehouse than a terminal really. My legs were beginning to pack up underneath me. They were always the first thing to go wrong when I started to cluck. They just seemed to shrink, and become ultra-stiff. Then, bit by bit, the rest of my body tightened. In the meantime, my bowels would open up, and I would become incontinent, and that begins to get smelly and nasty. It is a very anti-social thing to withdraw from heroin.

The official at passport control asked where I would be staying.

'The Ocean Spray,' I told her. Was it my imagination or did she grimace when I said that? But she just stamped my passport, and I was through. Coming out of the terminal building was like walking from an air-conditioned refrigerator back into an oven. Outside there were people waiting for family or friends, and I made my way over to the taxi rank.

'Taxi?' I asked the first driver I came to.

He nodded, and asked me where I wanted to go.

'How much to the Ocean Spray Hotel?' I asked.

'$20 dollars,' he answered, adding 'US' after a moment.

Although not a flea pit, the Ocean Spray hotel was quite far out from anything going on in the more built-up areas of Barbados. This was probably why the smugglers liked to use it. It was a good walk to the nearest rum shop and the small supermarket that stood next to it outside Oistins, a small fishing town in the southern part of the island.

The taxi pulled up, and deposited me outside the reception area. I booked into my room for a week. I was shown to a ground level room accessible from the gardens in the front with a great view of the sea. I could plainly hear the sound of the surf washing over the beach outside. At first it was very relaxing, but as the day wore on it began to get frustrating. The more my cold turkey kicked in, the more annoying the bloody sound of the surf became; wish, wash, whoosh. A couple of times I found myself at the window ready to shout at it to fucking well shut up, before it dawned on me that I was going off my nut.

I bunged the suitcase to the side of the table. I didn't even bother unpacking. Here I was in a beautiful place, a paradise island, but I was really in my own personal hell. I couldn't wait to lose myself, to escape reality again, even though I was in the sort of place people dream of escaping to. I just wanted to get out of it, and fuck the consequences. The consequences were shit to me anyway, whichever way I looked at it. I had an underlying feeling that I had run out of my nine lives and that my Judgement Day was coming, and that right soon, as the saying went. I had this overwhelming feeling that all of the horrible things I had done in my life were now finally being weighed in some great scales and my judgement was being prepared. Time and time again I had slipped through the nets and gotten away with all kinds of wrongdoings, but I felt that though the wheels of karmic justice ground slowly, they did ground exceeding small too, and my time was approaching when I would have to pay for all my sins.

My response to this wasn't to repent though; it was to go out and destroy my mind and body. After all, I was worth nothing anymore. I went out and made my way up to the rum shop I had spotted on the taxi ride in. I spotted a couple of likely-looking lads sitting outside, cheekily grinning as I came along, showing the perfection of their pearly white teeth. One of them had a red bandana on. I asked him if he wanted a beer. The bar was a really simple affair, with an electric refrigerator right under the counter where the beer was kept; only one brand, the local brand, Banks.

The young lad I had sequestered introduced himself as Kehn. We knocked back the beers and I asked him if there was anything to smoke.

'Only the green stuff man.'

'Balls to that,' I said. 'Where's the white stuff? I want the real thing!'

At first he was reluctant to get me linked with any of the local crack, but after a few seconds pressurising he relented, and took me along several long, quiet side streets, lined with quaint bungalows. Each looked as though it had been individually built, and to no one specific plan; almost as if each house had just simply grown there, on its own patch.

He took me to a small house. We entered a room he called the galley. There was a table with what looked like voodoo markings on it; a stencilled pattern of curves and spirals. There were a few seats dotted around, and rough planks formed the floor. His cousin produced, from inside a white handkerchief, a set of pearly-white stones. They were pure white, unlike the yellowish ones we used to get back in London. There was always a great debate within the crack-smoking fraternity over the relative quality of the white or the yellow. As for myself, I don't know. I just used to blast away.

On the way back to my room, Kehn and I stopped to pick up a small brandy bottle, which we knocked back, and began to prepare for smoking. There is a particular brand of brandy that crack smokers prefer, because the bottom of the bottle can easily be knocked out with a nail, to turn it into a crack pipe. A metal wire is then pressed together to act as the filter, and this is pushed tightly into the stem. The piece of crack is put upright on the very tip, and melted with a flame. The crack melts straight onto the wire. At this point, the smoker inhales from the bottom of the pipe. The smoke is thick and black as it moves through the chamber, and enters the lungs. It goes from there to the heart, and from there to the head, and creates a powerful rush. They say that the first rush of coke is your best. For me, it was almost religious, with a massive kick of sexuality and the feeling of having just won the lottery at the same time.

Unfortunately, those little few stones ran out, just as the party got started. Kehn had a good blast, too, licking his lips in preparation for his next, but unfortunately the larder was now dry. Only it wasn't. I still had a fucking great pile of money on me, didn't I? I peeled off another $20.

'What could we get for that, Kehn?' I asked, holding it out under his face. Automatically his hand reached out and took it back. Moments later he was off out the door, on his way to 'Silver Sands' where we could get a better deal.

He wasn't gone long. The withdrawal symptoms had receded, but I was clucking, and I knew there wasn't any heroin to be had for love or money. The only thing I could do was hit the crack, and hope that I would get through the worst of it before the money ran out. I nearly did it too.

***

For the first two or three days, Kehn ran almost non-stop between my room and whoever was supplying us in the mystical kingdom of Silver Sands. Every ten or 20 hours he grabbed a short sleep, or I might, but effectively he was on call. The feeling of it each time was sweet beyond belief. It wasn't just that the stuff seemed to be stronger than it was in England, it was also that the misery of my withdrawal seemed to highlight the beauty of the high. That lovely crackle of the white marble pieces as the flame hit and melted them into a wax-like substance, running like cream into the wire mesh, and mystically transforming into thick black smoke. The kick of that high was unbelievable. With that singing in my veins every tiny shred of pain and setback in my life was instantly wiped out and was replaced with a religious awareness of God and my destiny in His great plan. It all seemed so clear at the time.

Soon all of that great wisdom and supreme ecstasy would fade, within minutes, to be replaced with the mockery of me crawling on the floor, searching for any crumb of crack I might have missed, desperate to hold onto that high, but increasingly unable to. With trembling hands, I would scrape out the insides of my crack pipe. An hour's delicate work would yield enough black stuff on the wire mesh to chance another hit. Maybe it would work. For another ten minutes I would be spun back into the beautiful Garden of Eden I had been in before. And then it would wear off again, to let me down even harder.

There comes a time when, no matter how much gear you do, your brain cells are unable to process any more. It normally takes about two or three days of non-stop use to arrive at that point. I went out and got a bottle of local rum, knocked it back and fell into a troubled sleep. I woke some time during the night with the deep need to vomit. I just about had time to make it to the waste paper bin before emptying my guts. The stink was unbelievable. I couldn't handle any cleaning up though. All I could do was try to get back to sleep on the hard bed. I turned over, trying to get some respite, but unable to find any. The sweat was rolling off me. I recognised the stink from my last cold turkey. It was the smell of ammonia, which builds up inside the tissues of the heroin addict while they are on the drug. It starts to breaks down, leaking out as soon as they start to come off. It is a nasty smell. Really chemical-like. Having a shower is one of the best things you can do when you are clucking, but the thought of dragging myself to the bathroom was too much. All I wanted to do was curl up into a little ball and hope and pray that the dawn would come soon.

I don't know how long I lay there, but I gradually became aware of knocking on the wooden slats of my window. I hauled myself off the bed, and I looked into the face of a black version of Charles Atlas. This guy had what was probably the most perfect physique west of the Greenwich meridian. He hardly had any neck at all, but his shape was an almost perfect V from the top of his shoulders down to the pencil-slim circumference of his waist. He was dressed in a deep red T-shirt that looked as though it had been sprayed on. He wore a pair of dark glasses. Around his non-neck hung a stylised golden and ancient-looking crucifix.

'My name is Mike,' he said, looking through the slats at me. Was that supposed to mean something to me? Who was this fucker? I opened the door for him and he just walked in, as though I was supposed to know him. Then it dawned on me that he might well be the person I was supposed to link up with. I hadn't even thought about it from the moment I smoked my first pipe.

'I'm from Corinne,' he said. Or Mons as I knew her.

He sat down on the bed, and gave me a straight look. The kind that said many things, but here and now meant, 'You'd better not be fucking with me, kid.'

He then moved over to the suitcase and opened it. He started pulling out all the pairs of white underwear and vests. Inside was a birthday card. There was a handwritten declaration of love or admiration on it. I spotted the words: 'To a very special person' before he saw that I was peeping and took it away. Then he started in on the pairs of socks. I hadn't bothered sorting through all that stuff after arriving at the hotel. I had gone straight out on the razzle. Imagine my astonishment when he pulled a thick bundle of notes out of one of the pairs of socks! They were all $100 bills, and it was about two inches thick. Counting it slowly, with the occasional glance in my direction, Mike was making his way, inexorably, up to $5,000. There, it was all there. I hadn't realized that I'd be ferrying cash over to this place. $5,000! I began to wish that I had searched the case before this guy had arrived. The notes were all fresh as a daisy, too. Crisp and absolutely tidy, like a middle class family on their way to mass. If I had found that money, I would just have got up, walked out of there, and made my way to the airport. From there, the nearest flight to Pakistan, just to get my hands on a big bag of heroin. It would have been a dream come true. But it was not to be. Looking back, I am very lucky I didn't find it. I would not be alive today if I had.

Satisfying himself that everything was in order, he made to get up. I wasn't going to let him go without getting some gear. He'd just picked up $5,000 on the basis of my work, so I felt that I had earned it.

'Could you bring me some white?' I asked, 'if you don't mind of course.'

I cringed at the whining note in my voice but he nodded, and went out the door without saying a thing. He did return a bit later, with a small wrap of both white and some green. They were wrapped in a page torn from the Bible: the page at the end of Revelations where it talks about the divine punishment on the head of anyone who takes any pages out of this prophecy. It was like an evil omen.

All I wanted to do was get out of my face, but the money was beginning to run low and the stuff was neither getting me quite so high nor for anywhere near as long. I was due to be getting on the plane to come back home in a day at this stage, and. I was still waiting for the drugs to turn up. I decided to give Mons a ring. It seemed to take forever to get through to her. Apparently there had been a mix-up, but it was sorted now, and the guy would be over to deliver in the next day or so. There would be no problem changing my flight. I could just hang out on the island for a few more days.

The next morning, I left my room early to look around for Kehn. First, I checked his place. Looking through the window to his bedroom I could see that he wasn't there. The morning before I had turned up at six in the morning and awoken him, nigh on forcing him out of bed to go score for me. Then, I made my way along the deserted road. Here and there, a dog chained up in front of a house would growl at me, warning me to keep my distance.

By the time I got back up to the rum shop, the cluck was starting to hit. I had to sit down, it was so painful standing up. I had just parked my bum by the side of a bus stand when Kehn came along on his bicycle. I gave him one of my few remaining $10, and he sailed away, off to Silver Sands. I scuttled back to the hotel room, to wait for him there.

Later that evening, I was able to drag myself up to the rum shop between pipes. There was quite a crowd there, so I sat outside on the steps and looked up into the warm Caribbean night. I could almost touch the stars. The crowd inside were from a neighbourhood close to my own, in Tottenham, north London. We got chatting and they invited me up to their room. When I got there, I noticed a suitcase standing in the middle of the room. If I had leaned closer I would have been able to read the name and address on the label that hung from the handle.

Just then, one of the fellas asked if he could come and see my room. I could tell he wanted me out of there for some reason, and took him next door into mine. He looked around for a moment, said goodnight and left. I was still standing looking at the door, slightly bemused, when there was a loud knock. I opened the door to find two guys standing there. One held the suitcase I had seen standing in the other room. He saw me looking and moved the case behind him. Both he and his friend wore dark glasses, even though it was night time, and walked straight into my room.

The suitcase they brought in was soft-backed with a reinforced backbone.

'What do you want to do with the other one?' the first guy asked.

'Probably best for you to take it away,' I said, 'I've got no use for it.'

So the elder of the two picked it up.

Just then I heard Kehn appear from nowhere and call out, 'Terry!'

'Not now, Kehn,' I replied.

He might have stayed outside, peeping in. That seems most likely. All he would have seen was that I had a couple of visitors. Even so, as a local man, he would have sussed what was going on. This didn't particularly bother me at the time, even though I had a kind of 'fated' feeling about all of this. Almost as if I was an actor going through his script, powerless to change what was happening or what the outcome would be.

All week I had the sense that I was being watched by different sets of people; probably the smugglers, and certainly the police. In hindsight I was probably the best decoy the smugglers had come across in ages and in my drug-fuelled daze I had played my part perfectly, albeit unwittingly.

I hit the elder guy for an extra $100.

'I have got debts to pay, before I can check out of here,' I complained.

He moaned a bit, but in the end I got a few more bob for a drink that night and a relatively decent smoke.

**

The next morning I was up and ready to roll. I was a bit tired, physically and mentally, and needed help in getting the big suitcase wheeled up the long slope to the rum shop. There, the friendly rum shop owner offered to give me a free lift to the airport. After a beer, we were off, the Range Rover we were in doing over 100 miles an hour as we careered past dozens of other vehicles travelling in the same direction.

When we got to the airport, I pulled the suitcase out of the back, waved good bye to the rum shop owner, and walked into the terminal building. It was cool here, and also much darker. I looked around at all the other holiday makers and realised that I was still wearing the same clothes I had arrived in. I hadn't even had a wash or a shower in all that time, either.

When I went to check in, I burst out laughing when the girl behind the counter asked me if I had packed the case myself. I couldn't help it. The thing was empty inside, yet still weighed a ton on their scales. When she looked at my name on her screen, she suddenly jumped back. Keeping a sharp eye on me, she went to a little room at the back marked 'Security'. As she returned, I saw a very worried-looking guy come out, take a sideways glance at me and then scuttle off. The girl continued to check me in. My suitcase went over into the luggage area, where it was immediately put to one side, away from all of the other suitcases. The girl returned my passport to me. Just then, it became difficult for me to stand up. I needed a cigarette. I crumpled to the floor with my back against a pillar, lit up the fag, and took a deep breath. I closed my eyes and rested my head against the pillar behind me. When I opened them again, I saw two men approaching me. They showed me their police badges. A sudden heavy sinking feeling hit me right in the guts. I knew they had me. They knew it as well. My body felt as if it weighed about three ton, and I was now moving in slow motion. Each step seemed to take about ten minutes. We stopped and they recovered the suitcase. Now I had to wheel this thing along, as we made our way to the customs inspection area.

There, they told me to put the suitcase on a giant X-ray scanner. The operator ran the case through, but was unable to find anything wrong with it. He must have seen something the second time he tried. He shrugged to one of the cops, who then pulled a knife from his inside jacket pocket, and started tearing out the inside lining. Yards of black cloth peeled out of the innards of the case, and underneath it all was a large piece of sheet metal, tailored to run around the inside rim of the case.

'The work that must have gone into that!' the first policeman marvelled, struck by the artist's determination and craftsmanship. By now several more large, burly men, clearly security, police and customs types had congregated. The cocaine was concealed inside the metal outer rim of the case.

They all lined up to take a photograph, with the broken-open case in the foreground. Unsure of what to do, I entered the picture, but one of them waved me away to the sidelines. They all puffed out their chests for the picture that would be coming out in the newspaper the next day.

'We can get you 25 years for this, sonny,' one of them said.

I felt weak, totally gutted. What the fuck had I done with my life? It looked as if it were all over bar the shouting, now. I had to lie down. 25 years or not, I was going to lie down. I wondered if I wasn't close to fainting. Maybe I was. I wanted to smoke a cigarette, and tried lighting one up, but it was snatched from my mouth just as I took the first drag on it and inhaled.

They tested the quality of the cocaine then, but on the first test it came up purple, which indicated that it was negative. Blue indicated the presence of cocaine. Their faces when that purple colour came up was a real picture, and in anybody else's shoes would have been hysterical. I had a vision of standing up, dusting myself down, and waltzing out of there, but it wasn't to be. They tried again, with a much, much bigger sample, whereupon it went a very light blue. Deep blue would have meant it was good stuff. 'Mine' was probably mostly made up of crushed sleeping tablets. The tiny amount of cocaine mixed in was probably only there to ensure I did actually get arrested.

I knew then for sure that I had been well and truly set up. It dawned on me that I had been sent as the decoy, while on the same plane some ten or 20 drug mules were now heading back to London with suitcases full of the real thing; cocaine up to 95% pure. I felt gutted. I thought back to the moment when my suitcase had been put well apart from the rest, and knew they had been waiting all along. My mind went back to picture all those dodgy looking women in dark shades who had been on the plane, who all had identical looking suitcases. Identical to mine too. I tried to do some mental arithmetic. If there had been 20 mules going through, each carrying three kilos, that would equal 60 kilos, worth £20,000 each, and that would work out as one and a half million pounds wholesale. Someone was making a lot of money out of this batch, and whoever it was, they were surely cutting in someone in customs to apprehend me and ignore the rest.

I was hauled to my feet. With one guard on either side of me, we marched out the door into the main concourse. There were dozens of tourists all lined up, ready to go, looking at me as I was marched past them. It was obvious that I had been busted for drug smuggling. They put me in the back of a police car. A young black man sat in beside me. A ring glinted on the third finger of his right hand. I squinted to get a better look; it was engraved with the Masonic square and compass.

I leaned a little closer to him and extended my right hand. Unsure of what to do, he took it in his, and I gave him the Masonic handshake. He gave me back the right handshake. What a different kind of life! How had I managed to go from being a respected member of the order, to getting busted for drug-smuggling in this god-forsaken place? It was beginning to dawn on me how far down the ladder I had fallen.

My young companion and I worked our way through the traditional greeting and then sat next to each other, laughing about what could potentially have been a very miserable experience. He turned to me. There was such an expression of sadness on his face.

'So, how did you fall from the light?' he asked me.

I wished I knew. I had no answer to give him. I had no answer even inside my own head.

Two more policemen got into the car. A barrier was raised for us to pass through, and then we were out on the open road, with a police jeep behind us, its light flashing. I could feel the heat from the Barbados summer day hitting me through the windscreen, and took a deep breath as I wondered what I was in for. Probably a good kicking, I thought despondently, as I considered just how massive these cops were. I wouldn't survive a kicking from this lot. And as for Freemasonry, you can't use that as a shield for carrying out illegal or unethical activities, or as a licence to evade any negative come-back from the repercussions of your actions in life.

We drove back to Oistins, to the police station there. We all got out, and they took me into the entrance hall. As I looked around, I had the strangest feeling that I actually recognised some of these people. I was sure that I saw big Mike of the red T-shirt and the two guys who had delivered the suitcase of coke to the hotel. They were still wearing their sunglasses. Maybe I was tripping from all the coke I'd been blasting away on.

I was bunged into a cell right at the back. It was tiny, like something from the Crimean War. There were only two or three cells in the entire police station anyway. At first I thought it was already occupied. But what I took to be a body curled up on the floor, turned out to be a pile of food bags containing slowly mouldering items.

There were two thin strips of foam, both soaked in the sweat of innumerable other men and initially cold to the touch as I lay down on one of them. Not to worry, I thought to myself. I knew my body heat would soon bring out the smell of all those other peoples' sweat. Hopefully, I wasn't going to be here for too long. The best thing to do, I reasoned, would probably be for me to make a full confession, and plead guilty to whatever they wanted to charge me with. They had me bang to rights, so I might as well minimise the agony and get it over with. You hear tales of people trying to get out of it, by pretending 'they didn't know.' They end up waiting for one hell of a long time before they even get to trial, sometimes years, and then they get an even bigger sentence when they are found guilty.

As I was lying on this foam mattress in the cell another fella was brought in; a tall Rasta man, his long dreadlocks reaching down to his waist like thickly-coiled ropes.

He just lay down and went to sleep. That seemed the best thing to do. So I followed his example. If I wanted to escape reality, the only place I could do it now was in my dreams.

CHAPTER SEVEN

BACK IN PRISON

That night, the police got me out of the cell and took me to the front desk. I looked out at the warm Barbadian evening and wished that things had worked out differently. If I had got through, I would be halfway to London by now. I thought of myself sitting on a plane, looking down at the deep blue of the water as the sun set over Barbados behind me. But no, it was no use thinking about 'might-have-beens'. If I wanted to get through this, I had to discard all that sort of thinking and get up to date with what was actually happening to me. No, it was no use trying to run away. They would only catch me. I barely had the strength to stand up, let alone outrun some of these really tough and athletic types. I was just beginning to go into real cold turkey, which up till now I had partially staved off by smoking crack. Sweat poured out of me and I stank. The heavy ammonia scent of my body starting its purge filled the room.

I was formally charged, and then taken to room with a table and three chairs. Two respectable-looking guys were there before me. They introduced themselves and told me they were case-workers from the British Embassy, and that they worked with Prisoners Abroad. Having been nicked before, in Greece, I knew what the routine with these boys was going to be about. Did I want anyone contacted? Blah blah, the same load of old bollox they always come out with. They gave me a glossy leaflet on Prisoners Abroad before they finally left.

My my, we have been able to get into some of that nice funding, haven't we? I thought to myself, looking at the stylish leaflet. I remembered Prisoners Abroad from the old days, and back then they certainly hadn't been able to afford anything like this! It looked as though they were working much more closely with the Foreign Office than they did in the old days.

The next day, I was hauled before Oistin's Magistrates Court, which was immediately adjacent to the police station. The prisoners were lined up by the police. The first two were allowed home on bail. The next lad had stolen someone's bicycle. He got six months. Then it was my turn.

It was all a foregone conclusion. I'd have to do a little rollover and get my piece of time. No room for Perry Mason antics here. I didn't even have a lawyer, because I'd heard that any sort of appeal or defence may have delayed the case by up to two years, during which time I would have to sweat it out in prison anyway. In Barbados they don't count time spent in jail against your sentence either. So I thought it best to just get it over with.

'How do you plead?' the judge asked me. She was all business-like up on her bench.

'I plead guilty, ma'am,' I replied. 'To all the charges.'

I had been charged with not just possession, but intent to supply, and with trafficking, which were far more serious offences. But there was no point in stretching it out—far better to go and get it all over with in one swift bash.

She asked me if I had anything to say in my defence. I explained how I had been a successful person prior to my drug relapse, and that I had lost everything through addiction. I had run into a bit of debt and been misled into coming to her country to take drugs back to the United Kingdom, and that was how I had come to end up here in her court. She sentenced me to four years. Under the Barbadian system, that would mean I'd be out in three. If I hadn't felt so junk-sick I would have danced a little jig; to me that was a result! I was very lucky.

The next guy to go in was a man called Williamson, a Rastaman. His crime had been to steal bottles of a local-made syrup called mauby, and then go down the street selling them cheaply. The money he got from all this was to fuel his crack habit. He was a gentle soul, and was devastated when the judge gave him five years. He hadn't expected that. He had thought he was likely to get maybe a few months. Much of the crime in Barbados, I learned, stems from crack addiction. It really is the fuel that keeps the entire machinery of crime, punishment and attendant human suffering ticking over.

The cops escorting us from the courthouse were really pissed off that I, a drug-smuggler, was given a lesser sentence than a man who had stolen a bottle of syrup. I was bundled into a police van, along with two others, and off down to the centre of Bridgetown we went. I had not been into the centre of Barbados' main town at all in the week I had been here. We parked up round the back of the main courthouse. From the bus, I could see a chamber where a dozen or so other prisoners were hanging their hands and pushing their faces up against the bars. They were trying to get water to drink, but the guard just ignored them. They all seemed very weak, hardly able to stand. As they were being ferried to and from court for their hearings, each man was practically carried by the two guards accompanying him. The guards ferried them along at a gentle pace, more like nurses in a mental hospital or infirmary than the prison officer-types I had seen before. Now and again, I could see them say something to their prisoners, some words of reassurance or comfort I hoped. What was going on in that prison? I thought to myself.

Then it was our turn to go upstairs. They took us one by one. When it was my turn, I was handcuffed to a burly guard, and led up along the narrow set of steps. Inside it was cool, but very cramped. There was nowhere to sit and I could hardly stand. The officials there didn't seem to have seen anything like my condition before. One of the screws whispered something into the ear of one of the ladies there, and she looked at me, nodding slightly. Then I was given a chair to sit in. It was apparent I wasn't well at all. I was shivering, with great convulsions running through my body. Sweat was pouring off me, forming rivulets down the side of my face. I suddenly felt freezing cold. When they were ready for me, they stood me up and put my back against a height-marker. They made a note of my height; 5'8". Then they rolled an ink pad over my hands and took an imprint of each fingerprint, each one in its own little box. They took my photograph next. It was just like you see in the old films; I was given a little placard with a number on it, and had to look straight ahead. A woman with a digital camera put the thing straight in my face. Then I had to look to each side, for two further photographs.

They brought me back to the van. I was hungry, and asked the screws for some food. I hadn't eaten in days. When you are smoking coke you don't generally bother, but it was all starting to catch up with me now and I was as hungry as a wolf.

'Why don't you order a fish cutter?' another guy said.

'What is that?' I asked him.

'Fish inside a bread roll.' I realised that in revealing my ignorance of the meaning of the word 'cutter' I showed just how new to the island I was.

The screw brought back a cutter and a really cold lemonade for each man. The cup was half full of crushed ice that lasted even when the last gulp of the drink was gone. Then it was time for us to be on our way, and another couple of screws climbed in as reinforcements. As we sped along, they put the siren on, just for a laugh really. For some villains it makes them feel important, like they are some big-shot gangsterman, even if they are really in for robbing some young girl. We arrived at a colonial-style building, coming up the drive through a set of stone pillars, painted black and white. Ahead was a great green gateway, which opened to receive us. On the side was a painted sign that read 'HMP Glendairy'. I couldn't believe it; this couldn't be the prison. This place was ancient.

The van we were in moved slowly forward. Guards in brown uniforms came out of the shadows and surrounded us, like soldier ants checking out the arrival of some other insect into their nest, sniffing us, using their antennae to check we were giving and receiving on the right wavelength. The main screw in our van got out, and handed a list of our names over to one of them. He got back into the van as behind us, the outer gates closed. In front, I could see the inner doors leading to the interior of the prison opening up.

Thankfully, they had switched the siren off by now, but we still seemed to be the object of a lot of attention as we drove through the courtyard to the reception area. We filed out of the van and were directed upstairs.

***

When you come off any heavy drug, it is important to reward yourself for each little victory you achieve. You need to give yourself a great deal of reassurance and encouragement as you go along. I was afraid. When you are weak and vulnerable it is natural for you to feel afraid. I was surprised at just how frail I felt. Other people around me seemed extremely powerful and aggressive. They could sense I was in just the right position to be fucked over.

I made my way up the stairs. A prison officer had appeared from somewhere, and was watching over me. Was he checking I was ok or making sure I didn't try and disappear over the top of the wall that was on the other side of a simple wire fence? If I had been James Bond it might have been different. Just getting up the steps was a big enough challenge. The screw had a big pot belly. On the shoulders of his shirt, the letters HMP were printed in silver on a badge that could be easily removed when the shirt was cleaned. On his cap badge was a pair of crossed silver keys. I looked around the yard as I went up the steps. To one side was a main building, very old looking, with archways in between each of the pillars. It was three storeys high, and I could see inside the cells as I went up the stairs. Men were sweeping the insides of their cells, or hanging out washing to dry. Here and there, foam mattresses hung on nails driven into the wall to air out in the rays of the sun.

Just then the screw motioned for me to come back, and pointed me towards the Mess Hall.

'Get some food, fella' he said, pointing to a small serving hatch in the side of the wall. I went over and found a thin bony face looking back at me; the face of the man I was later to know as Mason. Without much ado, he poured some tea into a plastic peanut butter container. The peanut butter had been cleaned out, but there were still traces of it round the insides. Not that that worried me. All I wanted was something to eat and drink. Mason then gave me a thin, cake-like thing, which I later learned was called a lead pipe. I soon learned that the trick was to dunk the lead pipe in my tea. I would have eaten anything to assuage my hunger pangs.

When I finished my tea, it truly was time for going upstairs. I noticed three extremely tall fellas, dressed in the prisoner uniform of blue denim, but with red bands on their right arms. These clowns obviously thought they were Nazis in a film or something, the way they were ripping apart my luggage and the possessions of the two other new inmates I had just come in with. One of them had taken one of the new guys over to a small side area where he made him strip. He ripped up his trousers, on the pretext that something was hidden in the lining. He made the new inmate squat up and down, as if there might be something hidden in his arse and this was going to dislodge it. It was all one big piss take, and I could see immediately the way this place was run.

The officers were delegating as much work to these clowns as possible so as to give themselves an easy time. One of the Redbands tried writing down my name and details in a big book, but he found this too challenging and after getting me to spell my own name about three times seemed to give up. What type of place was this?

Now and again, the occasional screw sauntered in, like a holy cow in the backstreets of India, drifting around looking for something to eat. They didn't seem to know what to do. It was like a big holiday camp, where if you were a prison guard you could just walk about willy nilly as you wished, as long as you wore your cap on your head. The Redbands were the ones doing all the running.

It took two of them to rip my towel in half. After tearing it, one of the Redbands stood there for a moment, slightly confused. You could almost hear the little wheels in his head spinning as he tried to work out what came next. Oh yes, give one half back to the new prisoner. He held both halves up, one in each hand. From the slightly pained expression on his face, I could tell that he was asking me to choose which half I was to inherit. I made my choice, then the remaining half was thrown into the bin.

I was issued with a toilet roll, a small soap, a toothbrush and toothpaste, and allowed to keep back just one shirt; the green one I was still wearing. All my other clothes and possessions were then put into a black plastic bin liner. This was taken to the storeroom, where whoever was in charge could plunder its contents to his little heart's content.

I had hoped to bring my last packet of tobacco and papers into the prison. It was all I had to smoke. But no, this was too likely to get used for smoking weed, and was taken off me, and also put in the bin liner. I would be surprised if they lasted a single night in there before being redistributed to some more deserving person—one of the Redbands perhaps.

Then, an officer took me down across the prison yard and into the main building. I was dismayed at what I saw. This was quite an old building, probably built in the mid 19th century, when Britain built most of its prisons, but it looked like nothing had been done to it since. The design and sense of antiquity reminded me of Highgate Cemetery. We went along a small corridor, and then through a set of iron gates into the Back Prison.

I felt a variety of emotions as I walked through the place, trying to take it all in. From the behaviour of the Redbands upstairs I already had a pretty good idea as to how bent this place was, and that it would probably run on favours and bribes, but I was coming in with nothing, so what chance did I have? I knew I had to keep my defences up and not get too pally with anyone, otherwise I would be taken for a clown.

On the other hand, I always found that if I was a bit cheery, people tended to take a chance with me and start chatting. I tried to give off an air somewhere in between hard and cheerful as the guard brought me through to the back of the prison, but my face dropped when we got there.

It was like stepping back hundreds of years in time and finding yourself in the middle of a Crimean War battlefield. There seemed to be hundreds of prisoners, all heaving and striving to get out, and I was amazed at how many people they had actually managed to squeeze in. There were four chambers, two up a set of symmetrical steps, one on each side, and two down. Each section had its own gate of thick-set bars, and through them I could see men, young and old, crying to be let out. It was like a scene from Dante's Inferno, when he looks at all the condemned souls living and suffering in purgatory, or one of those Hieronymous Bosch paintings of Hell where everywhere you look there is some new scenario of degradation and suffering taking place. Yet what really caught my eye was the way in which everybody, amidst this chaos, seemed to be going about their business, as if they were beyond caring. It was a place for lost souls.

After years of destroying my body and soul, sending myself into spirals of destruction and my own personal torment, I realised that I had finally reached my destination: 'Welcome to hell,' I said to myself. 'I've finally made it.'

★★★

The screw escorting me held me by the arm as we entered the lower chamber. He got the other guard to open the gate; clearly there was a division of labour here, with different keys assigned to different screws. Inside, it was like being underground. I was taken down a long dark corridor. A dim electric bulb covered in layers of protective wire provided lighting every few metres. Along the way, men were playing dominoes or backgammon at tiny makeshift tables. Occasionally a head would look up from one of their games to see the new white boy being brought in.

What struck me about the place was how young the prisoners all seemed to be. Most seemed in their 20s, but many were younger than that. I wondered if the government of Barbados wasn't trying to deal with its, as I found out later, quite substantial unemployment problem by bringing their surplus young population within the walls of this institution, whether they deserved it or not. Which is basically the way many third world countries deal with their social problems—it is easier, and cheaper, for them to hide the problems behind bars and big walls then actually tackle the issues at hand.

The deafening roar hit me like a wall of noise. It seemed like everybody was shrieking at full volume, like tortured souls in the fires of Hell. Faces were lined up against the bars screaming down at one solitary guard who was running up and down stone steps letting men in and out of selected corridors. The poor man looked rushed off his feet, and I wondered what the point of this was. If they were supposed to be locked up, why were they letting these guys in and out in such a haphazard way? Alternatively, what was the point of locking them up at all if all they had to do to get out was scream? This was madness.

I wondered if there were any others from Britain. Then the words of the British Embassy man came back to me: yes, there were about 20 other Brits here, but spread out, not all in one place or part of the prison. I was more or less alone in this madhouse.

The guard led me down to what looked like the mouth of a cave, with a double set of bars and gates in front of it. Over it were the letters D&E. What was this? Was this my cell wing? The guard led me through and locked the gate behind him, then tightened his grip on my arm and looked me in the eye, as if preparing himself for a struggle he was more than used to with new prisoners being led down this corridor. If he was trying to scare me, it was working. What the hell lay ahead?

From the outside, this place looked like an ancient dungeon, but once I walked into its interior I was able to appreciate it in all its glory. It was like a tomb. And people had to live in here? Immediately on the right was an open doorway which led to an improvised shower area. Water was running down the walls onto a huge crowd of men who walked around washing and drying themselves completely without inhibition, some of them stopping to stare at me as I walked past. The corridor was pitch dark, but I could almost see it in their faces that they thought their dreams had come true. Most of these guys would have been stoney broke, and they must have immediately seen me as a rich, white source of cigarettes, amongst other things. They were sadly mistaken.

It occurred to me that this place probably played a central part in the lives of the inhabitants of this small island. Almost everybody must have known someone who was here, or worked here, or was still here, and stories must have passed around, and grown and grown until little meaningless anecdotes turned into sagas. I felt a weird sense of being like a writer sent here to record and document the place as it was, because something big was going to happen to change everything. I put it down to my imagination running wild, and my subconscious trying to give some sort of sense to the reality that I was stuck in this hell hole.

***

I was shown to a cell, number seven, on the left, and went inside. It was like being thrown into a grave. Immediately, an overpowering stench hit me like a cold hard slap. A large plastic bucket with a wire handle stood inside the door. In it was a considerable amount of piss, with something else floating on top, a little wrap of something in a folded-up newspaper; obviously a turd. The stink was unimaginable. All over the crumbling walls were additions of cement piled up over years, much of it covered up by small photographs from magazines—here a picture of a machine gun, there a picture of Pamela Anderson in a lewd pose. Opposite me was a set of two crudely hewn bunk beds. They were nailed to the wall. Large nails that looked old enough to have been used at the Crucifixion acted as pegs to hang clothes from, and were stuck out of the wall at various heights. Small items of clothing hung from them, but there wasn't a single breeze, so the boxer shorts and t-shirts would be there for some time. Right at the top of the cell was a tiny opening with several sets of bars criss-crossing it, through which I could see a thin sliver of sky, which was darkening. On the walls, there were various inscriptions, invocations, and messages.

I looked around for a place to sit down, but there weren't many places to look. There was really only the floor, which was bare rough concrete, but it was smoothed off by the passage of inmates' bare feet down through the decades.

The screw sailed off somewhere more interesting just as a cheerful-looking character who introduced himself as Troy Wiltshire walked straight into the cell.

'But you can call me Baggis,' he said.

He seemed genuinely pleased to meet me. I didn't have anything to smoke, though, which disappointed him.

'Tell you what,' he said, after a moment's pause, 'I could get a cigarette for that soap, and maybe another one for that toothpaste.'

'What about the toothbrush?' I asked, perhaps a bit too enthusiastically. A slight frown came across his face. No, not a good idea.

'What will you use to brush your teeth?' he asked me.

'Fuck me teeth,' I said back, and he kind of shrugged, and took it all. If I wanted a wash, I could always beg up a sliver of soap from someone. I knew my way around prison. And I could really do with a smoke.

Baggis popped out for a few minutes, and came back with a couple of smokes in his hand. I immediately knew that he'd kept at least one back for himself, maybe more. He handed me the two snouts, and then went out to get a wick so we could light it. Notice the 'we' word creeping in, now. Having thieved about half of what was due to me, the bastard now wanted to make out that it was normal to share a smoke with your cell mate. Whenever I had any smokes it was the norm, but whenever he got a parcel it became difficult to even find the fucker.

Baggis didn't want to wander around with a cigarette in his hand. That would have attracted the attention of a host of unwanted admirers, all keen to take a pull or two off 'our' smokes. Instead he came back with what looked like a mop end of slowly burning coil. It turned out to be thinly-rolled toilet paper, made into what we called a wick. He handed me the cigarette, and I went first. Lighting the end from the wick, I felt the rush of nicotine as it hit my blood. My muscles relaxed, and there was a brief but distinct rush inside my head. Then that was it, my half was done, and reluctantly, I handed what was left to my new-found companion. He pulled hard on the cigarette, so much so that it actually glared up at the lit end, and within two pulls, was down to its cork. Even then he didn't stop. Another strong suck, drawing cheeks inward so that they almost touched, and then the cork itself was halfway smoked up. As he exhaled, it smelt of burning newspaper.

It was getting close to lock down time, and the screws were coming down, one on each of the two sides of the narrow corridor. I could hear them making their way down door by door. There was a short pause between each lock up for the screw to make sure that the right people were in each cell.

Another lad appeared in the doorway and came in. He was quite young, and clearly a bit out of it. He didn't seem to know where he was, or what he was doing. His name was Jamal. I couldn't believe that three of us were to share this tiny cell. That meant I didn't even have a bed. The screw peered in to count us, and then shut the door. It was made of thick wood, really heavy and solid. Like a door from a mediaeval dungeon. At the back of it were many carvings, names inscribed, and symbols. Over the next while those signs would become very familiar to me.

I looked around for where I was supposed to go. Obviously, as the newest man in the cell, I would be squeezing in somewhere. I wanted to sit down again, anyway, and made to sit on the bare concrete floor. It was jagged and unevenly cemented, with cracks running through it and pieces that were barely clinging on. Baggis was already lying down on his bunk, but could see my predicament. He got up, and swung himself over the side. Reaching down to Jamal's foam mattress, he proceeded to rip it in half, straight down the middle with his bare hands. He offered me the choice of halves, so I picked one.

This was to be my bed, and comfortable it was, too, in comparison to the floor.

***

That night I lay and listened to the sounds of the great beast that had swallowed me up, and through whose entrails I was slowly moving. What parts of me, I wondered, would get eaten away, get digested, and what parts would remain, to be excreted, back into the world, once my sentence had been served?

Jamal suddenly went into a fit, or a kind of hysteria. Baggis jumped down, and held him, almost in his arms. Oh great, I thought. But it was not an erotic embrace. It was almost like a healer taking hold of someone possessed by devils. Baggis was speaking some words to him, and somehow what he was saying seemed to be getting through. Somehow Baggis intuitively had a knowledge, and understanding of what Jamal had been through, of the shock and trauma that he had witnessed that had pushed his mind to this dark and lonely place. I guess sharing a cell like this with him had made it a necessity. Bit by bit, Baggis was able to bring him back. I could make out some of what he was saying, now that I had become accustomed to the rhythmic pattern of the words, over and over again, rising and falling like the crest of a wave. It was something from the Book of Psalms, although I couldn't place which one. And it seemed to be working. It took over an hour, but eventually Jamal seemed to slip off into a light sleep. Maybe it was a light hypnotic state, but Jamal was resting his troubled mind, and was even starting to dream. Baggis let him go, and climbed back up the little wooden ladder that had been nailed to the rough sides of the bunk, and went to sleep. I hoped this wasn't a nightly occurrence.

The next morning I came to and heard the sound I was to hear every morning while I lived on the left hand side of the Back Prison: the sound of wood doves cooing. It was a lovely sound; coo cooo coo cooo, but it woke me to a horrible place and was gradually becoming supplanted with other sounds as the prison came to life. The day began gradually. At first I heard the cells of the workers being opened, so that they could get ready for their jobs. These were always given the first chance to get into the showers. After the corridor was open, it was Hell as there were about 150 men on this side, all rushing for shower space of about three taps, depending on which ones weren't broken or fucked up that morning.

On this first morning, I needed to take a shit, and, as there didn't seem to be any other way of going about it, I stretched myself up and parked my arse over the rim of the bucket.

'No, no!' came the cry from Baggis, 'Hold on! I've got something for you!' and with that he leapt off his bunk and was down alongside me with a sheet of old newspaper in his hand.

'What you do, is this … ' he began, instructing me in the first degree ritual of shit-taking in Glendairy Lodge.

'First, you lay the paper on the ground.' He showed me, opening the paper into its full length of a double page, alongside the bucket. 'Then, you squat onto the middle of the paper, and take the shit. Then, you wipe your arse, and put this paper into the middle of the heap. Then, you must wrap it all up like a small parcel and fold in the edges, so that it will not open when you put it in the bucket. Also, whoever takes a shit must be the one to empty and clean the bucket, when the doors open. That cuts across whoever's turn it would normally be. We take it in turns to do everything; clean the cell, carry out the bucket, wash the clothes.'

This was all well and good, but I knew something he didn't. I was still coming off all the crack I had smoked.

'But, I think I might have diarrhoea,' I said, lamely.

'No, no,' he countered, 'you'll be alright.' I didn't think he'd heard me, but by then it was launch time anyway. I whipped off my shorts, and squatted down, just as a big burst of liquid shit came flying through me. It squelched all over the paper, spraying as far as the door, making a modern art rendition across the floor. Baggis looked at me with a mixture of contempt and admiration, then, out of embarrassment, looked away.

I cleaned up as best I could, but I knew that for the next two to three weeks things were going to be difficult for me, at least as far as using bucket paper was concerned. What could I do? There was nowhere else to go, and this was the only 'facility' we had to share between the three of us. I told Baggis that I was coming off not just cocaine, but heroin. Things were going to get a lot worse before they got any better.

Baggis said something then, a Buddhist expression, by way of offering support, and was surprised when I responded in kind. My time with hippies and alternative lifestyles had given me not only an interest but also a working vocabulary as far as these things went. I felt I had impressed him.

Baggis helped me clean up along the floor, wiping out stains of my crap that I couldn't or wouldn't see. I asked him what he was in for, and he brought out a newspaper cutting. It showed him being carried along by a massive black policeman, who had both his hands around Baggis' neck. Baggis' expression was one of great disdain, and it seemed in the photograph as though he was struggling to breathe as much as anything else. According to the story attached, he had been on trial for robbery and had attempted to escape by using the open window of an upstairs toilet, and shinning down a drainpipe. He had made it to the back of the courtroom, but had been apprehended again, and, after having been brought back to court, was given 15 years.

I went back to sit down on my piece of foam, and Baggis clambered back to his perch. I looked up, and noticed a small window that presumably only Baggis could look out through.

'What's outside?' I asked him.

'You can have a look if you like,' he replied.

I really had to pull myself up along the rickety ladder that was in reality only a few strands of wood hastily bashed into the sides of the wall. Using the outer side of my left foot, and the inner side of my right, I made my unsteady way to the top, then, with a heave, I was there. Looking down, it suddenly seemed as though I were about 20 feet off the ground. I felt a bit unsteady.

I looked out through the window into an open area and a medical building. It looked nice out there. There was a small patch of well-tended grass. It looked completely peaceful. I looked through the three different sets of bars that had been thrust across the window space over successive eras in the prison's history, to where a beautiful breadfruit tree stood. Its limbs rose upwards gracefully, like the mystical tree of life you see on really old Persian carpets. At the top, a light breeze made the branches rustle in the wind. They swayed slightly as if they were tired dancers after a long night out on the town. Further down past that, I saw some other out-buildings, although I didn't know what they were for. They looked like workshops of some description.

Suddenly, there was a noise from the other side of our door. As I looked, I thought I could see an eye looking back at us, through the 'bull's eye' or 'Judas hole' as it is sometimes referred to.

'Tally,' said Baggis, as the eye outside moved off. Several times a day the screws tried to get their tally, or the total numbers of prisoners added up together, and square it against the number that their records gave. It sometimes took several attempts to get the tally right, often resulting in frustrating line-ups in the hot sun while they continued to get it wrong.

Cherchung, click, cherchung click, cherchung CLICK! Louder and louder came the repeated sounds of doors being opened by the screws coming down from the gate area along both sides. Then our door sprung open, and swung inwards.

People were already milling around outside, moving up and down, going about their business. Little things would keep people busy, such as who was getting a visit that day, or who was getting a parcel. What might be in that parcel was always a matter that occasioned considerable consternation, especially if cigarettes or weed were due to come in with the other goodies.

I managed to get some energy together and headed off to the tiny room that had been converted into a shower area, right up at the top of D&E by the gate, and on the left. I got to a tap just as the rest of the gang arrived. There must have been about 30 of them, and not one of them was looking pleased to see me. I wondered, as I swiftly dipped my ammonia-smelling body under the running water, if I was about to get kicked to death in there.

'Morning fellas,' I tried cheerily, but not one face moved a muscle; every face seemed to be carved from granite. I noticed a piece of soap lying on the floor, and as I leant over to pick it up, I suddenly remembered the joke about prison life, where you never pick soap up off the floor of the shower, especially when you first come into a jail. It was too late though. I already had the small piece in my hand and in doing so had inadvertently flashed my white arse in the air, unfortunately in the direction of this posse of hard-looking characters. I didn't want to fuck about, but I didn't want to come across as nervous, either. In prison, such a course of action invariably creates the very problems you might be trying to run away from. If I were a much harder man, I would have played it much harder, but I am not, and never have been. I have to admit I was shit scared.

Nudity is something I have never been that comfortable with, least of all in front of other men. In all my time in Islamic cultures, it is one thing that almost never happens. Modesty, or the covering of one's private parts is considered an essential element of everyday civilised life. Another element that was to become a part of my predicament, was the size of some of these guys' equipment. Looking around at the other guys in the shower, and then looking down at my own excuse for a dick, I suddenly realised the truth behind that old adage. These black guys all had the most amazing physiques. They were like body-building champions, but whereas a white man would have to virtually live in a gym to get similar results, these guys just grew like this naturally.

I finished off, taking my time to rinse down. I didn't want to seem as if I felt under pressure. In prison you have to start as you mean to go on and that means being a bit hard, even a bit harder than you really are, or at least than you actually feel. I stepped over the little wall at the shower entrance, and walked naked into the corridor. My place was immediately taken by one of the black guys. The noise from the shower room was deafening. The younger men, especially, were screeching to one another as loudly as they possibly could, often deliberately imitating monkeys. Growing up in Wood Green, it was always considered an insult of the highest order to label a black guy a monkey, but here it was different. The monkey was regarded as a creature of cleverness and ingenuity, and was imitated, if only in fun, with an element of respect amongst the local men. I subsequently met two men with monkey labels: Monkey Man and Rass Monkey.

Both were proud of their titles, having earned them the hard way.

I towelled off in the corridor, not wanting to hang around any longer than I had to, and then slid back into my shorts. My oversized trainers were still the only shoes I had, so I put them back on. With the combination of heat and water, I could see that they were far from the most ideal form of footwear. I looked at what the other lads were wearing and saw that they all had slip-on shower shoes, the cheapest kind available in all the tourist shops. I made a note to try and get hold of some. But how?

***

I wondered what the routine was for the day. Nobody had told me and the guards didn't seem too pushed to make us do anything in particular. It was like a free-for-all. When I got back to the cell, I found Baggis hard at work wiping the floor off with a piece of damp sponge. He had just finished when Jamal came back with the bucket in his hand, and put it back, nice and clean, on its little wooden stand. Then he stepped outside, and in a little air vent on the outer side of the door placed the cleaning items he had used; a piece of sponge tied to a stick, and a pot for carrying the water you used for cleaning the bucket. It would be my turn tomorrow. I already felt like a bit of a tourist. I had shit in the bucket, but Jamal had carried that out. And I hadn't done anything in the cell, either. I promised myself that, the following day I would do something, even if it was only to wash my clothes. You had to keep yourself busy, specific tasks that had to be done if you wanted to stay on top of it all. If you started letting things slip, not cleaning the floor, or letting your clothes get dirty, you would attract the negative attentions of others and they would start taking the piss out of you. But it wasn't only that. You did it for the sake of your own morale. You had to get busy and do your work, even if the only 'work' you could do was keeping yourself and your cell ship-shape. Over the three years I was moved around from cell to cell and had to share with various different people, but this philosophy always stayed the same.

Breakfast time brought the next challenge. At the far end of the corridor I saw a small team of lads in white overalls and caps appear and start putting up a trestle table. The top of the table was metal, and looked well scrubbed. On top of this the men in white struggled to place a great steel urn. I smelt tea, sweet and hot, the aroma trailing down the corridor. I could see the bread, too, dozens of little rolls, all boxed up, fresh, or as fresh as fresh can be in prison, anyway.

I said hello to the first guy I saw, and greeted him with a Muslim blessing. I don't know why I did, I was nervous, but as with Baggis, I was more than surprised when he replied with a blessing himself. I was very lucky; I had inadvertently found a bond between the first two inmates I spoke to. He introduced himself as Donald Stanton, after we had both given our Muslim names.

Donald spoke with a slight American accent. I told him where I was from, and what I was in for. He seemed to know some of the details already. It was great to be making friends already. I felt elated that things were working out for me.

'You're going to need a bowl, for food, and a cup, of some kind,' Stanton told me.

'Where do I get them? I asked, rather naively. He gave me a look and made as if he was going to say something, then thought better of it.

'I'll see what I can do,' was all he said.

'I'll have a hunt, too, maybe someone's got a spare one,' I answered.

Then the leader of his team appeared. He was a really black-skinned fellow that everyone called Blackie. He stubbed out a cigarette that he had been pulling on—no sharing for him— and flicked it clear of the serving area.

The cry went up: 'Tea and bread! Get your tea and bread!' and men started appearing from the entire length of the corridor, rallying to the battle cry and congregating in a queue by the gate. Blackie started giving out tea to the men, while I went and got my old peanut butter jar. At least it had a screw-top lid, I thought to myself, as I lined up.

'Not so close man!' the guy in front of me nearly jumped into the air. He was a little fella, only about four feet something tall. I found out later that his name was Malcolm Forde, and he was a long-term prisoner there. Ten years on that sentence done with ten or so to go. He was making out that I'd 'bounced him'—that is, rubbed up against him in a sexually provocative way. I instantly knew that this little bastard had to be stood up to. Here it was; my first test. He was getting me to show my mettle. I raised my fist into his face, and snarled, showing some of the absent and broken teeth that the years of my most recent drug relapse had cost me.

He seemed suitably impressed. In his mind, he had me down for a nutter, best left alone. Not worth fucking with, especially if he might get bitten. As soon as I saw him take all this in, I relaxed, and smiled.

'Only joking,' I said, cheerfully. He turned around, and got ready to take his breakfast, fast realising that he was barking up the wrong tree if he had thought he was going to be able to bully me. I only hoped the rest of them considered me not worth the trouble either.

Later that day, Stanton came back with a pair of old shower shoes. Now that was what I called brotherhood! I accepted them, and we talked for a while about where I had been. In talking with Stanton, I realised that I had never really had the chance to talk over some of my experiences in

Afghanistan or Pakistan with anyone, or even to take time
out to properly review them.

He seemed amazed to meet someone who had travelled
those places. It occurred to me that I had a few travelling
stories that were worth telling, if not for any heroic role
I played, then at least for their rarity and individuality.
Stanton would drop by periodically after that, with a couple
of cigarettes or even the few spare peanut-butter packets
they would get together for those that got a special diet.
Sometimes he would ask me to write letters to his various
girlfriends. He had one in the States by the name of Fanny,
with whom he had had a son, also called Donald, and a
Chinese girl somewhere on the island. His sister had been
in the New York Police Department, but had been killed in
the line of duty.

Around this time, I found out that another lad, called
Tyson, had a pack of playing cards. This was a good chance to
get in with the lads, and make something of my time here. I
would borrow them, from time to time, to do tarot readings
for the lads who could afford to pay me the five cigarettes
that I was charging. Tyson, who was a body-building freak,
but with a definite interest in mysticism, asked me to help
him learn the tarot. I wrote down the meanings of each of
the cards, and within a day he had memorised them, along
with the way of laying out the cards in a spread called the
Celtic cross. Whenever I got a smoke out of doing a reading,
I made sure that Tyson got one too, because friends were
important in here, although naturally, I kept back the bulk
of my earnings for myself.

Quite a few of the lads came forward for readings while I
was down on that corridor, and all of them seemed pleased
with what I was able to tell them. There was Christopher
Smith, from St Vincent, who didn't believe me when I
told him that he would be going home on his appeal, after

having been given 14 years at his first court appearance. He had to wait an extra year for it to come, but go home he did, and without the help of any lawyer. I did a reading for Stanton. What I said seemed to affect him. He paid me a lot of cigarettes and then asked if I could do magic. At first I wasn't sure what to say, but when he pulled out a further ten cigarettes I suddenly remembered that of course I could do magic. He asked me to put a spell on his Chinese girlfriend. She was going to leave him, he said. She wasn't going to wait for him any more.

'Can you get her back for me?' he asked, as he handed me the other half of the packet. Jamal and Baggis were in the cell too. They liked to watch me do readings sometimes. They went totally silent now. I could almost hear them holding their breath as they realised that I was going to be able to give them a whole cigarette each. Already I was earning my respect, if not as a master magician, then at least as someone who could trick this guy from the kitchen out of a packet of cigarettes and provide a smoke that night.

***

The guys from the kitchen were notorious for messing with the prison's food, and were indicative of just how corrupt I learned this place could be. They would sell it off for their own personal gain, either right under the screws' noses, or often with their consent. The kitchen guys were known to be rich. For a few cigarettes, the universal currency in prison, they could provide you with extra meat, extra fish, canned sardines, big thick wedges of cheese, extra milk, or extra peanut butter. Well, after Stanton had paid me with a full packet of cigarettes, I felt that I had better give him something of value. After all, my reputation as a juju man was now at stake. I could hardly continue to trick people out of further smokes if I wasn't at least seen to be doing something mystical for Stanton, in return for his smokes. So, after cell doors were closed that night, we kept the light on for a bit, and I let the guys have a smoke each. It was appreciated, and I now felt more like a partner in the cell and less like a tourist. When we finished our smokes, we put the light out. I lay on the floor and looked at the thin strip of light under the door. As the evening wore on, I visualised this Chinese girl coming back to Stanton, and when the screw came for tally I was so entranced I didn't even notice him.

The next day Jamal and Baggis set the corridor ablaze with accounts of my magical prowess. When would Stanton's girl come back to him? The strangest thing is that she actually did, though long after he had given up on it ever happening. But who knows, maybe magic is like that, I can't say. Stanton never gave me the full and unlimited canteen he promised me, but I did get a bit of a living from him for writing his love letters. He was a bit of a lady's man. The letters I wrote were always considered to be the best in the entire prison, although several times I would have to do a rewrite if Stanton thought it needed changing. I was happy just to keep busy, and earn a little something along the way.

***

In the evenings the noise level along the corridor would increase as people milled around in the massively overcrowded area, hemmed in by heavy stonework extending in every direction. One night, I looked up to the next balcony, and saw people enjoying an almost party-like atmosphere. Almost everyone had a cigarette, some had several, but these were unlit and intended for sale or trade. I saw Biggs, a big Jamaican lad doing 25 years for running coke through the island, walking up and down with a packet of cigarettes in his hand. It was so dark in this corridor that I could see the whites of his eyes in stark relief. I went up to him and asked for a smoke.

He rolled his shoulders and made a half turn away.

'I can't do it man,' he said, clearly enjoying the chance to say no to someone gasping for a fag.

'This here has got to go on roll-on. I need to buy one roll-on. You got a roll-on?' A roll-on is a deodorant. It is obvious that the last thing I had was any fucking roll-on. The frustration was massive. If I were stronger I would have just knocked this bastard down and taken the fucking snouts. But I couldn't. While the drugs were still in my system, I might have had a James Bond fantasy that I could take this guy, but as the drugs faded the real world began to impinge upon the fantasy world. Inevitably the real world starts to win. It is a phase everyone coming off the gear has to go through, and it can take quite a while to make it through. It is not pleasant at all to come face to face with your own limitations, especially after living in the cocaine-inspired fantasy-land of delusion for so long. It was bad enough being stuck in London and having to face reality, but here, it was almost as if every day I woke up with the new realisation that my reality was my being stuck in a rotting, putrid prison 4,000 miles from home.

I was stuck for a smoke, and glanced around to where I might be able to cadge one. I saw one fella who indicated he might be interested in a card reading, and asked him if he was ready for it. He paused for a moment, thinking about it, then nodded his head.

'Come,' he said, and we toddled off down the lane to his cell.

Inside it was like the Hilton, with carpet on the floor, and big wooden lockers he had brought in with him. How did he manage that? This guy was coming to the end of a seven-year sentence, and had contracted HIV somewhere along the way. He might have been held down and raped by someone. If you find yourself in a headlock with a blade to the side of your neck there's not a lot you can do about it if someone starts sliding up your arse. HIV and Hepatitis C were very common in the prison, I was told. The combination of shared razor blades, dirty needles for tattooing, and unprotected sex made it inevitable. Men sell themselves for cigarettes, packets of biscuits or drugs in prison. This place was no exception, and every now and then you could hear the screams of some poor bastard being held down and raped.

I sat down and laid the cards out. I put my hand out for the cigarettes he was going to pay me. He smiled, and took out a few smokes. It wasn't much, but it would do. At least I could smoke that day, and I really needed to. My withdrawal was really getting to me and I was suffering. My skin felt like it was crawling off my body. I got him to shuffle, and concentrate his thoughts into the cards. Originally this pack had just the basic 52 cards, but since Tyson had been learning the tarot we expanded it to the full complement of 78. When he was finished, I took the cards from him and laid them out in the Celtic cross pattern. I looked through the cards but I wasn't sure what I saw, let alone what I was going to tell him. It looked as though he was coming straight back to the prison after he left. It was too depressing to say that directly to him, though. Surely there was something else there in his cards? I tried to talk around what I saw, but he had already sussed that I was avoiding the truth. I could see it in his eyes, just as he could see it in mine. This was dangerous. I was alone in his cell with him. I didn't want him shooting the messenger. In the end I just told him to play it very carefully when he got out. There. That was the least negatively-loaded way I could find of expressing it without being an outright liar.

Later that night, I lit up my well-earned smoke from a wick, and pulled on it. After waiting this long for a smoke, you would have thought that the satisfaction would have been immense. But it was not. It was all a big anti-climax. What a waste of time. There was barely any sensation from this smoke at all, certainly nothing to write home about. I made a vow that before this sentence was done I would have stopped smoking. I knew it would take time, but the decision had been made and I was determined to see it through.

Though this was a major struggle for me, in a way I was helped out by the corruption that was rife in this place. For some, all they had were their cigarettes, which acted as currency in prison, yet those who could usually kept whatever they wanted to themselves and held back on supplying the inmates with what was rightfully theirs. The British Embassy was bringing in two cartons of cigarettes per month for each British inmate. This was paid for by money sent by the Prisoners Abroad charity. Time and time again my cartons kept vanishing. I discovered that a small group of British inmates had managed to insinuate themselves in a series of fairly strategic jobs in the prison. One was up in the library, with a guard called Miss Coombes, where all phonecalls could be controlled. Another was over at reception, where all the cigarettes were supposed to be logged in a book. This system inevitably broke down because it relied on some level of integrity from whoever was writing down the designation of the cartons to the individual prisoners. A little cabal arose in which these guys and their friends could divert other inmates' cigarettes and divide them between themselves, leaving one or two people—whoever they thought they could safely pick on—completely without any wherewithal for the remainder of the month.

It wasn't just that they were cigarettes, they were far more important than that because they were the main trading item within the prison. If you had no cigarettes, you had nothing to exchange things for, and had no way of getting hold of things like soap, or some decent food from the crooked kitchen staff. You could end up walking around for the month half-starved, sharing an infected razor with someone, and gathering up diseases because you had nothing to wash with.

My cigarettes kept going missing, but each time I tried to phone the Embassy to find out what was happening, the guy in the library would get Miss Coombes to block the call. On the rare occasion when I did manage to get through, all they could tell me was that they had definitely sent them, and they couldn't tell me why I had not received them, suggesting that I take it up with the prison administration. When I tried this, the prison officer at the gate would be told by another member of the cabal that I had been given my cigarettes and was only trying it on in an attempt to squeeze more out of the Embassy, so my protests were always ignored.

These bastards were thieving off me, and laughing about it every time they made their way back to their cells with not only their own share of cigarettes, but an extra helping courtesy of me. Stuck in the dark and dank wing where I was, I was powerless to track any of them down and confront them, but I knew who they were. These British inmates were the worst human beings I had ever come across, and I had come across a lot of very unsavoury characters. Thieving off fellow prisoners is considered to be about as low as you can get, but these scumbags really took the cake. The worst offenders were lucky they were released when they were, because they would have been ripped apart eventually, for all the bullshit they were getting up to.

Some of the inmates immediately traded their cigarettes for weed, and even crack, which found its way into the prison quite easily. They would even rush across the yard to intercept the guy whose job it was to carry the cartons to reception where they were supposed to be distributed. Mostly they wanted their cartons all at once, so they could score as much crack as they could, for a one-off smoke that very night. The desperation of this brought back terrible memories for me, but as I began to clear crack from my system, I could see clearly how shocking their addictions were, and then, how shocking mine must have been.

They would trade everything they had for one night of smoking crack, then hobble around for the rest of the month poncing off whoever they could mug a cigarette from. Some would wash other inmates' clothes—three cigarettes for a set of clothes—while others would hassle their families in the UK, or their extended families as was often the case, in Barbados or Jamaica, into sending parcels. They might get a pair of trainers, which they would immediately try to sell off. Everything they could get their hands on went straight out on drugs. These guys astonished me. They didn't have the ability to say no, or even to think it. I thought I had seen some really bad cases of absolute, resolute and unrepentant addiction in my time, but these guys were even more hardened than anything I had come across.

It was with horror that I realised that I could so easily have become one of them. In a way, I had already started to descend into that life, and only stopped when I was sent to prison where thankfully I had enough time and enough sense to realise that this was not a way to live.

Thankfully, I had never reached the depths some of these guys had reached and would never rise out of. I discovered that many were selling themselves to known 'Bullermen', who took out all of their sexual frustrations on whoever they could force down or pay enough to. One in particular had shacked up with a guy called 'Most Wanted' Jones, who would later come to be seen as the main cause of the riot that would bring the horrors of the prison to the media's attention. I decided there was no way, no matter how hard it was, that I was going to go back to drugs. In prison, it was just too dangerous. It always involved exploitation, beatings, and endless trouble, and I had had enough of all three.

CHAPTER EIGHT

LIFE IN GLENDAIRY

In Glendairy, the lads who had fried their brains with too much cocaine were known as the 'Paros'. Most cocaine users in Britain can safely sail through several years' worth of weekend usage and emerge more or less intact, mentally. In Barbados, with cheap strong cocaine, this is not the case. I was surrounded by drugs in the prison. Every day someone offered me a little hit. I would remind myself that I was now off the bus, wanted to stay that way, and thank the bastard that offered me the smoke. Bit by bit, I realised that saying no earned me some respect on the corridor. Mostly these dealers got a different response, from junkies all too eager to do anything after a blast to maintain that high. I've been there. An old wolf can smell a new trap.

I was still clucking a month into my sentence. I felt like I was being tortured every day. I was in so much pain, I was sweating severely, I could barely walk and I just wanted to curl up and die, but I knew that with each passing day I was getting closer to my destination. My body was on a massive drug-clearance exercise, and I knew that this was the only way for me to go. Eventually, I was hauled up in front of the prison doctor. Apparently my 'behaviour' had been noticed by one of the prison officers. I was walking like a crippled man and they wanted to check me. If I wanted to lay on the old junkie con and get some drugs from the doctor, this was my chance. I was sitting on a small wooden stool by one of the biggest, burliest screws in the place. When I tried to draw closer to the doctor, I realised that the stool was bolted to the ground. I couldn't move it. I took a deep breath, and told the doctor that I was a registered addict in London prior to coming on this run, but that I had already made my way through most of this cold turkey so, thanks but no thanks, I won't be needing any of his 'help'. I had seen some of what his help could do back on D&E corridor. The Paros walked around not knowing what day it was, long lines of saliva running out the sides of their mouths as they shuffled along, lining up for their injections once a week.

As I came out from that meeting, I felt as if I had passed some kind of a test, and although no-one said anything, or did anything, there was a kind of unspoken sense of having earned the respect of the other men on my corridor. As I was led back from the medical unit, the whole of D&E had already been shut down, and everything was really quiet. Prisons, when they are locked down, are usually really peaceful places. You could almost be in somewhere like the cloisters of Oxford or Cambridge. For some, prison is a place of refuge and safety, where they can be accepted, even admired, and sleep without being afraid that someone is going to get them. Listening to many of the guys' tales, I heard that on the outside a lot of them used to sleep with a gun in each hand in case one of their drug dealing competitors decided to raid them.

***

We used to see a fair bit of the girls from the Female Prison. Sophie Daniels was the one I liked and cheered for. She was a big girl, tough as old boots, but beautiful in her big beefy way. She was in for killing her boyfriend with an electric fan, although exactly how she did that I'm not sure. At first she was sentenced to be hanged, and the whole island held its breath until her appeal to see if the judges were really serious about hanging a woman. Any kind of hanging, these days, looks bad internationally, which is why Barbados still hasn't gotten around to hanging the 20 or so men on Death Row. But hanging a woman would be diplomatic suicide. So, while her appeal was lined up, Sophie busied herself studying. She improved her writing skills, and even got a certificate at a ceremony in the Mess Hall for religious studies.

When Sophie's appeal came up, she got lucky, and was allowed to go home right then and there. Some men complained that there was now one law for women who kill their partners, and another for men who do the same.

One of the other girls was from Switzerland. She was actually very attractive, with a big bust, slim waist and lovely curved hips. Her hair was long and dark, and ran down to the middle of her back. She was loved and admired by just about all the men in the prison. In fact, all of the girls were. Some had admirers who made deals with the kitchen boys who took the cooked food into the Female Prison to smuggle in love letters and blooms from the prison gardens.

The Swiss girl, I heard, got caught by the art teacher up in the toilets of what used to be the art room with her pants down. She was meeting in there with a local man to get screwed, and she was found in a compromising position. This girl was rumoured to have been a favourite amongst many of the guards and was quite often brought before them, only to have the door closed behind her. By a strange coincidence, she managed to be let out years before her time.

There was a course going on at that time run by a really old guy who we would see walking around every Tuesday.

One night he went on local TV to talk about the appalling lack of sanitation in the place. After that, we didn't see him in the prison any more, which was sad, because he was speaking the truth—the conditions really were a disgrace.

They were actually fucking gross. That human beings were kept under these conditions even to this day makes me sit here and breathe deeply, staring at the fucking floor. It is something that is very hard to get around; that there are places like that still operating in the world today. It is ironic that one of the worst was operating in a place most people would associate with heaven, bliss, and luxury. Glendairy was the very opposite. Everything was improvised. The buckets men used to piss and crap in, sitting in the corner of each cell, were really the tubs which the margarine had been brought in, with a piece of wire threaded between two holes punched on either side of the rim. Every morning, a vast long line of men would scuttle along the tiny corridors, all carrying huge heavy buckets full of unimaginable crap in a conga line towards a 'shit well', where everybody just dumped the contents. You can't even imagine the stink off that place. That was, of course, assuming it hadn't become clogged up and sealed off. Then we would have to carry the buckets to some skips that had been brought in. This was always far worse, because the contents of these buckets would all too easily spill when you had to raise them up this way over the side of the skips to empty them. Needless to say, here and there fights would inevitably break out when splashings of fellow prisoners occurred, all watched over cheerfully by screws who stood well away to one side and gloated at the prospect of seeing a bit of blood shed that early in the day. It was impossible to get these buckets properly clean. You could maybe buy some disinfectant, which was obtainable, but at the price of, say, about ten cigarettes, which was frankly a heavy price to pay.

The food containers, similarly, were completely home made; again made out of smaller Mello Cream containers, cut down to size and fitted with a lid over the top. We had to wonder where the money to buy actual food containers was going, because this couldn't have been the intention of the justice department. There weren't even any seats in the Mess Hall where you could sit down and enjoy your meal eaten out of an empty plastic container. One or two people were able to buy a metal bowl—I had one for a time, but it could have ended up costing me dearly. A guy called Azariah, nicknamed 'Grandpa' stole it from me. This was the cause of a lot of underlying tension between him and me that surfaced later on. He had traded me a metal bowl in exchange for a smoke, and one day wanted to borrow it back from me, to collect some food in. I didn't like that idea—after having had hepatitis once before, in Afghanistan, I wasn't overly keen on repeating the experience. So I told him where to get off. He didn't like that, and while my back was turned he went to the bucket I kept my meager possessions in and, taking the lid off, took out my metal bowl, and then scuttled off with it to get himself some food. I was livid. But I knew he was a bit too tough for me, so I bided my time.

My chance for revenge came a couple of weeks later. I just sat there, while he would merrily smile into my face and continue to eat from my former food bowl, the cheeky bastard. He had this habit at the very end of the day, of taking out a big tub of Nivea body cream and lathering himself all over with it, especially his legs. It really seemed to make his day. Well, one evening while he was in the shower I went and dipped my hands into his cloth shoulder bag, and took out the tub of cream. Wallop! Straight into the big dust bin round the back that went. What a satisfying feeling it gave me, too. Well, the next step, now that I had well and truly 'lit the fuse' so to speak, was to vacate the area. So, I nipped over, nice and easy, to the other side of the Mess Hall. Keeping myself fairly well hidden, I was dying to see his face when he came back and discovered that his tub o' cream, just like my metal bowl, had mysteriously grown legs and walked away. Well, back he came, full of the joys of spring, straight out of the shower, all fresh as a daisy. Reaching into his bag with his right hand, his face was a picture; slowly, at first, a look of vague concern, then, faster and faster the change over, till it became a mask of rage as the penny dropped and he realised he'd been fucked. It was a classic. Slowly, like a German machine gunner, he swivelled his face around across the Mess Hall, trying to work out who'd done him. I ducked down, keeping my gaze firmly on the TV and trying desperately to look engrossed in the children's programme—I think it was a 1970s version of Sesame Street—that was showing. I could feel the blast of hate, like a furnace door open, coming from his direction, but hopefully he wouldn't suss it was me. After all, he had no proof, eh? Maybe it was the same pixie that had had that metal bowl away, eh? Fuck me, though, I could still feel the fucker glowering at me. No, no, it had to be my imagination, surely. I began to wonder about the wisdom of fucking with this nutter. Maybe I had just gone and really fucked up. Nah, I thought, brazen it out. After a while, I couldn't resist any longer. Something on the programme made me laugh, but as soon as I did, I realised I was the only one who had done so. One or two of the lads sitting nearby looked over at me to see what was quite SO funny, but it was when my eyes turned along a bit further just to check that Old Grandpa wasn't watching that our eyes met and I knew he was. Oh fuck, he has sussed. Right then and there I knew that unless I was really careful, I might find myself paying for that tub o' cream big time.

***

Otherwise Glendairy was an absolute toilet, and I thank the gods it eventually went up in flames. Heaven knows it needed to be demolished. Running up the sides of it were great cracks that just shouted out that they were going to fall down and crush a few people; the corridors B and C had had building inspectors round several times to check the safety of the place and it had been condemned by them—no less than five or six times—yet the place was still used to house prisoners. It was only when Hurricane Ivan came close to Barbados that for a couple of days all the men quartered on B and C were temporarily accommodated in the Mess Hall, in which all the gates were boarded up with sheets of hardboard, and their shit buckets and beds carried across for the duration of their stay there. This was just in case the building blew down under the pressure of the intense winds. It was a genuine concern, too. That same hurricane went right over the nearby island of Grenada, and totally devastated Richmond Hill Prison, from which hundreds of inmates actually escaped, and many were shot by police who were sent in to stop them.

Lt Col John Nurse had been a desk jockey at the tiny Barbadian Defence Force before taking up the job of superintendent at Glendairy. Dazzled by delusions of his own military greatness, his main concern was walking around like Idi Amin with his red cap band on. He was usually flanked by a couple of hefty guards. When he appeared in all his glory, 'inspecting' the prison, everyone immediately had come to attention until he had passed.

On one occasion Nurse held convocation in the Mess Hall. Every inmate, except those on H&I, the wing where all the men on Death Row were kept, had to be there. He made a speech about how the prison worked and how we should behave and then stated that we as prisoners did not have any rights. We inmates were going to have to take everything that was coming to us. We all knew it, but I couldn't believe he was actually saying it out loud and admitting it.

Having said that, while I was in Glendairy, Nurse allowed teachers to come into the prison for the first time, to improve the prisoners' reading and writing. Classes would take place in the Mess Hall. Here and there, small conglomerations of up to 20 or 30 men would sit round a single blackboard on an easel. It was elementary beginnings, but a very encouraging sign. He did try to improve the educational facilities in the prison, while that option was still there.

At one point I even made a small contribution to teaching. I taught algebra! I put the algebra questions to them as if they were for bales of weed, rather than mysterious 'x's.

'So, if you buy 100 kilos of weed for $1,000, how much will one kilo cost? And if you sell the 50 of the kilos for $1,500, 30 kilos for $2,000, and the remainder you have to throw away before the police come, how much profit have you made? By putting these sums to them in this format, I found that I had a team of budding mathematicians on my hands. It seemed so obvious to link their desire to understand mathematics with something as practical as knowing how much money you are making in your business.

The problem was that as with everything else, these schemes were vulnerable to corruption, or at best were grossly unfair to the inmates if anything worthwhile came out of them. The art teacher was from Barbados but she had contacts throughout art galleries in North America. She was with NIFCA, the National Institute for Fine and Creative Arts. She was responsible for getting the work of talented inmates exhibited in the outside world. For this, the prison would take a hefty slice. Nurse felt the need to defend this on more than one occasion during his periodic appearances in the Mess Hall. They even took a chunk to pay for the electricity the inmates used while they painted! Every inmate in the entire prison was summoned to come and hear him talk. On those occasions the Mess Hall was so crammed there wasn't room to turn around. For some men, these inequalities were such that they refused to paint anymore. One such man was Coronel, the chief Colombian, who was doing about 20 years for flying a plane over Barbados and dropping half a ton of cocaine into a field in the north of the island. The trouble was, when he came over personally to pick it up, his car was followed and the police caught him while he and his men were attempting to get this load into the back of their car. From all accounts, the amount was so huge there was no way it was going to be able to fit in. He had a lot of talent, but he would rather give up than give his money to the prison.

***

The first time I met Nurse was when I had been in the prison a few months. By this time I had gradually learned the ropes and knew how to stay out of trouble. But I was still nervous because in a place like this, all it took was to be in the wrong place at the wrong time and that was that. Stabbings, beatings and rapes were commonplace, and you had to keep your wits about you. I was summoned to Nurse's office. Crossing the yard, I was taken to the white building at the very front of the prison complex. The screw knocked to announce our arrival, and we heard a muffled voice from inside. As I entered he held up a typed letter in one hand and asked me: 'What is this?' It was from a bank, about my overdrawn account.

'Seems to be a private matter, sir,' I said. For some reason the officials had included Nurse's name at the top, hence the letter being drawn to his attention. He gave me the letter, and asked if I intended to write back. I said I would, and took the letter.

'Aren't you working, yet?' Nurse asked me.

'Work sir?' I asked, as if it were the first ever time I had heard that word. Nurse said he would see if he could put something my way. I was actually desperate for work, desperate to get out in the sunshine and feel the air on my body, but to have shown my eagerness would have meant a knock-back.

Emptying the buckets in the morning was supposed to be a duty taken in turns by each man in the three-man cell. Yet this didn't always happen, as some men had a distinct aversion to doing it. Somehow I had this job allocated to me by some of the other prisoners, probably because when I came into the jail, I was so mind swept I didn't have it in me to refuse and I was easy to take advantage of. But there was another side to it. When I first arrived I was smoking cigarettes, and by carrying out another man's bucket you could earn a cigarette. Each morning I would busy myself carrying out about four or five men's buckets, and earn just enough cigarettes for that day. But it was demanding. Some men's buckets would be full right to the brim, and you had to be careful not to spill anything on the way along the narrow landing or down the uneven steps. It was disgusting having to carry these buckets out, the rim just inches from my nose, just waiting for them to spill over onto my arms. Also, they would be pernickety about how well their buckets were cleaned; some would hold it up so they could check to see that you had cleaned underneath before paying you. There was a specific way of cleaning them. Outside each cell, in a small recess by the door, each cell would keep its own home-made cleaning brush. This was normally a wooden strip with various rags wrapped around the ends of it. The implement was used to rub the inside of each bucket to try to clean it. After emptying the contents into the well we got some water to rinse the inside of the bucket. This was then emptied into the well, too. Then, you had to cast your small sprinkle of washing powder into the bucket, and use the home-made brush to get some kind of a lather going. Up and down, all around, inside and outside, and then just to foil the perfectionist bastards, and they were many, the bottom of the bucket, too. Then came the rinse off, and a quick swirl was normally enough to suffice. Then, back with everything to its owner, and, after getting the cigarette and depositing that safely for future consumption, off to the next one. You had to be a bit sharpish, too. You only had so long to get around your corridor and do as many buckets as possible before the screws got tired of it all and started shutting the gates.

After a little while, Mr Shorey from the prison admin came to my cell and asked me if I would be prepared to carry out buckets from H&I. I would have taken any job to get out of that hot cell. It was known I was doing buckets for 'money' on my own wing, and this would be allowed to continue if I took the bucket job on H&I. I would be allowed to do private buckets all day, if I so desired, anywhere in the building. This meant, theoretically, that I could earn as much as a packet of cigarettes a day, as long as I was prepared to put the work in, and go round all the corridors, soliciting bucket jobs. I would also earn Barbadian$15 or so from the prison itself. This was what many of the other bucket men on H&I did, and it was possible to build up your list so that at the end of each day you could afford a blast of weed, or even crack, but I no longer wanted those expenses, so after a while, relatively speaking, I became an incredibly wealthy man inside Glendairy.

Slopping out three or four cells was enough to fill the buckets we carried. We would then have to carry these

Above: As a boy in London I inherited my family's desire to see the world and went to a Nautical School until I gained entry into the London School of Economics.

© *John Alexander Donaldson*

Above: The long road up to Glendairy Prison in Barbados, where I was to spend three years in horrendous conditions.

Right: Superintendent of Prisons, Mr John Nurse on one of his inspections of the prison.
© *Carson Cadogan*

Above and Below: Chaos reigned as Hell came to Barbados. Riots and a fire swept through Glendairy as prisoners looked to settle scores all around me.
© *The Nation*

Right: The women's prison was evacuated first, but after a few days penned into cages in the blistering sun, we were brought to another location.
© *The Nation*

Above: Mia Mottley, then Attorney General and now Deputy Prime Minister, with then Opposition Leader Clyde Mascoll, were shown first-hand by John Nurse the devastation after the riot.
© *The Advocate*

Below: After all my years abroad I am finally home again in London. With my feet firmly on the ground, I hope to help others overcome their addictions.

massively heavy buckets right the way down the length of the corridor, pausing at each of the gateways so the screws could unlock and let us through. Normally we didn't have any rubber gloves. Some of the bucket men didn't even have shoes. The prison didn't supply us with any sanitary equipment. It was up to each man to somehow sort out his own arrangements. How were we supposed to do that? There was no way of getting proper equipment within the prison, and all the Embassy seemed to do was offer you cigarettes once a month. We had to be careful not to slip up on the slippery floor or spill any of the buckets' contents. Getting it on your hands could be dangerous for obvious hygiene reasons. For the first couple of months doing this work I had to stop about three times on each trip en route to the shit well, where we emptied the buckets, round the front of the building. It was heavy going, and the fumes coming up would sometimes nearly overcome me. I had to carry an empty bucket around with me, to sit down and take a breather every now and then. I just had no energy, and I was beginning to feel woozy whenever I exerted myself, but I put it down to the ongoing withdrawal symptoms and the general filthy stench of the fumes I was forced to inhale. This was another factor that helped me to decide that I was going to try to give up smoking cigarettes for good. I was out of breath too often.

I started to visualise my coming off cigarettes as a great big cloud of steam coming out of me, and somehow it worked, because I found it easy to ease off gradually until I was only smoking one a day, in the evening. The more I eased off, the more stress-free I became, and I started to feel better about myself, not because my health was improving—I still felt pretty bad most of the time and was becoming tired too easily—but because I was giving up another drug, and one I felt was the real gateway to other drugs. Almost every person's first drug is a cigarette. I realised, years too late, that taking any kind of drug was a one way road into all manner of chaos and trouble. The sooner I turned around and started to go back out of this street I had come down, the better I would be. Getting back to where I had been might prove to be very difficult, even impossible, I thought, but the sooner I made the start, the sooner I might 'get there'.

I knew it would be difficult because I am well aware of the trouble drug users, even cigarette smokers, feel when they fail. It is very difficult to deal with setbacks and disappointment. Believe me, I know. Disappointment had led me to where I was. I had been trying to deal with the come down from being so high all my life, in a world of make-believe, only to find out that I wasn't some great macho guy, but a muppet. But if I needed reminding of my worthlessness, all I had to do was look around me. So I stuck with it, and once I got to grips with it, my efforts proved worthwhile.

I still collected my two packets of cigarettes from the British Embassy, which had now stopped being nicked, but I used them to pay for other things, such as other peoples' boiled eggs in the morning. With my newfound wealth I was even able to buy luxuries like a cucumber or tomato brought in from outside.

Down amongst the condemned men on H&I, I got to meet a lot of interesting but desperate people, and I felt outraged at the dreadful conditions in which they were forced to spend the remainder of their lives. The only thing they had to look forward to in life was the end of it, when they would be brought out and put to death. Some of these men deserved a lifelong sentence, undeniably. They had committed horrible, horrible crimes. Some may argue too that they deserved to be put to death. But they didn't deserve to live like this for years on end and then be put to death.

Barnes had a cell to himself, about halfway down the corridor on the right. He had done 25 years of a Queen's Pleasure sentence. His sister had left him in charge of her two kids one evening, and he had killed them both. He tried to hide them in the freezer. When she came back he said he hadn't seen them. He was never getting out. Somehow Barnes had managed to stay in excellent physical shape and still looked pretty much as he did in the ancient newspaper article about himself he had kept all those 25 years, and which he carefully unfolded in front of me to read.

Barnes would sometimes ask me to write letters for him, which I was happy to do, especially if there was something in it for me. Usually I got paid in cigarettes, which if I didn't want, I could at least use to trade for something else. One such letter was a request to the prison administration for 'new handcuffs, new chains, new shackles, and porno magazines for the library.' I pointed out that they couldn't stock those types of magazines, but he started to get annoyed, so I asked and stuck out for another cigarette, which I got. Then, after drawing in a deep breath, I explained to him, with a hint of a wink, that they might be prepared to stock magazines of women wearing swimsuits. He liked this, and started regarding me as some kind of a genius after that.

Further down the corridor was Elephant Man, Frank White. He must have weighed about 30 stone, and had been sitting in there for about five years waiting for his trial. He was up for murder. He had enticed his homosexual lover to come with him in a car out to some deserted area, where he had stabbed him several times, and just left the body dumped on the side of the road. He had then driven off in his friend's car, in which he was arrested a couple of days later. Amazingly enough, his lawyer later managed to get him a blinding result of only about six years. In Barbados allowance is not normally made for the period of time a defendant has spent on remand, but this was still a really good result for this guy. I never liked him though.

Another fucking loony was Taxi Man, so-called because prior to his arrest that had been his job; just mini-cabbing, really, without any licence. Taxi Man was a young man, still in his early 20s, and his crime had been to kill a man at a night-club. When the case came to court, it came out that Taxi Man had been trying to pull somebody else's woman while dancing, and her boyfriend had intervened. Taxi Man then smashed a bottle of drink on the floor, and began cutting into the man's neck. According to the words of one witness, 'He was jookin', jookin' wild!' (jookin' means stabbing).

Taxi Man looked terrible in the write-up the newspapers had given him. Sullen-faced, he had said nothing in his own defence, except, 'May God be my judge.' The judge put the infamous black cap on his head and handed down a death sentence, finishing with the well-known words, 'And may the Lord have mercy upon your soul.'

Taxi Man was brought into the prison, as are all those sentenced to death, by a special squad of court bailiffs all wearing the old red British uniform and white pith helmet. The police van they brought him in entered the prison compound with its lights flashing and siren howling, and the entranceway to the Main Prison was sealed off by a detachment of police that they had brought along with them. Taxi Man was whisked up those five steps and along the narrow corridor that led into the Back Prison, through the metal gate at the end, and down the steps and right into H&I.

Inside H&I you were immediately hit by how different it was from the rest of the prison. It was dark, very cool, and very quiet. The section was divided into two parts; the front and the back. The front contained men doing solitary, but for breeches of discipline, such as raping or stabbing. On either side of a narrow corridor some six feet wide, were two sets of ancient, heavy wooden doors. Each man inside could look through the grill at the top of the doors and talk with the others, if he wanted to. Here were prisoners such as Trevor Eastman, who was a known arsonist, having flamed Blackrock Mental Hospital and as a result found himself incarcerated in Glendairy. I would take numerous books down to Trevor when he was in his rare reading moods.

Next to him was Dangerous Ground. I had been warned about getting too close to him whilst slopping out, as he could suddenly turn. Officer Carmichael, himself known as a hard man was, I always noticed, particularly vigilant and ready with his truncheon at hand whenever this prisoner's door was unlocked.

After him was Jah Hool, who was a very quiet and very serious Rasta man, with great dreadlocks running several feet down the side of his head. Whenever he emptied out his bucket he would first have to tie back his dreadlocks, so they wouldn't get in the way of the mess. Jah Hool was famous, inside as well as outside the prison, for being a rebel. Tales would abound as to how he would light up spliffs right in front of police, and fight them if they tried to arrest him, usually resisting successfully too. He was in H&I for stabbing another prisoner who had grassed on him.

Grazettes was next in the line. He was on H&I for raping another prisoner. Grazettes and I had played chess when I first arrived, and I never saw any of the behaviour that he apparently exhibited towards the younger men; with me he was always totally respectful. He used to call out to me as I went I to do the buckets, asking, 'How are you, Mr Bond?' but because of what he had done it was a long time before I could find it in me to speak to him again, let alone be friendly. For him it was as if nothing had happened. Nothing at all.

Billie Jo was next, and it was for him that my assistant bucket man would smuggle weed in. I would distract the guard at the crucial moment, and my assistant would spit the weed into Billie Jo's cell straight from his mouth onto the floor.

Then you came to the gateway that separated the front part of H&I from the back. You had to wait until one of the screws unlocked the gate, which was set into a wall of bars and concrete. As you stepped through, you were dazzled by the bright fluorescent bulbs, which were kept on constantly in the back part of H&I. This was where all the condemned men were kept.

Toffee, whose name was spelt like the sweet but pronounced with a slight emphasis on the last syllable, was an elderly man who had been waiting there some 17 years. His cell was first on the left. Toffee never ate his cheese cutter in the morning but would always put it in a paper bag for me to take away. But the state of his shit bucket was something else. Most of the guys used to shit straight onto a sheet of newspaper, and carefully wrap this up, and put it in the bucket. Not Toffee. He would shit straight into the bucket, and then expect me come into his cell, pick it up, and then carry it out into the corridor. There I would have to empty it into the much bigger buckets we had for collection, and bring back his bucket to where it normally stood.

Further along were Jeffrey Josephs, and after him Lennox Boyce. For some reason they had killed a girl. They were appealing the death sentences they were given. They were always really cheerful and happy to see me. It was their chance to chat with a genuine Londoner. They used to put on mock cockney accents and sometimes give me some of their food as a tip. I remember once Josephs asked me if I had ever seen the Queen, and I was able to tell him about the one time when I actually met Her Majesty when she visited the stall owners on Gabriel's Wharf.

On the other side of the corridor was Anthony Mears, who had killed some guy because he was 'queer', and then Mr Lickerish, who had done away with his wife and, I think, child, in a state of mind most of us, hopefully, will never know anything about. He was very scholarly, and we would regularly talk about *The Lord of the Rings*, and other matters. I felt that Mr Lickerish was a powerful driving force for the revolutionary ideology that was emanating quietly around the prison but I could never be sure. He was a black man's Lenin. But he was also a murderer, I had to remind myself.

Downstairs was the more underground section of the prison, where men had been waiting for 15 and 17 years to be hanged. These men would all keep busy on their schedules each day, keeping fit, cleaning out their cells, doing their reading and writing, learning their Spanish lessons. They weren't just sitting there doing nothing. The routine in H&I was always chock-a-block. Straight after breakfast there would be visits from medical orderlies, administration officials, and so on. After this, those men who had visits from relatives or lawyers, or who had to go make a phone call from the library, or had to go see the doctor or dentist (if it was Thursday), would be shackled and handcuffed, and led off to wherever they had to go.

The solitary cell was right at the bottom of the lower tier of cells, and here was a place I never wanted to end up. If the prison itself was like Hell, this was the very heart of it, the inner circle. It was no better than a torture chamber, and I can't understand how a place like this could possibly be allowed to operate in the modern world. Many a time I would be carrying out buckets down that end and the screw on duty would open the double set of doors for this cell, to let me clean inside. The outer door was thick and solid. It had no opening set into it, not even for air to pass through. Inside was a door made of heavy bars, criss-crossed, like multiple letter Xs. Yet another big key was required to open it. Often I would see someone I knew inside, and say hello. Sometimes I would ask the screw if I could give the man a cigarette, but the answer was always no. The man inside would be totally naked, in case he tried to hang himself, which was always a distinct possibility. His clothes, including his underpants, were kept in a little pile outside the door for when he was returned to the outer world. Inside this cell there was just a horizontal metal rail running from one side to the other. The prisoner could be shackled to this bar to restrain him, so he couldn't even move around that much. It was almost totally dark, with just the tiniest piece of light coming in through a glass window, which led out to the outside world. Rats and cockroaches would run wild around the inmate inside the cell. In the corner was a really filthy bucket, dirty from years of never being properly cleaned. It leaked so that when a man urinated into it the piss would run out across the floor, and the prisoner would have to stand there in his bare feet, in the middle of the pool.

***

I could only stick with that job for four months, but got reassigned to the garden, under Miss Daniels, who was a real sweetie. It was great to be out in the sun, and away from the dark and dreary cells full of killers and their shit buckets. In between shifts I would sit underneath the five palm trees that flourished in the middle of the courtyard in front part of the prison. I brought my bucket, or portable seat wherever I went. Underneath these trees I could experience the pleasure of some shade and chat a bit with some other passing inmates, as they made their way back and forth to the workshops or the small medical unit. Sometimes the word was out that the storeroom had some new toothbrushes in, or even some razors, and there would be a rush to get hold of some of these treasured items. The severe shortage of razors meant that virtually everyone in the prison was sharing, which may well have been the way I caught Hepatitis C round about this time. Hep C and HIV, as well as many other blood-borne diseases, ran rife through the prison.

Once again there were rackets going on where people in positions of power took advantage of the circumstances. The bastards in charge of the barber shop would rarely, if ever, do their assigned job and use the electric razor to shave your head or chin unless you paid them. The fee was normally two or three cigarettes. The guards would always look the other way and let these clowns have their little rackets.

It wasn't until I got out and had returned to London that I was diagnosed with it for the second time. I am very fortunate that I live in a country where I can be diagnosed, and where society is prepared to pay the money required to cure me, but the poor lads in Barbados who might eventually discover they have the virus don't get that help, and maybe that is why they aren't tested.

Apart from my health, I was beginning to find my feet and could afford to have things done for me, such as have my clothes washed, or maybe buy some new sandals, and when word got out that I had quit smoking as well as the harder stuff, I sensed a strange sort of admiration and respect for me coming through. I could overhear people ask my cell mates if I had quit 'for real', and many didn't, or couldn't believe that someone who had been so far gone when he arrived could now be winning a battle against all narcotics. People would come up to me to test me, saying, 'You've done really well so far man. Now reward yourself with a smoke.' But I would always decline, remembering to thank them anyway, just in case I offended anyone I would later regret, like I had done with Grandpa.

CHAPTER NINE

CRIMES AND PUNISHMENTS

I n Glendairy, radios were not allowed and the only
television in the entire building was way off in the
Mess Hall, so many evenings we would tell stories. Men
would be galvanised into using their imaginations to stave
off boredom and make the evenings pass interestingly. Each
man would take his turn to tell his stories, many of which
would revolve around him being the fastest draw, the most
charismatic, the most daring robber, or lover. I was disgusted
and outraged at some of the stories, particularly those
involving rape. This is a horrible crime, but it was made even
worse by the fact that some of these guys were telling their
stories like they were badges of honour. They were proud
of them. It made me furious having to listen to these same
stories night after night, told in such a monstrous way, but
I kept my opinions to myself and tried to picture myself as
a journalist getting a unique insight into the minds of these
criminals.

What really amazed me was how such a mish-mash of
criminals could be thrown together in such a way, as if all
of our crimes were seen as equal. Murderers, rapists, child
molesters, burglars, handbag snatchers; they were all poured

into this big criminal pot-pourri. I had smuggled drugs, but I was rubbing shoulders with dangerous killers. And what about some poor bloke who went down for shop-lifting? He could end up in a cell with a guy convicted of violent rape and murder.

Monkey Man's stories would normally revolve around his rape conquests, although amazingly, and sickeningly, he never actually perceived them as rapes, or violations of some other human being. Instead he thought of them as 'surprises', and couldn't see anything wrong in what he was doing. When I shared a cell with him, back on F&G, he seemed to welcome having an audience that was non-judgmental. At least, nobody judged him out loud. It was a rarity, as far as I was concerned, to come across someone so upfront, proud, even, of his 'conquests'. In fact, I was to find this amongst many of the other rapists throughout Glendairy; they seemed to welcome the prospect of telling their tales, often in graphic detail. To be honest, I was shocked.

Many of the Monkey Man's stories may have been exaggerations. In prison there are no 'small men', only top-level gangsters, hit-men, international men of mystery, and so on. Monkey Man, though, was on remand for two rapes, around Oistins on the south coast. He would sit up in trees, and swoop down on women as they passed below. Hence his name. Wearing a hood, he would then pin the woman down and put a knife to her throat. After robbing the woman of her gold, he would then rape her. He was finally caught when he gave his girlfriend a gold chain that had belonged to one of his victims. A jeweller recognised the chain when the girl tried to sell it. Up until then, Monkey Man had committed dozens of rapes throughout Barbados and he had got away with them all. He never wore a condom. You would think that he would have been caught long ago with DNA but when he was charged they didn't have the technology to use DNA evidence in Barbados. Monkey Man had been charged with rape several times before, but each time the fact that his face was covered allowed him to get away with it. Incredible, but true. Each time he was charged he would be back on remand, only to get away with it time and time again. But on this occasion that little gold chain had betrayed him. He was found guilty and given 15 years.

Franklyn Yarde was another one who relished telling his rape stories. He would 'go a-creeping' around people's houses late at night. 'It's how I get my kicks,' he would say, time and again. Franklyn had committed untold numbers of rapes in Barbados and probably several murders, if he was to be believed. He had previously served a sentence for rape, doing 8 years, but this was his second offence. He had kidnapped a young, mentally-handicapped girl and taken her to a sugar cane field. He tied her up and raped this girl repeatedly before stabbing her and leaving her there to die when he had finished. Somehow she was able to recover enough to free herself of her bonds and get away to get help. Franklyn was given 25 years for that rape, and, some two years later another case came to light, in which he was again found guilty and given a fresh 25 years. I remember the day he came back from court, moaning about getting a fresh 25-er to pull down. To the younger, more naïve lads on the corridor, this man was a hero. Many of the young men would listen to what Franklyn had to say on any topic, and were influenced by him. I thought he was the scum of the Earth and just being there in his company sickened me. But I had no choice. I had to sit there and listen. To walk off to my own cell would have been a huge offence, and I would have made some serious enemies.

There were other stories that appalled me too though. I had learned the hard way that corruption was rife in the prison, but I was shocked at the level to which it permeated society in Barbados. It seemed that, far from being a paradise, there were many instances of gross injustice and inequality. In my week-long drug haze when I had first arrived, I had managed to read the local newspapers a couple of times, and had been surprised at how many court cases seemed to involve what looked like harmless old black men, given six month sentences for possession of 'smoking apparatus', while someone better off got a fine. I myself had gotten off lightly, possibly because I was a white foreigner from a wealthy country.

I had noticed when in court that the judges never seemed able to resist making smart comments at these poor men who were obviously suffering from addiction. I had also noticed several articles in the newspapers about policemen accused of rape, especially of much younger, i.e., underage girls. The inmates told me how this was common, yet that bail was always granted. Wouldn't that make it all too easy for the accused to start putting pressure on the girl and her family to drop the case? The inmates also told me how common 'accidents' involving these people seemed to be, and how in the weeks after they press charges family members find themselves getting knocked down late at night, or more usually, have their houses burnt down. Being made of wood, they tend to go up in flames very quickly, so the message gets across.

My own story of being set up, and how I suspected involvement from the officials was met with knowing nods. They had heard it all before. It all boiled down to economics with cases like mine. People were paid off so that more money could be made. Smugglers sacrificed one mule to ensure 19 others got through unchecked. People in positions of power might not even like the idea of being in cahoots with drug dealers, but in a society like that in Barbados, it would be one of the very few ways of making any real money. If hard working, honest men and women want to send their children to a good school, or be able to afford any of the things middle class families in Britain take for granted, then they have little choice ultimately.

Inmates told me stories of local men being subjected to suffocation, and beatings, in order to get them to confess to crimes they were only suspected of having committed. On the one hand, the police in Barbados are very poorly funded, and don't have the resources to conduct expensive and resource-consuming investigations in ways European forces can. They operate under an extensive informant system, which means that criminals and police are inter-linked by necessity. The police know who is up to no good, yet when they swoop it is often difficult to prove that it was such and such a person who committed such and such a crime. But they know roughly what has been going on, and use coercion to get to the bottom of it.

One way they do it, I was told, was through the extensive 'dope holes' throughout the island. These are crack houses where smokers can go at any time to curl up and blast away at their favourite drug. Women also call around to offer themselves in exchange for drugs. These places are usually run by people who are duty bound, for one reason or another, to furnish their contacts in the police with information they might require. For instance, if Mr X, a known smoker, is seen smoking thousands of dollars worth of crack, the question is asked: Where did he get the money from? Once the money has run out, the dealer tips off the police, who will then arrest him for a robbery of a tourist, and thereby 'clean up' the crime. They know he has robbed someone, but the person who was robbed may not even have reported the crime.

***

I was moved over to K&L. A few days later, Franklyn and another lad called Sandeford were moved into the same cell as me. I wasn't too happy about it, because it meant I was back on the floor, and back to being the subordinate in the cell. I had to do what I was told, or there would have been dire consequences. Sandeford was one jealous bitch, but a bit too nifty for me to try and wallop on my own. Luckily I resisted the temptation to whack him. He would probably have killed me, and got away with it, too. The first thing Franklyn did when he moved into the cell was nail his wooden safe to the wall, high up next to his bed, and right over my head. The dust rained down on me. Not that he cared. I started sweeping the mess up. I came to admire Franklyn's complete inability to consider anyone else's needs other than his own. On more than one occasion he would suddenly spring up from his bed, and swoop down to the ground. He would open a double page from one of the old newspapers we kept specially for this purpose, and peel his boxer shorts off. This was the signal for me to get up and make space for him to have a crap. If I had stayed there, he would just have defecated right next to me, over me, even. He just didn't care. Then he would spread the newspaper out onto the floor, squat down and let a huge turd fly out onto the paper. It was always hot and steamy, and the smell of shit would fill the air.

Sandeford, however, worked a different system. He preferred to wait until after lock-down before taking his crap, although sometimes he could be coaxed into taking one just before, as long as I was around to carry it out for him and clean the bucket out in the yard. His method was to put some newspaper down inside the rim of the bucket, and then sit on that like a potty. Then, he would wrap it all up any old way, and point to it for me to take away. Carrying out shit buckets at lock-down was never popular with the screws. Their chief concern right then was in getting men back into their cells, not letting them back out into the yard where the shit buckets were emptied into the well. In addition, many of the men disliked it, as it meant the smell of shit would linger in the corridor after lock down. There would often be some comments from the lads for pulling this one, which meant tension levels started rising. You would often have to wait at the gate for ages before getting an officer to ok your request to empty the bucket. Sometimes they refused, which meant that you would have to carry the shit back into your cell where it would keep you company all night long. This meant double humiliation; once for doing the shit in the first place at a time when access to the toilets outside was no longer possible and then for having to take it back, often to the loud protestations of the very man who had given birth to it in the first place. Sandeford would often start shouting when I had to bring it back, to make it look like I was the 'shitty bitch' and not him. There was nothing I could do though, as these guys were in it together, and one word out of place, or one refusal to do their bidding, and I was a goner. I couldn't wait to be moved again.

Soon after Franklyn got his second 25-year sentence, I moved in with *Charlie*, a mixed race guy born in Barbados, but brought up in Reading, England. *Charlie* had owned a shop in Reading, and been the manager of a decorating firm. His mother was Barbadian but his dad was Scottish. He was in for inadvertently killing the love of his life after he snapped. She had attacked him with a bread knife when it turned back on her somehow. He had been going through a breakdown of some kind. The doctors said it was a one-in-a-million chance. But unfortunately for everyone it happened, and at court he was given Queens Pleasure, which means forever.

It was great having *Charlie* as a cellmate. He knew what I was on about when I talked, for one. He was on my wavelength. We would talk in the darkness after lockdown and our minds would roam through all kinds of subjects. Sometimes we would talk about our innermost feelings in ways that neither of us could ever reveal to outsiders. In some ways we were closer to each other than many people who are married, and in a totally straight way. *Charlie* was always very good at talking with people. I noticed more than once this ability of his and how he could get through to difficult people. One of these was the Jamaican spiritual healer Michael Johnson. This healer had cured my bad back by passing his hands over my back and my sides. He then got me to drink some water into which he had put the power of one of the psalms. So imagine my surprise when I overheard *Charlie* getting Michael to talk all about the problems he had with girls.

Sometimes *Charlie* would hum a soft gentle tune, maybe something he had taken from the Supremes or the Three Degrees. In some strange way, I felt something deep in me being healed, even though *Charlie*'s thoughts were probably on how many cigarettes he could blag off me the next day. It was like the scene in the film The Story of the Weeping Camel in which the nomads strap a harp onto the back of the camel. As the wind moves through it, the sound it makes heals the camel of the experiences it has been through. When I saw that film, I remembered *Charlie* and his soft, haunting singing, the actual tune of which you could never quite get.

Once we got hold of a magazine from Reading, with all the beautiful properties in it. We looked at one amazing place. It had pillars by the door, its own paddock, stables, and conservatory. We imagined ourselves somehow coming to own such a place and what life might then be like. It was only a dream, but it was all we had to hold on to while we were stuck in this cavernous dump.

Men were paid a certain salary, according to the work they did. For the four months I was working the buckets I was paid Barbadian$15 dollars a week. This was high by prison standards. Later, when I transferred over, with Mr Shorey's help, to the job in the gardens under Miss Daniels, my pay was adjusted to only Barbadian $5 a week. All these monies were fastidiously paid into our accounts. But, surprise, surprise, when some men went to collect their pay from the office on their release day, they were told that they had already spent it. This happened even in cases where the men had deliberately not touched their money so that they definitely would have something to come out to and get their life started again.

Some of the prisoners got involved in building things like the new rehab buildings, the brand new set of toilets round the back of the Mess Hall and the library. At no time was any protective clothing or equipment given to these men. They even had to supply their own boots or else do their jobs in flip-flops. Men would work 150 feet up on some of the worst scaffolding I've ever seen, barefoot and bareheaded. Sometimes men would commit suicide by leaping from the heights of C Corridor, and smash their bodies to pieces on the hard concrete below. There were no safeguards or deterring barriers to prevent this from happening. Men would get hurt doing their jobs. They would have to wait ages for the person on duty to make the relevant phone call and get permission to call an ambulance from outside so that the injured man could get emergency treatment. Other injuries would occur in the woodwork and tailoring shops and the gardens.

Apart from the ever-present threat of violence, with so many dangerous people just roaming around, and being injured while working, there were many other areas of concern. Being poisoned was a big in-house paranoia. All someone needed to do was pay the kitchen staff enough to put something in your food. If that happened, and happen it did, then you were in for some suffering. Suicide was common in the prison. Ratrace hanged himself in his so-called safety-cell in the security part of A Corridor. He must have been hanging right after early-morning tally, because we had all been let out already and were swarming out from the shower towards the Mess Hall for our breakfast, when suddenly the screws started getting jumpy and signalling for us all to go back. They weren't too serious about getting rid of us, though, and we decided to ignore them. They seemed to accept this compromise, as long as we didn't get in their way. The cell door to Ratrace's cell was already open, and the screws were swarming in and out of it like flies around shit. From somewhere a stretcher appeared, and this was carried into the cell. After a while, a body was carried out, wrapped in blankets, and strapped to the stretcher itself. Ratrace was in for murdering five local girls. He was caught when the police found his mobile phone at the scene of one of the murders. When the police brought Ratrace in to the prison, he was totally off his face. He didn't know where he was. There were two police officers, one on each arm, steadying him as they took him straight to his cell on the security section in the Front Prison. Mr Sealey, the senior prison psychologist, was rushed straight in to see him, but none of that stopped this guy from committing suicide. Apparently, those responsible for his safety 'forgot' that blankets can be ripped and shredded and turned into makeshift ropes. He hung himself from a set of bars high up in a window in a solitary cell.

***

Just before lunch one day, I saw my first escape attempt in Glendairy. I was standing on the steps of the library, waiting to make a phone call to the British Embassy. All of a sudden, we heard gunfire. Several officers came rushing around the side of the building to unlock the gates that led round the back of K&L. Some guy had managed to get up on top of the roof to K&L. He got as far as the spot just above the gallows. From there his progress was halted by the vigilant officer who stood beneath with the 12-gauge shotgun.

The guy on the roof, realising that he now stood no chance, threw up his hands in surrender, but the officer below was having none of it; he was enjoying his moment in the spotlight and he wanted to bag himself a bad guy. He kept firing shells up to try and hit him! Eventually, the other officers were able to persuade their colleague to desist and they set up a ladder to bring the prisoner down. His plan had been to throw a makeshift rope across to the other side of the exterior wall, and drop down from there. He nearly succeeded, and probably would have, too, if he had not been grassed up, as I heard it, by one of the Bullermen.

The gallows were set right at the back of H&I. The sergeant-in-charge had his desk right in front of the door. One day, I asked to have a look in and, surprisingly, the officer let me. The gallows went up some fair height. The condemned would have to climb about 15 steps up to a platform. There the prisoner would stand on a small wooden trap door while they tied the rope around his neck. The wooden support from which the rope was attached was thick and new-looking. It was replaced when the government of Barbados reintroduced the death sentence, having abolished it back in the late 1980s. As I stood there, I thought about all the hundreds of Barbadian men and women who had been executed there, and I said a silent prayer for them.

***

Just before I left Barbados, a group of English guys were brought into the newly-relocated prison at Harrison's Point on charges of kidnapping. The brother of one of these guys had stolen a winning lottery ticket from his old mum, and run away to Barbados with his girlfriend. This guy then rustled up four helpers, who all thought they were going to be 'dogs of war' and go and sort things out. Only after they kidnapped this man and his woman did the police catch up with them. The judiciary in Barbados is really going to hammer these guys. They are only too aware of the massive rise in kidnappings in neighbouring Trinidad and Guyana. They want to put the message out to other potential kidnappers and tourists that kidnapping is not going to be tolerated in Barbados. Kidnappings are going to play a much greater part in criminal activity in countries such as Barbados in the future, simply because they are so easy to get away with. The white people who go to places like this are, relatively speaking, extremely rich.

One convicted murderer told me of his plans to carry out a number of kidnappings when he got out. He was looking forward to it. He also told me of other people he knows who are considering the same thing. Admittedly, in prison, there is more that is said than is ever done, but when he was talking I felt that what he was saying was more of a prediction than a personal objective. These days, when it is possible to go on the internet and see any number of beheadings and killings being carried out in the world, the possibility of a massive expansion in the kidnapping business is a distinct reality.

Humpty Dumpty was a Guyanese prisoner who was particularly wide at the middle, hence his name. His real name was Gilbert, and he suffered from a heart condition, which worried him, and prompted him to go over to get his blood pressure checked at least once a day by Miss Hippolyte, the nurse in charge of the medical unit. He was interested in Freemasonry, and often used to talk with me about the comparable fraternal societies, such as the Mechanics, and so on, and what their 'distress signs' might be. In the Caribbean there is the idea amongst laymen that all a Freemason has to do to generate money is sit in a public place with their legs crossed in a certain way, and members will see them and know that they are short of a few bob. Local legend has it that once that 'sign' is given out, the money comes flooding in for the brother-in-need. With Humpty Dumpty I could never go into any specifics concerning the 'signs or tokens' of mutual recognition, but I did enjoy talking in a general way about spiritual matters with him. He died of a heart attack in the Mess Hall. One minute he was there, the next he was not. It occurred to me that day that it would be absolutely awful, the worst possible fate, to die in these surroundings. I did not want to die in this place.

How people get their names is quite a subject. You can't just think up a name and call yourself it. Mostly they are simply discovered and immediately assigned to the person concerned. Taxi-man, Taxi-priest, False-priest, are some of the slightly spiritual-sounding titles I would often hear being called out by people who had just had visits from family outside. They and the people who had just been given their parcels. Many of the items in their parcels got sold off: the biscuits, the bottles of mauby, the packets of flavoured milk-shake powder and spare flip-flops were the first things to go. These items tended to end up in the hands of people like Starliner or Yankee, as these inmates were specialists, knowing where something can be sold for the best price. These guys would have that magic charm to be able to get through the interconnecting metal gates separating each corridor and past the guards manning them. Selling these things was a profession in itself. These guys would always try and chisel the person whose goods they were selling, with anything from an outright blag (i.e. hijacking the goods) to chipping as big a piece of money off the resulting amount. All payments would be in the form of cigarettes. These would then be re-packed and put into amounts of ten and 20, ready to be swapped with dealers for weed or crack. Sometimes intense arguments would blaze up over these transactions.

Quantities of weed would make their way into the prison, brought in strapped on the backs of prison officers. Other amounts were thrown over the prison wall, which was unguarded along the outside and surrounded by forest in most parts. Those organising for the drugs to come in would do so on mobile phones, in conjunction with their associates outside the walls. It was like an office for some of these guys, and it is hard to believe that the guards didn't know what was going on. Especially those with something pungent strapped to their backs.

They had to make an effort to look like they were on top of all of this though. Now and again, John Nurse would shut down a complete corridor, and, cell by cell, search for drugs and mobile phones. A party of officers would appear at the end of our corridor, all wearing white plastic gloves. Then, they would unlock each cell, one by one, and order us out.

Charlie and me and our cell-mate Archie would traipse out into a deserted corridor, and hang around by the railings. We would have to drop our trousers en route so an officer could make sure we didn't have anything strapped to our balls. Some times the guards really put some energy into it, and would climb up onto Archie's bunk. Once they even took a hammer to it! The insides of bedding, shoes, bags of clothing, all would be rummaged through and left scattered all over the cell. On the rare occasions when they really meant business, an officer would climb up into the crawl space between the ceiling of the cells and the roof. To get into this area, the officer would have to peel back a wire screen that normally secured this area from access by prisoners.

The searching would always slow the day down. My cell was up at the beginning of the corridor, and was usually the second one to be unlocked, in a corridor of 80 cells. This gave me a head start getting down to the shower room before the hordes from my corridor and the other corridors managed to get out and down there too. It was a nice feeling to be stepping out of the big shower room just as the rest turned up.

Officer Paris was often a member of the search teams. He was the only prison officer in Glendairy, at least in my time, to shoot another guard and still retain his job. The shooting was recorded as an accident, but it showed that prison guards were allowed to bring their own personal weapons into the prison and walk around with them in their pockets. This was dangerous for all concerned. In hindsight, it would have been an easy matter for two or three of the lads to have grabbed hold of someone like this and taken his weapon off him. If this was attempted, maybe the guard would panic, and somebody would get shot. No reprimand was ever made of this officer and he continued working in the prison. He was always grinning to himself, with his chin strap down under his chin, always ready for action!

This shooting incident happened immediately after the performance of a play, written by an inmate, Lestor Bullen, which featured the lives of several members of a gang on the island. It was, apparently, very realistic, and ended in a shoot-out with the police surrounding their hideout. The sound effects were especially powerful. They were taken from a computer shoot 'em up game, and were played over loudspeakers. The heavy blasting sound of the guns got the audience incredibly excited, and when the play ended, it was difficult for the men to simmer down. When we all returned to K&L corridor, several fights broke out. *Charlie* and I stayed in our cell. We knew this kind of thing could get out of hand and end in someone getting seriously hurt. We didn't want it to be us. Archie had already climbed up into his bunk, from where he would look out the barred window at the countryside and the lights around the prison. Looking down the corridor, I could see things were getting out of hand. A bit of a to-ing and fro-ing motion started off, like a rugby scrum or a tug o' war. It was at this point that several officers went down the corridor with their clubs. For some reason Paris then pulled his gun out and let off a couple of shots. Fearing that a possible massacre was about to take place, *Charlie* and I slammed shut the door to our cell and at that point started feeling a bit more secure, so we never actually saw what happened. We just heard the next day that one of the officers had been injured by a gun. And none of the prisoners had guns.

***

Mr Sealey, the chief psychologist and drug counsellor in the prison, ran a drug rehab programme that I managed to get on to. I spent 15 months on it, attending three mornings per week for the whole of that time. It was one of the best things I have ever done. I will never forget some of those rehab meetings. Some days we would sit there and watch videos about the effects of drugs and alcohol, some days we would discuss experiences that we had been through.

One of the subjects covered was the Medicine Wheel. This was a circle, drawn up on a flip chart standing on an easel. In one quarter was the word 'associates'; in the next quadrant was the word 'companions'; then 'friends', and finally 'lovers'. The point of the Medicine Wheel was to show us that many of those we had regarded as friends weren't our friends at all. It was designed to help us break free of the delusion that the people we had known as addicts were our friends. This may seem like an obvious point to those who have never been inside the world of drugs, but inside there is the connecting thread, a feeling of being special between drug users, a feeling of being part of an elite group. That's what had made me drink that phy when I was 13, what made me smoke and trip my way through college and then Asia and Europe; I felt like I belonged to this special group that was somehow above morality and society. If you suffer from an inferiority complex, that feeling can be so influential in bringing you back into the fold, even after you have done a drug rehab program somewhere. It was this sort of thing that Mr Sealey's program tended to focus on, and I found it very powerful in helping me to re-programme my own mind, something I realized was vital if I was going to successfully overcome my addiction. To stand a chance of having all that rehab actually work when I came out into the real world, it was vital that I started off by admitting that what I thought I knew hadn't worked, otherwise I wouldn't be back here in prison would I? A modicum of humility was necessary if I wanted to move forward. It is a question of making yourself small enough. I have seen so many junkies sitting in rehab meetings, so cocksure that they knew more than the therapist. Invariably all these clever-clogs would end up in shop doorways with track marks down their arms soon after their release. To a very large extent, Mr Sealey's program was a de-programming exercise, which, in my case at least, actually worked. I found it amazing to sit down and watch through all those videos about the different drugs. I learnt more about drugs and their effect on the human brain than I had ever done before. I am not saying for sure that I would never have ended up an addict, but I am sure that the chances would have been greatly reduced if I had that kind of knowledge before starting out on all that drug-taking so many years before. I only wished it had happened sooner, but then in my time there was never anywhere near the kind of drug education that there is these days. Or if there was, I never saw it.

Most of the guys who managed to get out of their cells and off their corridors were into having these little denim bags made up, in which you could carry round your few bits and pieces during the day over your shoulder. My bag cost me ten cigarettes from a guy I knew in the tailor's shop, and had an extra pocket on the outside in which I put my soap, dish, flannel, and toothbrush and toothpaste. Inside the bag, I had my metal bowl, spoon, toilet roll, small chess set and board, and whatever book I was reading at the time. It meant I could have my stuff with me at all times, because if I left them down I might not see any of them again.

The Mess Hall went through a number of changes while I was there. It started off with rows of metal-topped tables, all balanced on trestle-type wooden stands. The old-timers, like Charlie, who was a Bullerman and as mad as hell, would all have their preordained places, but, if you knew how to move, you could get yourself co-opted onto one of the top tables. I started off sitting down with Charlie at lunch, which surprised a lot of people, because normally Charlie would only have one of his chi-chi men as a guest. Chi-chi men were 'receivers' for the Bullermen. There were many looks from side to side when I sat down next to him, on his invitation. But Charlie had heard that I was, or at least had been, a Freemason. Charlie was on so much medication he hardly knew up from down. He was getting increasingly psychotic as his release date drew closer. He had done about 12 years when I met him, and he was released a couple of months later. He seemed to like me, though, and took me down to show me what the Farm looked like. As we went up to the wooden gate, separating the Main Prison from the little path that led down to the Farm, where much of the prison food was produced, he put on his red band, even though the guard on duty at the gate knew his rank. Taking me through, I heard the screw say to him, 'What, having some white meat today, Charlie?'

'No, not in that way,' he replied, obviously embarrassed, and hurried me along before I could place too much credence on what had just been said. There were sides to his personality that he felt ashamed about revealing. Charlie started showing me all kinds of weird signs of mutual recognition from other fraternal organisations. There are many societies such as these and in a country like Barbados they still abound and flourish.

Barbados is like a little England but set way back in the past. The police still wear the white pith helmets and red tunics at the High Court, the kind you see being worn by the British soldiers in the old Zulu film with Michael Caine. On ceremonial occasions, such as the march past by the prison officers on Independence Day, they all get these uniforms out and parade in them, even on Barbadian television.

The prison is probably the most important institution in the island, employing more men as guards than there are serving in the Defence Force, and nearly as many as in the police. On an island of 250,000 people, virtually everyone has someone in their immediate or extended family inside as a prisoner or as an employee. That's why what was brewing and what was about to happen in Glendairy affected the entire country, and made everyone sit up and notice what the place was really like.

CHAPTER TEN

THE RIOT

The Assistant Superintendent of the prison, David Broomes, had been a senior policeman before he came to Glendairy. I remember one day when the British Embassy came to call, and the main thing on Broome's mind was not the awful conditions in which we were forced to live, but working out whether he should keep his cap on for the visit or leave it off. His cap was not quite as glamorous as Nurse's; the rim being of silver rather than of gold. At the start of the meeting, he sat there with his cap off. It sat in a prominent position on the table with the crest facing out towards the embassy staff who had come to visit us. As the meeting progressed, he seemed at first to fight the urge to put it back on, but eventually succumbed and placed it squarely on the top of his head.

Contact with the outside world, for those not conducting the delivery and distribution of drugs on their mobile phones, was almost non-existent. Especially for foreign prisoners like myself and other Brits. We received visits from the British Embassy periodically, usually only every three to six months. Usually they would tell us things they thought we wanted to hear, but there would be very little actual work done towards making sure we were managing ok, or towards securing our transfer or release. Appeals just didn't happen for us. As far as I was concerned, they were supplying us with cigarettes, and that was that.

Our main visitor was Greita Taitt, an extremely kind and sensitive lady. Greita was from Barbados, and would normally come along with someone else from the Embassy. I remember on one occasion she turned up with a real nerdy-looking white man just out from England. In the meeting, *Larry*, another Londoner in for smuggling drugs, asked about getting transferred to a prison in the UK. This new man started talking about how the 'Treaty' between Barbados and Britain was nearly complete. This process had been going on for several years and nothing had happened. My intuition told me that nothing was going to, but this guy was talking as though we were about to be transferred imminently. When *Larry* heard the words 'Wandsworth Prison' his face just lit up. Supposedly, this was where we were to serve out the rest of our sentences.

'Does anyone want to ask any questions?' this guy asked at one point. Poor *Larry* was almost on his feet.

'Greita,' he said excitedly, 'Can you get me a bag to carry all my stuff in?' expecting this transfer to happen within days.

This happened all the time. The Embassy staff would come in and do the whole: 'Never fear chaps, we'll get you out of here,' routine, and the more naïve young men would end up running around like headless chickens for a few days, expecting to be carted back to a nice and comfy, good old fashioned British prison, where they could enjoy their egg and chips and put their feet up to watch *Eastenders*. The way they promised these things, and the way they spoke to us, you'd swear they thought we were simple. But then again, watching these young guys being taken in every time, maybe they were right. The Embassy staff, kind as they were, must have enjoyed the odd chuckle on their way back to their building after each of these visits, so easily placated were the inmates.

I tried very hard to get the point across, on these visits, that the way we were being treated was a violation of our human rights. I explained about the lack of sleeping space, the horrible old makeshift bucket three inmates per cell had to use as a toilet, the shit well, the plastic containers and dirty jars we were supposed to eat and drink out of, and the general free for all that was the chance to get a meal. On top of this, I constantly described the ever-present threat of violence, and the fact that not only were we walking around surrounded by guys off their heads on crack, but we were actually supposed to share filthy, dark and airless cells with them, and with murderers and rapists. On top of that, the guards were allowed bring in their own guns from home, and the Redbands were just itching to have a crack at someone. They didn't need to be told any of this; they knew already. They would just put their hands out, palms facing upwards. On one occasion, an Embassy official actually said to me: 'Look, dear chap, what can we do?'

I said they could get me the hell out of there because my human rights were being violated, but that was the end of the conversation. Basically we were expected to just sail on through, do our time, regardless of the conditions, and then go home. As far as I was concerned, they were totally useless. The one thing my meetings with the Embassy did do was reinforce in me my desire to stay clean and well away from drugs. Some of the other prisoners I saw come in were like zombies, and would believe anything you told them, and the thought that I could so easily have become one of them tended to snap me out of any ideas I had of going back on drugs.

So with no practical help from my own Embassy, a complete inability on their part to improve our conditions or ensure our safety, I was left with no means of getting my message across or my voice heard. What could I do? Who could I turn to? Write to the Queen? They would never have let the letter out, even if I did. It hammered home to me that when you are on your own, you are really on your own.

***

The human rights violations and the corruption actually got worse the longer I was there. Broome and Nurse brought a squad known as the Dogmen in to try to control the flood of drugs coming into the prison. The Dogmen looked like real thugs. They dressed in grey boiler suits and walked around with dark glasses on. They were called Dogmen because their original remit was to control the dogs used in the prison for sniffing down drugs. These mutts were the most useless creatures under the canopy of Heaven when it came to finding drugs. They never found a thing, as far as I know. The Dogmen differed very markedly from the ordinary screws. They never associated with the ordinary officers. They kept themselves apart and behaved as though they were some kind of special unit, or 'death squad'. The ordinary officers, who were generally fairly laid back, didn't seem to like them either. At least some of the ordinary officers knew their men and were pretty good at averting any trouble they knew was brewing. But the Dogmen would stalk around the prison, three to a group usually. They would stride about in their big boots and grab hold of anyone they wanted to shake down and search. They seemed to enjoy intimidating prisoners, but there were rumours that they were intimidating the other officers too.

The Dogmen were rapidly promoted over far more experienced prison officers who had been at Glendairy for donkey's years. The drugs were still coming into the prison, but what started rankling the fellas more and more was the sudden upsurge in searches all along the corridor. The very screws who had brought in all the mobile phones and the drugs, serving as inmates' connections, were now the ones expected to go and hunt them down.

Sometimes the screw would have to say to his fellas in their cells, 'Look man, I need to find something!' and beg his clients for something to take back after a long and usually fruitless search of the corridor. Sometimes Broomes would order the shutdown of the entire prison, in an impossible attempt to prevent contraband from being transported from one corridor to another. Usually, we would get tipped off through the inmates grapevine the night before that a search was on for the next morning. There would be a little bustle that night with pieces of planking being taken up, and the mobiles and drugs being secreted inside the hidden compartments of the wooden lockers, doors, even the walls.

On the Farm meanwhile, one of the officers had seriously injured a prisoner by forcing him to climb into a wooden box. Then he kicked the box down the stairs with the prisoner inside before practically destroying what remained of it with his truncheon. Nobody heard of any action being taken on this, and the guard remained in his job, but it seemed to me that this was all hushed up and the prison's priority was more to keep things bottled up and out of the public eye than to get to the bottom of any injustice and solve it.

Another guard hit *Larry* in the eye with an iron bar when he tried to defend himself from a disturbed local inmate. *Larry* tried to get to hospital but was denied, as was his right to call the British Embassy.

Meanwhile up at the main building, all the younger prisoners had been moved to the right side of A Corridor, in accordance with a senior officer's desire to see all the younger fellas in one place. On more than one occasion, he marshalled them all together and marched them up to the library, where he could talk to them without interruption. Bringing all of the younger prisoners together turned out not to be a good idea. One of the screws, Officer Mayes, even said to me: 'If there is ever going to be a riot, it will be these young men who start it, and it will start on Corridor A.'

John Nurse had started a fence building programme throughout the prison. I believe that it was his intention to restrict the movements of prisoners from one part to the next. One set of these fences had been built in front of the prison, with the establishment of a caged area where football playing often took place. The other main area was on the inside of the back prison in front of the carpenter's shop and the medical building. Here, there were an additional two sets of fenced areas, erected so as to give the hundreds of men in the back prison the opportunity to exercise at least once or twice a week. There were men who had been years on D&E, and F&G and had been denied the opportunity to exercise, and had been kept in these dark miserable cells *ad infinitum*. It was a welcome addition for many of the inmates, but it also added to the sense of being caged in, even when we were outside.

Prison officers regularly got away with beating any prisoner who, in their books, made a fuss. In other words, insisted on his rights. Even getting off the corridor to see the doctor was a major difficulty. The inmates all knew which officers you could talk to and which ones would show you the end of a stick if you so much as opened your mouth in their presence.

Prior to my arrival in the prison an incident had occurred that gave even the British Embassy cause for alarm and highlighted just how out of touch with the world this place was, and how out of context with the idea of Barbados as a peaceful slice of heaven. The men on B corridor had gone on a food strike, which differs from a hunger strike. A hunger strike is when the prisoners refuse to eat at all. A food strike is when a number of prisoners refuse to take the food issued from the prison, but instead organise their own supplies.

The men up on B corridor had had enough of the food from the kitchen and arranged for supplies to come in. This was mainly in the form of food parcels from family and friends. This strike had been going on for maybe a week, when one evening, a posse of 20 or so drunken guards returned to the prison after a binge outside. They went upstairs to B corridor, and began systematically opening the doors and beating the prisoners inside each cell to a pulp. In addition, all the prisoners' furniture and belongings were thrown over the side of the balcony and trashed in a heap. The prisoners were then led downstairs into the yard where they were subjected to further beatings by the group of officers. Only one guard, Officer Wiseman, refused to have anything to do with any of this and even tried to discourage the others from their course of action. This incident happened just as Lt Col John Nurse was taking over from his predecessor, George Clarke. Nurse's response was to immediately suspend all the officers concerned, pending an investigation. But this incident happened years ago and the investigation is officially 'still continuing'. Some 20 officers have been charged, but this case is still meandering through the courts and is likely to go nowhere.

***

It was with 'Most Wanted' Jones that the trouble started and the nightmare began. He was a really big, powerful man, and had for some time been hassling the younger prisoners for sex. First he would offer them drugs and extra food. There was one particular 'pretty boy' who had caught his eye, and I heard that 'Most Wanted' had raped him. The matter was brought before a senior officer, Carrington, for adjudication, but Carrington could do nothing, so he allowed Jones to go about his business. This was typical of the way things were run in Glendairy. There was no justice whatsoever. Only in this case the young men on A Corridor decided to act for themselves. If Carrington wasn't going to dispense any justice, they would dispense their own. Now, by this time Carrington had moved his office from what had been a pretty strategic spot. His office had been in a separate building outside the main building, and by the wall where it was ringed by other officers and gates and fences. He had relocated to a refurbished section in what had formerly been a chapel, alongside the dimly-lit and poorly protected corridor which led from the front to the back prison. This corridor was only about two feet wide, and in theory, there was a guarded gate at either end. Carrington's new office was set in a totally unprotected area where there was absolutely zero opportunity for reinforcement, should the need arise.

The young lad, whose name I can't remember now, could not believe it when he realised that Carrington was not going to go against one of his Bullermen. In fact, it was a close thing that he was not put into security for complaining. He went back to A Corridor, where he was met by some of his mates. I had seen this lad around a few times. He did seem very young and from his looks I was not surprised that he had become a target for the Bullermen. When his friends found out that nothing was going to happen to Jones, they grabbed hold of their jukas, their home made knives, and led by a prisoner known as 'Badmouth', they ran to where Jones was still standing in Carrington's office. Jones by now had drawn his juka, and was ready and able to use it.

They young lads advanced on Jones. Carrington tried to intervene, but someone whacked him on the side of the head and he ran away out the door. Jones then threw a rock he had picked up. There were thousands of them just lying all over the ground in Glendairy, just waiting to be used as missiles. This rock missed the person it was intended for, but struck someone else who was passing in the corridor. The rock took out the side of his face, leaving his eye hanging out on its stalk, as he screamed in agony. It was like something out of a horror film. There was blood everywhere, all over the walls and floor. People were screaming and running. The pandemonium had begun.

Jones managed to lock his assailants outside Carrington's office, but he knew that the door wouldn't hold them back for more than a few moments. He turned around and began pulling at the set of iron bars at Carrington's window. Straining and heaving, he bent them back. Jones was through in seconds, just as the door crashed behind him. The gang of youths was right behind him now, but Jones escaped through the window with just moments to spare.

Just then, Lt Col John Nurse came onto the scene, flanked by a couple of soldiers bearing assault rifles. Nurse looked good, standing there in his red-banded cap. But all that parade ground servility was over now for us. He tried giving an order: 'Everyone retire to the Mess Hall.'

I attempted to follow that order immediately, but as I got to the Mess Hall, another senior officer, Sergeant Paine, for some reason, saw fit to lock it, and thus prevent anyone from getting through.

On the yard the situation was quickly getting increasingly out of control. One officer was lashing out, trying out some of his much talked about martial arts moves on any prisoner who came near him, even those trying to get out of the way. It began to look as though the soldiers and Nurse, with their shiny rifles, might even be get kidnapped, or at least lose their weapons. Nurse looked up and saw that big balls of flame were already whooshing out of some of the cell doors, up on B and C corridors, which were the first and second floors, and faced outwards over the yard from their narrow balconies. Even down on the ground floor flames were beginning to lick outwards and take out the contents of entire cells. Dante's inferno had begun.

Nurse made a quick exit, but Carrington reappeared and single-handedly made his way upstairs and began unlocking the closed doors to release those prisoners still stuck inside. Although a hail of stones greeted him, he bravely continued and was eventually joined by another officer. If he had not acted as he had, many prisoners would have died in the fire. After releasing the prisoners, Carrington then attempted to put out the flames in some of the cells, but the barrage of stones was too much, and, for his own safety, he had to vanish.

I had been standing by the Mess Hall, trying to get as far away from this fracas as I possibly could. I had stood by Sergeant Paine, one of the Dogmen, but one of the better ones. As the gang of youths came close, I thought that they were coming for us, so I screamed to him, 'They are going to fucking well kill us!'

Paine freaked out. His hand shook so much, he nearly dropped the key. It stuck in the lock and he shielded his body as if to protect himself from the rain of blows he expected. I stood frozen, expecting the same. But they did not come. Instead, all the youths ran past us, to the entrance to the tailor's shop.

By now, 'Most Wanted' Jones had made his way out and around the back of the prison, and was running along the inside of the perimeter wall, dodging a fusillade of missiles; rocks and stones thrown by a rapidly growing number of people. It was as if it were raining heavy pellets, a complete downpour. Jones was trying to dodge them and pick up rocks to throw back at the same time. But for every one he managed, perhaps two to three dozen were striking him. Blood appeared all over his body; his head and face were gashed into shreds of flesh. Then he turned and continued trying to run again. He went further behind the Mess Hall, hopping over two, then three sets of fences to evade his pursuers. At first the gang of youths were unsure what to do. They crashed through the first set of gates and then into the workshop. From the rear windows they were able to regain sight of their quarry. It was there that Jones met with a massive flurry of missiles. He went down. But even this was not enough. Several youths came and stood over his body, and picked up really big stones, too big by far to actually hurl through the air, and brought them down with a smash onto his head.

I could see a few officers were standing by themselves on the inside of a perimeter fence over by the Superintendent's building. They had sealed off the gate with a lock and were looking around. Unsure of what to do, I was standing just by the entrance to the kitchen at that moment, when suddenly, about a dozen men rushed in and started trashing the entire place. Mason, the chief cook, was standing there as well, dressed very nicely in his brilliant prison whites. As the men came in, he could immediately see that they were in no mood for parley and dashed to the side. Great pots full of white rice were overturned to the floor, and men dragged out stacks of knives, cleavers and cutting instruments from the kitchen stores. It was an armoury for what was to come. I was getting pretty scared at this stage. In the frenzy, I could see myself getting stabbed, just for the hell of it.

I saw men carrying great stacks of tinned sardines, handing them out to whoever wanted them. I looked through the bars of the Mess Hall gate and tried to see my friend and cell mate, *Charlie*. I saw him, but because the gate was still locked, I couldn't get in to him. He was sitting there, calm as a Buddha statue, opening a tin of sardines, and munching contentedly. He was doing the most sensible thing in the entire prison. I had shared a cell with *Charlie* for about a year and a half up until that time, and had always felt his presence a reassuring factor. His advice and wisdom was often invaluable.

There was a sudden rush, and a group of about 30 inmates made a mad dash up the steps into the reception building, where the cigarettes were kept. They soon reappeared, throwing great numbers of cartons about and onto the ground. People split cartons and stuffed packs into their pockets. Although I had had two cartons in storage up there, I had managed to grab back two packs, which was something. Some of the lads started getting greedy, and made off with two or three cartons for themselves, not wanting to share the booty.

Just then the sergeant in charge of the reception area, along with two female officers, came down the steps and walked away, with great dignity and a sense of resignation. They must have been terrified as they came face to face with an angry mob of convicts wielding knives and cleavers. But no one interfered with them. All respect was given them; all along they had been ok screws.

By now the smoke was really building up, and people were streaming out from the main building into the yard. All of the normally closed-up sections were now being opened, not by the screws, but by inmates who were just picking up the keys left lying on the ground, or even, in some cases, taking the keys off officers by force if necessary. Just then I saw Miss Coombes come trundling along, pulling her little trolley as she came. Her eyes were white with shock at what was happening. I didn't know it then but she had just been interfered with sexually by a couple of the real freaks of the prison. I asked Tanty, one of the Bullermen who survived the retaliatory beatings that were to follow, what had happened to her.

'Just her bubbies were played with, and also her pokey,' he told me, grinning inanely, as if this were supposed to be humorous. She made her way out to a gate. She went on sick leave, so I later heard. Probably permanently.

***

The air was hard to breathe, and we all wanted to get away from the fire. Things were getting dangerous. There was a collective rush down towards the gate that led to the Farm building. Within moments we were flowing through this. Tweety Pie was the screw on the gate. He just stood back to let us all pass without interruption. Tweety Pie had always liked to throw his weight about a bit but he looked very humble and anxious as we went past.

Everywhere I looked, violence was erupting. Payback was being meted out to grasses, Bullermen, anybody who had ever pissed off anybody else. While I watched these panoramic scenes of vengeance and violence, I hoped to God that I would be alright. I tried my best to remain calm, and outwardly looked like I was. I felt that as long as I didn't deliberately start anything off, I would make it through this ordeal. I hadn't grassed, or done anything against any of the major unwritten rules which we as convicts were supposed to conduct ourselves by. I did have a little run in here and there with a couple of lads, such as Grandpa, but I had to look at it this way: If Grandpa, or anyone else, wanted to come for me, ok then, bring it on. I would at least get some digs in before I went down. But what was traumatic was having hundreds of convicts running around with murder in their eyes. *If they didn't find their intended victim, would I be used as a substitute?*

The mass exodus down along the country lane took us past the garden area. I saw Miss Daniels looking out at this massive influx of people. Short and stubby, she looked decidedly disturbed at seeing so many people running free into an area into which access was always tightly controlled. She could see that something was wrong. She started making her way out while she still could.

The smell of smoke was heavy in the air, and then I heard the sound of shotguns being fired. Guards were shooting at the inmates. This wasn't good. It would be all too easy to end up in the wrong place at the wrong time, and looking down the barrel of a shotgun being held by a terrified, twitching guard. I made sure to keep on moving.

As we passed by the entrance to the female prison there was an initial surge of a dozen or so fellas to the gate, and they started trying to kick it in. I didn't know whether they wanted to liberate the female prisoners, or if their purpose was perhaps less altruistic. But just then some of the other inmates with more sense appeared out of the crowd and discouraged them.

'Not that, brothers!' they insisted, 'Not that!' And with that the matter was somehow settled. From inside the female prison, though, we could hear the shouts of the women as they called out expressions of solidarity to us. Some were up at their windows and were calling out to us, although it wasn't possible to hear the precise words.

As a group we surged along right down to the bottom of the lane, and made our way into the Farm. This was quite a big area, and included not just the prison's quarters, but also various other buildings, such as the sheds for the pigs, sheep, rabbits, chickens and ducks that were supposedly used to feed the inmates. Eggs and meat were produced in huge quantities down here, but precious little of it ever made its way back onto the plates of us prisoners. Most of it went straight out of the prison on deals with local supermarkets. Nobody ever knew where the money for all this went; that was anybody's guess. But it was a big and lucrative business, aided partly by the fact that, in Barbados food from supermarkets is expensive.

In fact the cost of living is very high, especially for the locals, who tend to get paid pittances for the work they do. Nobody really thinks about that, because the people who go to Barbados are holidaymakers, and they are usually wealthy people who meet other wealthy people and come home with the view that everybody on the island must be wealthy too. In reality, for those who live there all year round, by accident of birth and not by choice, have it very hard. But nobody wants to hear those stories about a paradise island, do they?

Similarly, huge stocks of prison soap, toothpaste, brushes, rubber boots, gardening equipment, cloth and computers would regularly vanish through the gates. Whenever we asked for a new razor blade, or for a repair to be made on our worn-out uniform we would be told that there were no more supplies. But where could they possibly have gone? There weren't enough inmates to go through the supplies they should have had, yet there never seemed to be enough of anything to last a week. Hardly any of the meat from the Farm ever came our way, except on the days when the prison had an official visit from the British Prison Inspectorate. Then all of a sudden we would get a first class meal. He would make sure the visitors got a sample too, of course!

In groups, the inmates forced their way into the Farm, pushing aside the puny metal gate and chasing the guards away. The guards scuttled up the steps to their office at the sight of so many prisoners suddenly turning up outside their gate. At one point one of them started shooting through one of the windows. But one of his fellow officers must have advised him not to continue, because he stopped doing it very shortly afterward. Doing something like that in a riot situation can really inflame a crowd and make them rush and kill.

People kicked in the cell doors that had been hastily locked, freeing the prisoners and bringing them out. I saw a great ball of flame rise up from the back corridor of the Farm building, giving off a massive shroud of black smoke.

When the place started to burn, many of the inmates were still locked up inside their cells. They were freed by prisoners kicking their doors down, most often with their bare feet. These great thick dungeon doors, that had all hung there for so many decades were all reduced to matchwood in seconds by the barefooted teenagers. I saw one inmate, Vino, come out of the building, with a knapsack on his back. His freshly-shaved head was already red and raw from the sun. He was laughing. He had been in his cell when the screws suddenly came around to start locking them all down. Bit by bit, he had smelled the smoke, and then heard a tremendous banging on his door. Thinking these were fellas intent on breaking in to give him a beating, he had picked up a length of wood he kept in his cell, and stood ready to whack them. When they broke in, imagine his surprise that they had come to save his life, not take it!

Well, now the inmates had control of the Farm, although we didn't know for how long. Some of the men started tearing up the dozens of chickens that had been slaughtered earlier that day, and sinking them into makeshift frying pans. One man even tried to eat a chicken completely raw, tearing into it with his bare teeth. Meanwhile, a single pig had wandered into the scene, probably wondering what all the commotion was about. At first someone grabbed it by its hind legs, and was holding it up over a boiling vat of seething oil. They were going to fry the poor animal alive! A Rasta man with more sense came along and stopped them. The poor animal squealed until they let it down. And it wandered off again.

Up in the sky we could see what looked like a great vulture flying around the area right above the prison complex. It was clearly a huge spy-plane from somewhere. We guessed that photographs were probably being taken and perhaps even a film made. One of the lads said that he recognised it as the plane that did the runs between Barbados and St Vincent. It was large and green and definitely sinister-looking; like a harbinger, an evil omen of bad times yet to come.

From over the wall, we could see people appearing on the outskirts of the nearby villages. They were standing at the edge of the outer perimeter, taking photographs. There were soldiers in place by now, reinforcing the minimal police presence that had sprung up around the prison. Only a bare sprinkling of individual officers stood in the no man's land between the two walls. They were facing us, and had their hands on their weapons. No one was in any doubt that they would be prepared to shoot whoever might attempt to escape.

Meanwhile we got on with the feasting. Someone commandeered my sitting down bucket and began filling it with fried chicken. It was soon filled to overflowing, and I was given a large number of chicken livers as a gift. They tasted delicious. I ate as much as I could, because the signs were that we would soon be going on to leaner times. While we were down on the Farm, no animal was harmed or killed. We only ate the chickens that had already been slaughtered and prepared for food.

After a while, a number of soldiers appeared at the ridge of the gate area and signalled us to stand back so that they could evacuate the female prison. With so much firepower aimed at us, we had no choice. Our part was over. They formed a line, with their rifles pointing towards us, as the gate to the female prison was opened and the women brought out. Many of them were overcome with the emotion of seeing old Glendairy burn down around them. The soldiers were reinforced with others holding tear gas guns. For a while it looked as though we were about to get a whiff of tear gas for our troubles. One of the gasmen was a really old copper. He was massively overweight and was huffing and puffing as he chugged along. A great strip of heavy silver cartridges strapped in a leather belt hung around his waist and he cradled a cylindrical cannon under his arms. You could tell he was itching to use it.

As when there were so many inmates rushing around earlier on, the fear returned. In front of me were soldiers brandishing M16s, while behind me huge clouds of black smoke were approaching, and inmates were still running around all over the place. For a while, looking around, I thought that yes, it was quite possible that I was due to die that day, and it could so easily have happened several times. I was filled again with the feeling that at any time, someone, anyone in fact, could strike me down and really bring me pain. But it was like a battlefield, and when it is all happening around you there is too much going on to start wondering about could-have-beens. I felt a resolve inside myself growing, telling me that I had been through too much, come too far, to get sabotaged at this hurdle.

CHAPTER ELEVEN

Caged

As I looked around I could see on quite a few peoples' faces the slowly dawning realisation that they were in for a rough ride, to say the least. Here and there you could see these Quislings looking around in the direction where the guards and soldiers were congregating, then looking nervously back at the other inmates nearer the prison who were scouring the place looking for targets. I stood and watched some of these bastards who for years thought they could get away with their incessant grassing and bullying, intimidating and pressuring younger inmates into having sex with them, and I thought: *Welcome to the Day of Judgement.*

After the girls had all gone, we were ordered to form a line. Each of us was searched and had to hand over everything we had in our possession, including the cigarettes. We passed by a series of police officers who searched us again. I had two policewomen, who went through my pockets and cleared me. They took my bucket, still containing chicken, and my small knapsack. All of this was now taken from me. I now had absolutely nothing.

I passed through the gates and lined up with several other inmates. We were then led by armed soldiers through the yard into a central caged area. Slowly but surely, all the other prisoners were brought up from the Farm and placed in this reservation. There was nowhere to sleep except the ground, nowhere to piss and shit. There was nothing to drink or eat, but eventually one of the officers brought out a hosepipe and ran water from it directly into our mouths.

The moon came out overhead, and happily most of the fires had been put out. I could see some of the thousands of bats, which had presumably been living in total peace underneath the roof's eaves, flying about, filling the night sky with thousands of jittering jagged sharp movements. They swooped, ducked and dived as they went in search of their prey; mosquitoes. We wished them a hearty supper. I found my old mate *Charlie*, and opened up a can of sardines, which I shared with him. It wasn't much, but it was all we had. The moon was large and luminous that night, and although there wasn't much space, we all squeezed in together like the sardines on which we'd been dining. There was literally no room even to turn over. Outside the wire there were soldiers patrolling. They kept reminding us that they were under orders to shoot anyone who attempted to escape. We all went to sleep, hoping that the following morning would bring some hope and some kind of order would be restored.

From around the far side of the prison wall we heard a whining sound. Then, what looked like a great dragon head appeared over the top of the wall. It was a mobile crane with a lifting platform. Two soldiers, both armed with rifles, stood on the platform. On the front of it was a single bright spotlight. It was like something from a science fiction film. As the night wore on, this dragon appeared and then disappeared several times. The soldiers on the top spent their time looking down over the scene beneath them.

As we sat in our corral, the prison building itself was still a hive of activity. We saw several bodies being carried or dragged out by soldiers with masks over their faces. The word was that Nook Nook, one of Carrington's grasses, had been murdered. I myself spoke with more than one man who claimed to have actually seen it happen. A tall Dutch inmate by the name of Ventro told me that Nook Nook had been caught trying to set fire to the carpenter's shop, and three men, two of them Bullermen, had been instructed to do away with him. They put a rope around his neck and tried to strangle him. When that didn't work, they took him out onto the unmarked cemetery area and hammered him on the head, killing him instantly.

Up above the carpenter's shop, the entire building for the officers' quarters had been wiped away in a sheet of flame. The concrete floor had saved the bottom level of the building. Inside, we could see some more sneaks, including the Colombians who had spent their entire time going around trying to impress everyone with stories of what big dealers they were. Everybody knew they were grasses that the Americans had 'turned' after capturing them in their boat with several hundred pounds of weed on board. It is hard to say exactly what was going on in their minds, but interestingly enough every one of them, apart from Coronel, was separated off from the bulk of the prisoners and put with all the other grasses, informants and collaborators as soon as trouble broke out. Looking back, it is probable that they did a deal with the American Drug Enforcement Administration when they got caught. Chances are then, that as they are free by now, they may well be busy at work trying to stitch other people up back in their own country. They had better be careful, because out there, people get 'inched' for grassing.

Inched means broken apart, inch by inch, with a set of bolt cutters, and scattered to feed the pigs. I imagine it to be a painful process.

Mobile electric spotlights were brought in to the prison, and with these the guards formed a ring of stadium-like light around us. It was bright, forcing us to cover our eyes or look the other way. Eventually we all tried to get some sleep.

During the night, I awoke, and went to what was now the pissing corner to take a leak. It occurred to me that there were no longer any guards around to watch over us. This worried me. *Where were they? Why weren't they here?* I suddenly felt very vulnerable, caged in, while the prison still wasn't totally secure. On top of that, we had just been left with there with nothing; no food, no water, no shelter from the elements. *Maybe somebody would come along shortly, and bring some tea in, maybe even some bread?* Even to see John Nurse again would be reassuring. Hopefully he would make his reappearance soon. But as the sun rose and the rays became hotter, it became apparent that this was not going to happen. It was by now getting devilishly hot, and we looked around forlornly, wondering what was going on. Was this a trap, to lure us out into the open so the soldiers could then start shooting us? It looked like that. As we had gone to sleep, there had been soldiers standing over us. *What had happened to them?* There were none here now. Not a single one!

Another hour went by, then another. Finally the men's patience broke, and people starting ripping apart the shreds of wire in the fence and pouring through. Everyone was desperate to get a drink of water, at the least. I went through the wire and over to the Mess Hall. By now the entire area looked as if a bomb had gone off. All over the ground were bars of soap, books, washcloths, shoes, solitary boots, you name it. The guards and soldiers had all disappeared.

I made my way over to where I could get a drink of water, from the taps in the back of the Mess Hall. It was glorious to feel the beautiful water going down the back of my throat and filling me. All around me were hundreds of men, many running up into the main prison to carry whatever they could raid from someone else's locker. Up on the second and third floors, gangs of men were busting open people's wooden containers and spilling out the contents. Some were forming semi-organised groups with the express purpose of looting other prisoners' kit. Like bands of pirates, they went merrily about their purposes, oblivious to the fact that it was extremely unlikely that anyone would be allowed to retain any of their booty when order was restored. But none of this seemed to cross the minds of anyone. By now, everyone was acting out of pure instinct, doing whatever seemed natural. In the face of catastrophe, I suppose it is a natural enough reaction and a way of coping with trauma.

A flurry of additional activity started at the top of the steps of the reception area. A team of four or five men had succeeded in dragging the prison safe all the way out, and were now preparing to throw it down from the top of the steps. We all stood back, and after a cry of one, two, three, down it came, tumbling over onto its side and resting face up, with its handle in the air. From nowhere the leader of this team produced a hammer and a chisel, and began to bang away at the lock. It took him the best part of an hour, but he managed to get the safe open and all of its contents were cleaned out. There were dozens of men walking around with golden rings on each finger, gold chains, other people's passports, Rolex watches. One fella had $5,000 in cash in there, and he was now cleaned out. Everyone lost everything. Mobile phones, wallets, address books, family photos; they were all gone now.

Outside, I could see a dozen or so lads recharging their mobile phones in preparation for the coming day. It was with these that they were able to make their calls to the many newspapers of Guyana, Trinidad, St Vincent and other neighbouring countries to inform them of the events that were still unfolding in Glendairy. I subsequently learnt that many papers in that region carried the story, and even a television network somewhere.

The next thing to happen was that the main building of the prison burnt down completely. Inside the main building there was a wooden staircase that led up to the second and third floors. In the back prison the entire roof was made of wood, tiled over with Perspex down the middle to let some light in. Along the spine of F&G it was clear, but down the length of K&L it was of a green material, which gave the place a weird yet strangely peaceful glow of greenish light.

Someone had started firing all this now, and it was going up fiercely. The smoke was making it impossible to breathe. We tried to look for a way out, but there was none. We moved downwind, in the only direction that was open to us, away from the fire and the smoke, but were met with a hastily-constructed ring of razor wire. Suddenly there they were—a line of soldiers, all wearing gas masks to protect themselves from the effects of the smoke. Many of us were wearing white vests, and we started taking these off, to indicate that we had come in peace and wanted their help. But they weren't interested in helping us, only in keeping us pinned down. The officer in charge of them came close to me, and I spoke to him, asking him for help.

'Anyone who crosses this line will be shot!' was all he said to me in return. Then he disappeared back to where his men stood ready to shoot us down.

The rehab building suddenly whooshed up into flames, as did the bakery, and other buildings. I had no clear idea as to which buildings outside my visual range were going but it seemed to be many. The air was so thick with the smoke that I had to lie down and just hold my vest tightly over my face. With my own saliva I was able to wet the entrance way to my mouth on the vest, so as to minimise the effects of the smoke. It was an imperfect mask, but it was the best I could come up with at such short notice. I thought I was going to choke to death on the smoke and fumes, but all I could do was keep my head down and hope that nobody panicked and made a charge at the soldiers. We would have all been shot dead.

It seemed to take hours for the fires to burn out. We eventually formed a kind of survivor's group in the middle of this new caged area. Some of the men climbed back into the main building and threw down some mattresses, which made resting and even sleeping, a little easier. Others, like Scoobeela, his tiny wizened form hunched over a pile of boots like a mad dwarf, concentrated on opening up the soles of their boots to hide drugs in them, aware that we would all be searched yet again, only this time much more thoroughly. He was sitting down beside me, carefully re-gluing the soles of one of these boots, hoping against hope that he might be allowed to keep his boots after the next set of searches. There were quite a few like him.

Meanwhile the Rastamen had gathered in one side of the area and were forming a half circle. They were facing eastwards, towards the face of the main building, and raising their hands, interlacing their fingers to form the six-pointed star that is their holy crest. One of them had resurrected the large picture of Haille Selassie and stood it to face the prison building, which for them was the ultimate symbol of Babylon. They were chanting 'Iya Bingi, Iye bingi,' over and over again, slowly, with meaning, with resonance.

Just then something strange happened. Up on the front of the building, for as long as anyone could remember, there had been a clock. The hands on this clock had stopped at 8.20. Without warning, it crashed down to the ground and broke, thus epitomising the breaking of the spell of the past and releasing us to move forward and be free of it. It was a poignant moment for each of us.

Beyond the gate, the officers had started moving some of the prisoners out on buses. One of the first to go was a Spanish guy known as Jesus. He had achieved a reputation in the prison for being the best blow job in the building, not that I ever tried him out, personally. For some mysterious reason one of the officers had take a shine to him and given him a plum job in charge of the storeroom. He was one of the first to get bussed out. He just skipped out as merrily as you like, without so much as a backward glance. He was lucky though, because if he had been selling himself he would have been badly busted up by the gangs when the washoffs started later on. He never even saw any of that, as he got bussed straight to Harrison's Point and allocated an outside job there. I would see him from my cell window, walking about untouched by life. There were others that the screws took out quickly, mostly known grasses and informants, lackeys and other arse-wipes. A lot of them were the Bullermen. All were collaborators.

When I saw people being taken out strategically, I knew there was a fear of reprisals and violence, and I started to feel afraid for my own safety. I had tried to keep from offending anyone in the prison, but you can never know when some crack head might take something you have said or done as a slight. I kept as far away from the other prisoners as I could, especially my so-called country men. I sat through the night with Vino, although from time to time I would even get paranoid about him, and who he might be in collusion with. At one point I thought he was trying to set me up to get murdered. We spent hour after hour together, sitting on pieces of cardboard, in the middle of the yard, telling each other jokes and just laughing the night through. He also went into a paranoia trip, thinking that he was just about to be attacked by someone. I kept reassuring him that this was not so. It's strange, but when you're paranoid, nobody else's paranoia seems real, only your own. To try and focus on something positive, and which would take our minds off anything sinister, I started imitating some of the characters from Viz magazine; Big Vern, and Cockney Wanker.

Stuck in this caged area, a few people started to seek out people they had disagreements with, or just didn't like, and more than one person was stabbed with a makeshift juka, or was beaten. Two British inmates that I had kept away from for a long time kept coming around, as if they were looking for a chance to get at me. I had to keep in the open, where there might be witnesses, or at least the chance to see something coming at me before it actually arrived. I had been getting weird vibes off these two for quite some time anyway, but everything seemed highlighted and in stark relief because we were basically trapped here together. All around me small gatherings of people were taking place, and amazingly, even in the midst of all of this chaos, some were smoking herb or crack. There must have been massive amounts of it in the air because in hindsight I'm sure it was these chemicals that were inducing the intense paranoia I was going through.

Eventually the opportunity came for us to go through and get on a bus. I stepped through the gateway. Officer Blackman searched me. After that, I was led along the area in front of the medical building and given a paper plate of stew and mash, along with a plastic spoon. Thank God. I was starving. With that, I was led into another caged area at the back of the prison. There were hardly any other prisoners in either of these two cages, as yet. *Charlie* had gone in just before me, and I went and sat down alongside him.

In the middle of this area was a single chemical toilet. I was glad that I had already emptied my bowels before stepping through the gate. Hopefully I would be good for a day or two. Taking a shit here was already beginning to look a bit grim.

As the hours wore on, this space filled up and it began to get very crowded. By about 2am it was chock-a-block, so the screws started leading people into the next cage. This too soon filled up to more than overflowing. The atmosphere was spooky. High above, the moon, past full and leading two bright stars behind it, like a pennant, sailed across the sky. It was marvellous, despite the discomfort, to be out in the open, actually sleeping under the brilliant night sky in all its radiant glory, feeling the warm air around my body. Above in the sky we could see bats flying around again. They would swoop and soar, swoop and soar, as they dived and hunted their prey. I drifted off to sleep, and when I woke up it was still night, but the moon and two trailing stars were much further over to the right in the sky, nearing the horizon. When they got a bit further it meant that the colours of dawn would soon start to appear.

***

The next day we awoke to the most brilliant sunshine, breaking through a bridal gown of purple, blue and mauve lace that was the remnant of the night before. To the west, I could see the moon, still leading those two single bright stars, one silver, one blue. To the east, the sun rose with a sense of gold and brilliance that I have never experienced since. It was fantastic. It was like a banner, a symbol of a new age that was dawning in each of our lives individually and collectively, announcing the birth of a new era for the whole of humanity.

But soon the beauty of this sunrise was replaced with weariness as the heat of its rays strengthened. It burned, it hurt, it wearied. We all started looking for a place to hide from the strength of its rays. Men began stripping off long pieces of cloth from sheets they had managed to bring along with them, and began creating wider sheets capable of protecting them from the sun. They strung the sheets along from one side of the cage to the other, gaining some protection.

Occasionally one or two of the officers would throw some bottles of water over the top. These were always grabbed quickly, and stored up. You never knew when you might be getting any more. When a fellow Brit asked me for some of my water, I told him to sort himself out. I wasn't there to wet nurse anyone who wasn't already looking out for themselves. After all, that had been his motto all along up until then. *Charlie* was my exception. *Charlie* and I went back a fair way, and when the food came along he tried to get extra for me when he possibly could, and I reciprocated. The first day in the cage was traumatic, and few of us were prepared to sit there and take much more of this bullshit. No word as to what was going on came through. Rumour after rumour ran and rippled through the prison.

Soldiers had us completely surrounded. They stood just a few yards outside the perimeter. At one point a number of us agreed that enough was enough. We stood up and told the soldiers that we were about to come over the fence. They replied that if we did, they would definitely shoot us. They said it in such a tone that made me, for one, believe them. The other lads jeered at them, telling them that they were traitors, and were like white men, ready and willing to open fire on their own black people. This seemed to take them aback a bit, and for a moment they looked at one another in uncertainty. But then, after a brief moment, that sense of resolution and purpose that comes with what some might call training, but to others is brainwashing, came back.

Later that day, Roland Yarde, a friend of mine from F&G days and a constant chess companion, suddenly jumped up, and made a rush for the fence. He succeeded in climbing over the top of it, and scaled own the other side. One of the soldiers, a woman from Guyana some said, knelt down and aimed her rifle at him. She looked to her senior officer as she did so, for confirmation that she was indeed to shoot. His order was for her to open fire. She shot Yarde, three times in the legs. He went down like a sack of old clothes. I thought he had been killed. His body certainly wasn't moving. At all.

Just at that point there was a tremendous rush forward as practically everyone in the cages ran to scale the fences. But the screws and the soldiers were up on their feet, ready for an immediate massacre, and itching for it, too. One was right in front of me, a big ugly screw whose name I think was Bourne. He was waving the wrong end of a shotgun in my face, moments away from opening up on me. I backed down. I didn't especially want to follow Yarde's example and become a martyr. Everyone hit the ground just then, and the screws seemed to relax a bit. They brought in a stretcher very quickly and assembled it around Yarde, as he lay there, motionless. Then they carried him away. He looked as though he were dead, like a bundle of old clothes that gets scooped up off the ground and carted off somewhere.

Meanwhile, throughout the day, someone was still inside the back prison continuing to set it on fire. From time to time flames would billow out of some of the cell windows as the arsonists repeatedly struck, setting fire to bedding and whatever they could find, determined to destroy as much of this hated place as they could for as long as they could. It was a question of the dog not being able to let go after the quarry had been hunted down. It was making life difficult for us outside. The longer they remained in there, the longer we would be forced to stay out here, helpless to move, being slowly burnt to a crisp while tensions and frustrations rose. Yet again we had to resort to covering our faces, lying completely still and straining to breathe through clouds of billowing and toxic smoke. Much of it smelt like plastic or rubber, and we had to breathe it all in. There were so many highly combustible materials in so many people's cells. Again and again the fire engine was called, and hosed down the noxious flames with great gusts of water. Then, off it would trot again, only to return an hour or so later when the arsonist struck yet again, albeit in another cell.

Come night, and the atmosphere became that of a ghoulish carnival. By now someone had pierced the intersecting wire separating the two cages, and we were able to move freely back and forth between the two as we wished. The sun had dazzled most of us with its constant radiance throughout that day, and it was delightful to feel the soothing power of the evening. During the day, we could see the sneaky faces of all the grasses looking down on us through the bars of the windows of the medical unit. From their expressions, it looked like they thought they were cute, that they were able to sit in the shade while the rest of us were stuck out in the sun. They were like little rats gloating down from a ship's rail at men who are beginning to drown.

A line of what looked like boy soldiers moved in a snake-like line and took up position around the cage perimeter. These were from the Regional Defence Force, men and women soldiers from Guyana, Antigua, and other neighbouring islands brought in just in case local soldiers proved unable to shoot their own people. John Nurse wasn't taking any chances in relying on his own men for this one.

We were trying to sleep on the unmarked cemetery area, where all of the condemned men who had been executed in Glendairy since its inception in 1832 had been buried, in unmarked and shallow graves, face down, so as to prevent them from rising again on the Day of Judgement. I remembered when Patrick Graves, appropriately named, had dug the graves for Josephs and Beckles, who had been on death row for years and had just received notice that their appeals were denied and they would be hanged. Graves dug the three-foot deep graves side by side just outside the tiny exercise area Josephs and Beckles used for one hour a day. As he had dug their graves, he uncovered several skulls. No-one seemed to know or care who they belonged to. The policy of the prison system in Barbados is for any condemned man's corpse to remain inside the prison walls after the execution. The family does not receive the body and are not allowed to give their relative a Christian burial. Their souls were destined to lie in Hell for all eternity.

***

Occasionally a small team of soldiers came along and threw some white bags with sandwiches in them over the top of the fence. There was a rush to grab what you could. Later on they brought in a slightly more ordered system of chaos and forced people to queue up in lines, but even here some of the locals would double back and pick up more than their share, even though it meant someone else would have to go without.

Every now and again there was a roar as someone got 'washed off' or badly beaten. Chuckie, one of the male rapists, got chopped up by a bunch of people, and preferred to risk getting shot by the troops rather than stay in the cage with the rest of us. I heard that at a later point a group of men got hold of him and ripped his balls of with their bare hands.

I managed to find a spot to get some sleep and drifted off.

The following morning we awoke to the smell of rain, and, looking up, I could see what looked like the body and head of a huge grey-black dragon coiling and uncoiling itself over us as it floated in and moved over the island. It began to rain. At first little spots began to hit us, then larger, until it turned into a veritable downpour. There was no protection or cover anywhere. Luckily, one of my friends, Stanton, came up with a small piece of cardboard, and somehow three of us managed to stand underneath this small piece of protection and get out of the rain.

Some of the lads had been unable to find any cover. *Henry* was one of them, but this was no time for sentimentalities. Everyone had to look after themselves and helplessness wasn't seen in a very good light. He started shivering when the rain died off. He didn't even have the sense to take off his soaking clothes to allow them to dry in the heat that followed the rain.

All kinds of emotions started flowing through me: anger, resentment, love. I don't know why but it was as though all these crazy emotions were suddenly let loose through me. I looked at the wire cages surrounding us and saw the raindrops sparkling with an intensity I had never seen before. Each raindrop was now like a tiny prism, refracting the light and the rays of the sun and shining like a myriad of diamonds. It was like a sign from the gods that we had gained their favour. Each of us was completely soaked, so we stripped off and hung our clothes out to dry. It was as though we had been baptised, like the children of God going through the Red Sea. All our sins were washed away.

The illusion didn't last. The portable toilet was still sitting in the middle of the enclosure, like Dr Who's Tardis. By now it was completely blocked up with shit and people were crapping into the polystyrene hinged lid containers our food came in and flipping these over the top of the opening of the portaloo, where it was building up inside. Eventually even this filled up so people would just go off to one of the two farthest corners and do their business there. These corners were ringed off with a makeshift string and covers, to try and provide some privacy.

The heat was becoming unbearable, and I began wondering if I was going to die in this place, so forlorn did everything look. It was as if we had lived to see the Day of Judgement, and now it was our time to leave this world. Now and again fights broke out, but by and large people were content to sit around, or sometimes go for a stroll, chatting with someone, listening to the rumours. Some tried selling me some of the knocked-off gold. Starliner asked me if I wanted one particularly exquisite gold ring. I forget how much he asked for it, but he was keen to get rid of it. With trembling fingers, he nervously pushed back his long dreadlocks and looked around anxiously. It's possible that he had been smoking crack. *Why would I want this ring? And what could I possibly offer him for it?*

After a while, a senior police officer with a very conspicuous gold watch on his right wrist came out and began calling out from a list of names. People were transfixed by this, and a silence fell over the entire area. One by one, the people whose names were being called moved over to the gate, and from there, were led out along the path back to where we supposed they would be shipped out on buses. Two soldiers, one on each arm escorted them along.

The screws were calling out the names of their favourites, mainly, although now and again someone was called out for a genuine medical reason, or just because they had been able to get a screw to put their name forward. My friend *Charlie* was able to get out this way, as he suffered from high blood pressure. As he went down the way I called out to him, '*Charlie*! I'll see you on the other side!' although as the words came out of my mouth I realised that my meaning must have seemed ambiguous.

Some of the grasses were being pulled out, and pretty quickly, too. Imagine my surprise when some of them turned out to be some of my country men. Actually, I must have been the only one surprised. Most of the local men knew about them, right from the start, and, with the knowledge of hindsight, I realised that they had actually tried to warn me.

The other grasses were led up from the carpenter's shop, where they had been sheltering. They were booed as they moved past, none of them even showing any surprise or shame at the reception they were getting. Then the grasses who had been holing up in the upstairs room of the medical building were brought out and off they went to a more comfortable venue.

The crowd inside the cages was getting restless, but soldiering on stoically through this period of difficulty. Eventually they stopped calling names and started on the remaining mass of us. Long lines were forming. People were desperate to get out. I saw Vino line up for several hours, before they took him out. Eventually the crowd inside the cages thinned, and those left discovered the joy of having a lot more space. Quickly, we had become used to having such a mass of people around us; it was even feeling quite lonely now that the bulk of our fellows had been taken away.

I hung back right till end, and at a certain point a strange thing happened. The wind changed. This in itself was unusual, because in Barbados the wind almost always comes from the east. It cooled and changed direction. Suddenly, there was a different kind of vibe in the cages. I saw Mr Lickerish there. His face was covered to hide his identity. If the screws had seen him there they would have tried coming for him, as he was a security prisoner, awaiting the noose. Thus, he had nothing to lose by attempting to escape. Many a time we had chatted and I knew that he was more than he let on. He was a real thinker, and as I neared I overheard him telling a younger inmate about Malcolm X, and Marcus Garvey.

'Terry,' he said to me, in a tone that was almost prophetic, 'This is your redemption.'

As he spoke he held up his hand and pointed towards the burned-out hulk of what had been Glendairy prison. On some deep level, I felt as if a great boulder had been rolled away, and I was now free to climb out of a tomb that I had been in, possibly for all of my life.

'You must write about what you have seen here, Terry' he said to me.

I promised him that I would.

Then an eerie silence prevailed over the entire scene. It was as if I had made, or become part of, a solemn promise, an oath, and the spirits of all those people who had died in this place over all those years had marked my words. Everyone and everything stopped moving. I had a sense of The Last Post being played by spirit buglers in some adjacent reality. Every man seemed to be standing still and to attention. I felt honoured, and humbled, to have been chosen to be the only white man deemed worthy to have been shown this, and to be present in the midst of it. I felt that I had been chosen by history to be part of this experience, to have stood and suffered with these men at this great turning point of history. This made me feel more special than any other event or experience in my life.

But there was another element; it wasn't as though my presence in this was something superfluous. It was a necessary ingredient. What I had been a part of was a gigantic spell, to redeem the past and change the future. It was like an act of inner cleansing. My being here in the midst of it was in fact a vital part of that—a vital part of a spell which had started when I took those first steps down into the underground corridor of the condemned section H&I and began carrying out the shit buckets for the men sentenced to die by hanging. I had been part of an event that I felt would eventually be recognised as a significant point in history of the 21st century. This symbol of inhumanity had gone up in flames. For me personally it represented being set free from the limiting and negative condition I had been struggling under in my life, such as my addiction.

Eventually, even this sensation passed away, and it was patently my turn to present myself at the gate for the forthcoming bus trip, to goodness knew where.

CHAPTER TWELVE

Six Roads

When the right moment came, I went over to the gate and was taken through, a soldier on each arm as if I was going to try and make a run for it. They led me down the path to where Officer Blackman was yet again, waiting to search me, a rubber glove on each hand and a long black torch in his right. He told me to strip. I did so, dropping my clothes straight onto the ground. I had to take off my shoes, and as I did so I saw the massive pile of shoes that that the guards had already collected; all kinds of boots, slippers, shoes, and sandals. Beside the shoes there was a pile of Bibles and other holy books, personal photographs of wives and daughters, letters treasured from years of imprisonment. My sandals went into the pile. I had to kneel with my forehead on the ground and pull the cheeks of my arse apart so Blackman could look up into it with his torch, to see if I had any contraband hidden. Currency, gold, passports, mobile phones, and even chargers had been found stuffed up various prisoners' backsides.

Then, I was told to put my shirt and trousers back on. I was handcuffed and taken to where a bus sat waiting. Hamilton *Pete*, my old mate who had faithfully washed my clothes and done many errands for me in our time together, was right behind me, and he boarded the bus immediately after me.

'Hey Terry,' he said to me as soon as he got on, 'Watch this.'

He stood and took a deep breath and with a massive grunt he strained his arms. With a crack the handcuffs popped open.

'Old party trick,' he said to me. 'Got lots of practice getting arrested all those times in the States!'

I was amazed, and not a little worried, at how many people the screws had managed to squeeze onto the bus. Built for about 30 people, there must have been about 70 or even 80 in there. I looked around for someone I knew, but all I could see were very young men, all from the Farm, which I rarely, if ever, visited. They were all talking excitedly about what they had seen and heard. But there was a deeper vibe here too, one in which each man knew that he had taken part in what was to become an historically significant event in Barbados—the storming of our modern-day Bastille Prison; Glendairy!

There was nowhere to sit, so I just sank to my knees, my hands behind me. I was squeezed tightly by my fellows from left and right. *Pete* squeezed in beside me. The screws locked the inner door, securing it with a padlock. Then we were moving, out along the pathway which led to the front gate of the prison, past the Superintendent's car park, past Miss Daniel's favourite rose bush, then right, through the gates. A sight that truly amazed us waited outside. There seemed to be hundreds of police cars out here, all with their lights flashing, red and blue, red and blue, red and blue. As our bus made its way down the drive to the main road, one of the cars moved out in front and another right behind, their sirens blaring into action as we manoeuvred into the road and picked up speed. I was glad to be out of there. There were times when I wasn't sure if I would make it out alright. At any given moment I could have been picked on by a disgruntled old cell mate, an angry mob, someone high on crack, or by an officer or soldier panicking in the mayhem. There was also the small matter of the fire and the billowing smoke that threatened to consume us all, and the risk of dehydration and all manner of diseases from being cooped up under the sun with no facilities for so long. I let out a small sigh of relief, as we moved off. I didn't know where we were going, but I didn't really care. It couldn't have been worse than where we had come from. Could it?

As we picked up speed it became too painful for me to remain kneeling, so I just flopped back and stretched out my legs. The shriek of the sirens announced to everyone on the island that that some really top-level villains were being transported. The lads in the bus with me were lapping it up; this was the red carpet, all right! We were being treated as if we were real terrorists or something, which for us was ironic, as the overwhelming majority of us had actually played no part in the disturbances at all, and had tried to stay well out of the way for fear of being killed or at least seriously hurt.

We spun through the highways and byways of Barbados that night, everyone being thrown from one side of the bus to the other as the mad driver took each roundabout at about 80 miles an hour. Luckily no one was hurt, but seeing the beautiful land of Barbados, albeit by night and under these uncomfortable conditions was a joy in itself. I smiled ruefully to myself that, when I became a very old man, I would one day look back on this 80 mile an hour drive with fond memories.

Eventually we arrived at what looked like a gigantic warehouse. It was ringed off with razor wire, coiled three rows deep. Interspersed along the outer edge was a series of sniper platforms with the silhouettes of armed soldiers illuminated against the night sky. The bus edged closer to the entrance and came to a stop. The inner door in the bus was unlocked and they started bringing us out, two by two.

When the guard saw that *Pete* had snapped his links, she started talking about giving him some kind of extra punishment, but, quick as an arrow, he was able to soothe her over with a tale of how it had happened inadvertently. She decided to let it pass, and we were brought out. She unlocked my cuffs, and I got down off the bus and went into a search area. Here, Officer Broomes, who I had known from my time on H&I, was busy searching. He checked me out and then let me pass. As I stepped into an inner cage area, which led into a great big warehouse, I was amazed at what I saw. It was similar to what I have since seen on television in the reportage of the Hurricane Katrina disaster relief operation in New Orleans, inside the big dome where they housed all those people, except here every person was a criminal and most of them were dangerous to be around. There was nothing separating us from the really dangerous ones, and that worried me.

There were hundreds of people, with dozens of beds going off in every direction. There was row upon row, with people sitting on their beds, either alone, or in small groups. From the side a disembodied voice seemed to be greeting each new arrival with the word that there was a shower: 'Over there! Use it! Now!' I did as I was told, even though I didn't have any soap or wash cloth. The feel of that naturally warm water running over my sweat-stained and stinking body was wonderful. The shower area had about half a dozen pipes on each side, and was full. Strangely, everyone was smiling; the vibe was warm and convivial, almost like a carnival. Maybe it was because we were all happy to have gotten out of Glendairy alive. Further back behind the shower room was the toilet area, where we had several plumbed-in loos, and a set of washbasins. Things were actually looking good, compared to our last couple of days. Here we had a roof over our heads, so we were protected at long last from the sun and the rain. What luxury!

I came back into the warehouse and looked around to see what was going on and who I might know that was around.

'Terry! Over here!' I heard from one of the beds by the side of the wall. Vino was sitting with a few others. I looked around hopefully to see if he could squeeze me in somewhere—even a piece of head-resting space would have done. But apparently this was someone else's bed, so after a brief chat I had to move on to make my own arrangements.

I went around and noted that the Muslims, along with Stanton, had congregated in one corner together, while the gangs had taken over the others. One was led by Jah Hool, who I knew from H&I. He smiled at me and I felt strangely reassured. He was sitting with his back to the wire of the inner enclosure, and around him were his son, also an inmate, and about 20 members of his team. In the other corner there was Rebel, Problem Child, and others, while in the other corner was Sandeford, my old cell-mate. Sandeford's crime had been to rob a poor black woman who ran a small store, but because she knew his face he wanted to be a tough guy and knife her to death. He and his accomplice had been able to get away, but the police sent out a message that they knew who had done the crime and asked him to turn himself in. He had been smoking crack cocaine at the time of the robbery, as had most of the guys in Glendairy immediately prior to their arrest. Sandeford had originally been sentenced to the noose, but after a year down on H&I he had been able to wangle his way out of that and into a commuted sentence of 30 years, and back into the mainstream of ordinary prison life. He too sat surrounded by his soldiers, who called themselves the Ant Hill Mob. As I moved along, I saw my old mate Baggis, who I first shared a cell with when I came to Glendairy. It had been a little while since I had seen him and I noticed that he had become a Rasta man, growing his dreadlocks quite long. We chatted for a while, and I moved on. I was trying to reacquaint myself with as many friends as I could, just in case someone took exception to me.

Later that evening the food arrived, and the officers on duty seemed determined to try to create as much confusion as possible. They were giving the food out willy nilly so that it was like a rugby scrum at the hatch where the food was distributed. Men were pushing and shoving, fighting to get in front of others and snatch as many of the little white bags for themselves as they could. Nobody seemed interested in making sure that the limited supply of food was going to be enough to go round. It was every man for himself and may the devil take the hindmost. It was disheartening to see men reduced to the level of beasts, and an absolute absence of unity amongst us. It wasn't as if the food was any great shakes, either—only a small bread roll with just a hint of cheese spread inside it, along with a slice of sweetbread. That, along with a small packet of orange juice, was the meal for the evening. And for this, men were prepared to totally disgrace themselves, even fight, for more than was their rightful share, even if that meant another man was going without.

At first I managed to get a large piece of cardboard, as all the beds had long since been taken, and found a space where I could squeeze in without anyone being too hostile to my presence. It started as a width of about three feet, then narrowed to two as the beds on either side edged closer, till finally it became only one foot wide, and even became a walk-through alleyway servicing a different set of beds. I eventually got fed up with about 30 people an hour stepping all over my space to get through, and decided to move somewhere less hectic. None of the British inmates were interested in helping me out. Even if I had a bed it would probably been taken from me once the gangs started turning up. In that situation there is little one man can do against a united and determined team of five or six.

I spread the cardboard piece out in front of the entranceway to the shower area, where there seemed to be some space. It was a pleasure to have somewhere where people weren't walking all over me. I took off my denim shirt and rolled it up as my pillow. During the night a cold draught seemed to spring up, and I felt its chilling influence as I tried to drift off to sleep. This was bad news. I got up and looked around for something I could use to minimise the cold, and, in the corner by the bin, found it. It was a sheet of plastic that had been used as a covering for one of the new beds. I picked it up, and, using it as a sleeping bag, slipped into it. Although a bit of condensation developed inside it through the night, it served me well and I slept beautifully through each night of the fortnight that I spent in the warehouse, but I couldn't help thinking how absolutely appalling these conditions were.

This place was part of an industrial area and was called Six Roads because it was located at a junction where six of the most important roads in Barbados converged. This warehouse had formerly been a place where fish was canned, but it seemed as though the operation had not been a great success. Barbados is periodically in trouble with one of its neighbours, Trinidad, over fishing rights, and this on-going scenario might have had something to do with the demise of the cannery.

Up above the general area, there was a sealed-off observation post where up to a dozen soldiers and prison officers would perch themselves and look down over the chaos that engulfed us. Mostly they just nervously fingered their automatic rifles as they peered down through the wire from their balcony. John Nurse came along, and was booed by some of the men. Keeping his red banded cap on all the while, Nurse spoke mostly on the need for the men to be patient. Then he left.

There was an explosion of anger. Many of the men had spent hours drawing up lists of items needed to make life bearable in the camp; colour television, access to the press, and domino sets. Brutal Bob, so-called because of the brutality of his sexual encounters whilst under the influence of crack on the outside, was very active in this side of what he called 'The Campaign', and in bringing about a sense of order in general. Along with two other men, known as Tanty, and Jet Li, he managed to get the men organised into two queues at mealtime, one for meat and the other for vegetarian. Many of the men tried to go back a second or even a third time for extra food, but if they got caught it meant an immediate beating. One fella, known as Earth, got caught several times, but no matter how badly he was beaten, he still went back to get more than his allowance. Before the fire, Earth had a star earner in the kitchen frying up rice and other goodies for his private customers in exchange for blow jobs or cigarettes. Now his empire lay in tatters. Earth sat by himself, his only companion one little multi-sexual-looking cocksucker freak from Brazil who used to open his legs in exchange for some weed and extra food. When I saw how badly some of these men like Earth were being beaten, I was content to sit down with my own white paper bag and just eat my own food, quietly.

Soon the screws were using a list of names to call people, to ensure that each man did get his own food and no more. It was a system that worked, thank God, and the food sharing became much more organised. Sometimes they would call out the list backwards, just to vary it a bit, which was at first confusing once you got used to the list being called in its original way. Then one evening one of the screws was caught hiding a big tray of prisoners' food so that he could carry it home for himself. There was uproar, and the officer was forced by Sergeant Scantlebury, one of the most principled and genuine screws there, to hand it over to the inmates. The screw in question was scowling as he did so, though; he was known from the Farm for hating prisoners and used to go around verbally abusing inmates as if drunk. Everybody laughed to see his discomfort. I think it was the first time I had ever seen a black man's face go bright red from embarrassment, or anger.

The next morning I was one of the first to wake up, and the vibe was so good! From a gap in the roof above a single ray of brilliant gold sunshine shone down, cutting through the dust in the air and hitting the ground just a few inches away from where I lay. The silence was broken when a few men began to rise to take their brief strolls around the place, before it got too busy. One of the men jumped up and pointed to another fellow.

'This one I caught fucking a sponge!' he shouted, but the collective response was one of amusement, not anger, so the accused was allowed to get away with whatever his transgression had been. From the sound of it, he had been masturbating through a hole in the bed mattress.

***

That morning, as part of the breakfast there was a banana and an orange for each man. These tasted like no fruit I have eaten either before or since. But as I was finishing, and about to throw the skins and peel away, one of the Rasta men came up to me and stopped me, putting his hand out for my bag.

I gave it to him, and he continued collecting everyone else's bag, too. When they had collected all the skins, a small team of men gathered together and began cutting away the inside of the skins using the edge of plastic spoons. They soon had little piles of a white paste-like substance in front of them. When they were finished, they brought their piles out into the spot on the floor where the sun's rays were striking, and used this to dry the paste. Every now and again one of the men would have to get up and move the pile of paste to keep it in the light, as the sun moved across the sky and the angle of its rays changed. Eventually though, one of the Rasta men was satisfied, and the little pyramid of what had become a white powder was taken away.

They used the paper from the white bags, and managed to seal this up as ready-to-smoke rollups, with the mysterious white powder inside each of them, instead of tobacco. One of the Surinamese inmates had managed to smuggle a tinder box into the warehouse which they used to get a spark to light up their rollups. The first spliffs were lit up and the men dragged deep off them. A weird vibe came into the air. Even though I hadn't smoked any, I could not help but breathe the smoke as it filled the air around me. My vision was affected; things looked a bit cartoonish, or two-dimensional.

During the day men passed the time by playing five-a-side football, using a home made football of paper for the purpose, or played chess or draughts on boards they drew themselves with borrowed pens, and pieces cut out of cardboard and polystyrene. Sandeford started a Fight Club, where men parried blows with each other, but not to the head, only the chest. We even had a wheelchair derby, in which we borrowed the wheelchairs from two of the invalided inmates and raced each other round a makeshift track. Brutal Bob was good as one of the riders, and usually won. Some men were even betting their food on the outcomes of these races, but then Barbadians are known as great gamblers. All in all, we were making the most of a difficult time, and getting through it, as a team.

That afternoon, though, something in the atmosphere began to change. There were hastily-convened meetings between each of the different gangs, with representatives from each talking with each other in what looked like high-level diplomatic manoeuvrings. Then, when I went to use the toilet, I could see why. Inside the gate a man was busy bending back and snapping off the thinner of the bars that had been hastily welded on to reinforce the door. These he was then handing out to other men, who were taking them deeper into the toilet area and scraping them up against the walls. They were sharpening lengths of wire into jukas.

As I looked round the toilet, I saw perhaps a dozen men busy at work sharpening up their jukas, wrapping the ends in a cloth to prevent slippage. I knew that war was on the cards. These guys had very serious expressions on their faces, totally absorbed in their work. I only hoped I wasn't one of the forthcoming targets. I was trapped in this place, unable to get out, get away, or even stand any reasonable chance of defending myself. A sick feeling began to float up from the bottom of my stomach. As I looked, I had no way of knowing if I was going to be stabbed by someone who I might have inadvertently offended, or crossed. It needn't necessarily be anything specific, either, I realised. Maybe someone was going to stab me up just for being a white man, or because at some distant point I hadn't given him a cigarette. I thought about this, and wondered who I was going to be able to rely on for any back-up, should the need arise. I realised with grim horror that I was on my own entirely. The other white guys were all too busy resting up on their own mattresses, not even wanting to share them with me, or even let me lie down or rest on the side of one of them. I knew that none of them would lift their voice, let alone a little finger, to help me, should I be attacked. If anything, they would probably sit there, having a laugh, squealing with delight if this were to happen.

That evening Mia Mottley, the Attorney General, visited the adjacent section of the warehouse where the other half of our population was being accommodated. Through an aperture, high up in the wall between the two sections, I could vaguely hear her voice although I couldn't make out the actual words. There was some applause for her when she had finished, but she didn't come into the section where we were. Some of the lads were able to climb up to the window and came back with the news that she was talking about parole, one of the greatest pieces of Barbadian legal bullshit and a never-ending roundabout of deceit that the authorities there have no intention of bringing into being. Yet, they bandy this word about when it suits them to.

***

The vibe that I had been feeling all day suddenly boiled over into violence. The fist thing I saw was a big rush of maybe a dozen men from one corner over to where one man was sitting, talking with some people on his bed. They immediately went to work, beating him, over and over again, the heavy thumps and kicks reverberating throughout the hall. It was horrific. I could hear the man's ribs crack and snap. Kicks from unshod feet were thrown in, again and again. The man screamed in agony, but the beating continued mercilessly. Eventually, it was decided that he had had enough, and he was allowed to make his own way over to the inner enclosure of the caged area, and sit down there, to await the screws coming to take him out.

Slowly, desperately, he dragged his broken body over to this area, where he sat down, tenderly. He called out to one of the screws on the other side of the gate, but they just continued to look back at him, as if they couldn't understand what had happened to him, or what he was saying. The screws just stood there, on the far side of the fencing, their arms and legs twitching nervously, the fear visible on their faces.

Then the wolf pack moved off rapidly to its next target, and finding it, started the same procedure. They moved as if they were each the different legs and arms of the same great beast. This was no collection of different people; this was a collective mind, a single entity that was moving amongst us like a giant spider, picking off whoever it desired. Now another man was suddenly encircled, and savagely and mercilessly attacked. One man had his long dreadlocks literally ripped out of his head, and was then thumped and stabbed till he ran into the inner sanctum by the gate where a collection of broken and bleeding bodies was rapidly accumulating. Many were unable to stand, and had collapsed on the floor inside this cage. Still the guards just looked on.

This was a nightmare. More gangs seemed to appear out of nowhere to start their work. Again and again they gangs moved through the hall like a brood of mythological giants, tearing apart whoever was on their list for some real or imagined transgression. It was a time to pay off a lot of old scores. Once again, the people who were mainly singled out were those who had been bulling, chichi-ing (receiving), shacking-up (prostituting), or grassing. Now and again, his nerves getting the better of him, a man would suddenly make a dash for the sanctum, even though he hadn't even been attacked, but simply because he suspected that he was about to get his payback. Occasionally a man was given just one or two blows and then allowed to run. Others got the living daylights kicked out of them, such as a young Guyanese boy, a seaman by trade and a notorious chichiman. He squealed like a girl when they beat him. I felt terrible, but was far too scared to say anything or intervene. One thing I learnt is that when you are really afraid and on your own, the next man's fate is nowhere near as important as you had previously imagined it to be.

One guy, Corry, who I had known a bit and even shared a cell with for a short while, suddenly found himself accused as a Bullerman. Apparently, he had pressurised a very young man, Weasel, into having sex with him. What sealed his fate was the gold cap in the front of his mouth, and he was immediately smashed into the ground. Amazingly, though, he was able to pull himself up after about 15 minutes of a devastating onslaught and negotiate with his attackers for a chance to get to the sanctum. Their hearts softened, and they permitted him free access. His bravery earned him some respect as he took his 'punishment' like a real man.

Then they were onto *Pete*, who was accused of being a grass.

'What?' he cried out, and then, 'Jah Hool!'

Jah Hool took one look over from his throne in the corner and with an imperial wave of his right hand signalled to the demolition team to leave him alone. I could see that *Pete* was greatly relieved. He had rarely come that close to such a hideous beating, and got away with it. But *Pete* was always a very resourceful person.

One of the more eccentric characters in the place was Azariah Phipps, Grandpa. He thought he'd try and get one of his old-time enemies in the prison dobbed in for being a Buller.

'He's a Bullerman!' he cried out, pointing to a guy who was actually one of the biggest suppliers of weed in the entire prison, a man who had probably the most powerful people in the prison in his employ. The wolf pack wasn't having any of this, especially when the accused man leapt up and started hitting his accuser. At this the wolf pack joined in, and Grandpa got the daylights beaten out of him in retribution for what he had just tried to put another man through. I subsequently saw the old fart glaring out of the sanctum over the next three days while these beatings or 'washouts', as they became known, took place. He looked hungry during that time, but would I go over and give him even a piece of crust? No fucking way.

It sounds terrible to admit to this, but it gave me a tremendous lift to sit there and collect my own food parcels, and slowly munch through them, while dozens of wankers were ripped to pieces by the sharks and the wolves. Now and again, I even looked back as the tasty food slid down the back of my throat, seeing their wild eyes frantically looking around all over the place. Some even called out to me, but I was too afraid to answer them. One of them had worked in the kitchen prior to all this. He had been such a bastard with the food sharing, wanting money all the time for extra food and never giving anyone anything. Well he could sit there and starve for all I cared. In fact it would be nice to see some of that too, I thought. Sort of adds to the experience. At this point something really evil seemed to get inside me, transforming my fear into a maliciousness that gained pleasure from seeing people who had taken the piss out of me get their comeuppance.

People like Badmouth were whiling away their time by going back into the area and pulling out these cruds, subjecting them to further beatings, just to keep the interest going. I later heard that Badmouth would get freaks like Sheep to stage fights with those already beaten, or tell them to repeatedly bash their heads against the walls until their heads made a deep satisfying booming sound and they screamed in pain like schoolgirls.

Others got washed off, too. One Jamaican man, Anthony Grant, from Ochorios, just got one kick in the back from someone and was then told to go and sit in the sanctum. This he did, but he wasn't very happy about it and glared back. I hadn't really known him before the burning, but in the brief interval at Six Roads I had talked with him a few times, and we had formed a kind of friendship. Whenever I went to use the toilet or have a shower, he would try to speak with me and beg me to bring him some food. I shooed him away out of fear for myself. If I showed this man any consideration it might mean similar treatment for me. Initially, I felt terrible, like a traitor, but at the end of the day I had to look out for myself.

Huckle Sweet was a notorious chichiman but a generally much-loved rogue. He was smacked on the head as his nominal punishment, but they didn't put him in the sanctum where he would have been without food for days, as the screws weren't opening up those gates and taking anyone out. Huckle was made to go round and tap every other chichiman on the shoulder. Each chichiman would receive a slap and have to go to the sanctum.

***

I soon grew tired of the malice I was feeling and just wished for it all to end, but the washouts went on for days. I would just try to go to sleep while it was going on, sliding back into my plastic sleeping bag and drifting off, while all around me men would be crying out like in some dungeon or ancient torture chamber. It was like having a series of bad dreams filled with the cries of lost and tormented souls.

My piece of cardboard was beginning to break up as the days went by, as each day I, like everyone else, would have to pick up my entire bed so the floor could be swept and wiped down. But I held onto all my pieces with ferocity. It might not have been much, but it was all that I had! I, like everybody else in here, had been reduced to acting like a wild animal defending his den.

The Jamaican Preacher man was busy, calling on all of us to repent and receive the Lord as our Saviour. Over the previous week he had gathered round about him about a dozen men for prayer meetings. His voice could be heard over everything else, calling out the name of Jesus in an impassioned tone. This man had become semi-famous in Glendairy through his highly emotional outpourings, normally just before lunch, in which he would be joined by Monkey Man's uncle, who was also a holy man and was in for running down a woman tourist, and then driving off. Jamaican Preacher was a professional cocaine smuggler, who still hadn't been paid for most of the 'jobs' he had done to the UK, and was already looking forward to his next opportunity to smuggle.

At one point, Jamaican Preacher man managed to get about 30 men all standing in a circle, holding hands and praying all night long. Eventually though, Jet Li went over and gave him a slap and told him to 'Fucking well can it.' Many were outraged at this act of impiety, but personally I found it slightly humorous. These Rasta men weren't taking any of this white man religious shit any more. Part of me could sympathise.

Meanwhile, the screws did absolutely nothing to discourage or dissuade the beaters from attacking the other prisoners. Not one single word was spoken against them. All they did was to stand up on their balcony and look down on the scenes from Hell, taking it all in. Neither did they try to get any of the injured to safety, or offer them any medical attention. It took them three days to open the gates. Half a dozen of the soldiers, from Antigua, stood there with their rifles raised and pointing at the heads and bodies of each of the injured men, as they were brought out of the cage, their hands cuffed behind their backs. They were stripped, and then flung in the back of one of the prison buses outside where they were left for the night. The next morning, the screws began driving some of these injured to the QE hospital. *That's right lads, no rush, eh?*

In the adjacent hall things were going the same way as they had been in ours. A man by the name of Jah Fire was the one leading the 'washouts' there. We had our scouts up on the window looking through at what was happening. On one occasion, one of them called out that Eggs was being made to shit himself. Eggs was one of the local fellas who used to come around and see me when I was on D&E and have his cards read. He would always bring me a couple of cigarettes, for which I was very grateful. It pained and saddened me to hear of this man being forced to humiliate himself this way. I was told that he was being done for being a Bullerman, which, now that I thought about it, seemed possible. You might have thought that, in all the chaos, someone there might have thought to take a whack at a white man just because the opportunity was there, but it never happened. No one was ever hit on the basis of race.

Very suddenly, three shots rang out from next door. We all held our breath: our scouts reported back that Bullets, a brilliant portrait artist whose work I had often admired, had been shot in the neck, and Packman had been killed. One other prisoner had also been gunned down, allegedly because he wouldn't stop beating other inmates. That incident seemed to cool everything down. The beatings tapered off and things began to return to normal. Thank God.

We were at Six Roads for about two weeks. Somehow I made it through.

Then, eventually, the buses started up again to take people off to wherever it was that we were going next. More buses came, and now whoever wanted to get out of this place and move on to the next was able to queue up and get away. Eventually things thinned out so much that Jet Li and one of his assistants came over to where I was sitting and suggested it was time to move.

'No one has harmed you,' Jet Li said.

I offered him my hand, but he rejected it.

'No I don't do that bitch thing,' he said, turning away.

He was quite a character, and went through some beatings himself, afterwards, from what I heard.

I quickly took a shower and lined up. I asked Vino if he wanted to come with me, but food sharing was coming up and he wanted to hang on for that. *Henry* was playing the fool and staying put on the mattress he had managed to get for himself, in a semi-open defiance of Jet Li's strong suggestion. As I queued, *Pete* was suddenly beside me and as the screw opened the gate we went through with the Jamaican Preacher. We three were the last bunch for the bus out of there that night.

Pete and I were made to strip as soon as we stepped out of the external gate, where there were many, many soldiers waiting. These troops were all from Antigua and Guyana. They were all silhouetted against the bright light from the searchlights arrayed behind them. Behind them, too, were rows of police, standing there with the red strips of their cap badges plainly visible on their heads.

'White boy,' one of them said to me, 'what you in here for, mon?' He cradled his automatic rifle across his arms. He was short but very stocky, and there were coloured badges of things like triangles all over his camouflage jacket. On his head he wore the camouflage jungle cap

'Drugs,' I replied.

***

When you are stripped naked, and made to sit in front of an armed man you have never met before, it can be slightly unnerving. I looked to the side and saw a line of police looking back at me. There must have been about 50 of them there, all senior officers, by the look of their uniforms and the red stripes in their caps. Great spotlights had been erected outside also, and cast an eerie, cold glow over the entire scene. I had to pull back my bum cheeks again, thus affording the most senior police officers in Barbados a view into my innermost parts. I hope I didn't dazzle too many of them.

Everything I was wearing was thoroughly searched. Even the bar of soap that I had acquired was split in two to see if there was anything hidden inside. I managed to keep hold of my water bottle. I knew it would come in useful wherever I was going, and in this I was to be proved right. When you end up in a completely new place, and haven't been able to take anything with you, it can take days or even weeks to rearrange around you all the bits and pieces you need to make your life right.

I was then given a new T-shirt, a pair of blue boxer shorts, and a pair of flip-flops. You can't walk too well or for too long in them, but then again this wasn't likely to be a problem we were going to be experiencing. I looked to the side and saw that *Pete* was going through the same thing. I managed to hold onto my old uniform, though, even though I now also had the T-shirt and pants. We were both handcuffed again, and put back on the bus.

The bus started off, and again I found my place on the floor. I wasn't able to see much of the scenery as we trundled along. Some of the lads were having a great time again, lapping up the notoriety that the flashing lights and wailing sirens seemed to confer. The rumours were that the new place was going to be like a prisoner of war camp, our version of Guantanamo Bay. We arrived quite late at night. There seemed to be several buildings inside this new complex. Massive fences of razor wire had been thrown up all around the complex, which was right by the edge of the sea. It was the former US naval base that we had heard so much about: Harrison's Point. A red and white painted lighthouse stood just outside the point where the wire fence ran out.

The buildings inside this great prisoner of war style camp had huge letters painted up along the sides; A, B, C. Our building seemed much bigger than any of the others. D Block was made up of two stories, but ran for some 300 yards. It was a fairly modern-looking building. Apparently they had been built to accommodate US marines some time in the 80s. It had last been used for the US invasion of Grenada, and since then had been allowed to fall into disrepair. Just right to house convicts with no human rights then. During our time at Six Roads, the authorities had been going flat out to fix this place up, reinforce it, and make it ready to deal with nearly 1,000 prisoners, but their efforts concentrated on reinforcing security rather than providing us with any sort of comfort.

Standing at the entrance way, as I was led off the bus, was a man who looked like the Chief of the Royal Barbados Police, so splendid and glamorous was his uniform. He looked briefly at me as I was led in, as he must have done at each of the other inmates being brought in, but didn't say anything. He gave off a vibe of being a very serious and dedicated man. There was definitely something special about him. He seemed deep in thought, and quite grim in manner. I was searched by one of the screws, and allowed to keep my old uniform. This was later to prove very useful. I was led upstairs and on the way saw two guards I had befriended; Officer Sobers and Miss Logi. Sobers smiled and said a few words to me, and Miss Logi's eyes flickered in recognition. I was led down a long narrow corridor, past dozens of cell doors, through gateways that unlocked as I approached and locked behind me. The officer guiding me along was Mr Shorey, who had helped me get the job as a bucket man on security. I had always liked Shorey's style. He was one of the academic ones, and was studying nursing. I was taken right down to the end of the corridor and the last door on the left was opened. The number outside read 13. *Lucky for some*, I thought. *Why not me?*

CHAPTER THIRTEEN

INSIDE CELL 13

I stepped inside, and was glad that I had take advantage of my last opportunity to get a shit and a shower at Six Roads before making this leg of the journey. The cell was about 30 feet long and 14 feet wide. On each side was a line of plastic mattresses, pushed edge to edge, and each accommodating at least one man. I was the last in, and it was already seriously overcrowded. Once more, we were expected to cram into this room and fend for ourselves. As soon as I walked in I could feel the stuffy, claustrophobic atmosphere.

I looked around for a friendly face, but it was dark, and the only light came from the corridor where the fluorescent light was permanently on. I looked up to the ceiling and saw a gaping hole where a lamp fixture had once been. Over at the window, there were two sets of metal grills in place, but the view was magnificent. I could see the sea, the lighthouse, and from here, the highest point in the prison, look down over virtually the entire camp. A ring of big spotlights and a wire fence, which looked like something out of the East German border post, had been erected around the perimeter. I couldn't help but reflect on this contrast—a scene from paradise away in the distance, with sea and sand and palm trees and luxury, but in front of that, hemming me in, all the trappings of hell. In my deeper moments I saw it as my paradise lost. Ever since I had set foot in Barbados, I had managed to create for myself a living hell through my drug-crazed actions, and had almost wilfully walked myself into a jail sentence in one of the worst prisons in the world, ensuring that I could see what I was missing, could see the delights of this island, if I just looked through the bars on my cell window and beyond the razor wire that kept it from me.

Then I heard a familiar voice. It was *Pete*'s. I breathed a sigh of relief. I was not alone!

'Just ease yourself in there, Terry,' he said, pointing to the bed on the end.

'You can sleep on the crack in the middle,' he continued, as if offering an explanation to the man who was already occupying the mattress *Pete* was pointing to.

That night nobody moved about much. Not that we could. We didn't expect any food, but it came anyway. There was a brief commotion at the gate when an officer and an inmate appeared. There was a cardboard box full of white bags and an urn of tea beside it. They had a set of paper cups to go with it. Each man collected his food and got a paper cup of tea, then returned to where he had been sitting. The trick here was to keep your cup, because you never knew when you were going to be able to get a new one.

The next morning I awoke, and from the window could once again see the beautiful bright blue sea out beyond the perimeter. Far out, there was a boat sailing across it, and beyond that what looked like a container ship sailing in the direction of Bridgetown. After looking out at that beautiful expanse of blue, I went down the narrow aisle of the cell and made it to where we had our toilet buckets. There were 30 or so men in this cell, and we had three buckets between us. I took a hearty piss into the one that still had a bit of spare space. The other two were full up already, and stinking. Where were the screws? The whole place seemed deserted, as if we had been left here and forgotten. I looked through the bars of the gate and was able to see into the cell opposite, number 12. By straining my head to the left, I could see a little way back down the corridor. To the right, I could see that at the very end of our corridor was a gate that seemed to lead to the outside. The sky was visible through it, and I got the idea that there might be a set of steps running down that side of the building to the ground.

Most of the men were still sleeping, and I made my way back to the middle ground between the two adjacent mattresses. The fella at the end was awake now. He was really thin, and seemed to be a bit nutty. It turned out he was an old crack freak, and had more or less done his brain in smoking that shit. His name was Dada. I asked him why.

'My daughter calls me Dada,' he said, in the voice of a seven year old.

It was obvious he wasn't the full shilling. He started telling me about his family then, but it sounded as though he had all the makings of a real tragedy here, and I got the feeling that I had heard enough. He spent his time just rolling around trying to get as blasted on crack as he could. One night, Lestor Howell, one of our slightly wiser and certainly more intelligent fellows asked him why he chose to smoke crack. Dada took a deep inward breath at that moment, considering his answer.

'Because I get satisfaction from doing it,' he answered.

There was no way he was going to change. He didn't have too long to go before completing this sentence, but given his predilection for smoking crack a return ticket to prison seemed inevitable.

We worked out amongst ourselves who was getting out and in what order. First out was a thickset man in for rape. He was pleasant enough to us, but I wouldn't want to be a child or a woman and bump into him late one night. He had a couple of weeks to go. Then, a week after that, it was going to be Dada's turn to go.

We were basically left there all day, every day, with nothing to do but talk and think. The screws came by each morning and fed us, but all we were getting were two fluffy bread rolls, lined with a thin smear of cheese spread. Still, it was better than nothing, and I downed it along with the paper cup of hot, sweet tea. Some days we got Milo, a kind of cocoa drink. On some days, we got a slice of real cheese with our bread, and because I had been on the special diet list before, I was able to get my milk ration back. Not that I ever drank it; it would always give me the shits, so I would pass it on to *Pete*, who either drank it himself or in turn would give it to one of the unfortunates that he tended to take under his wing.

We were told that visits were now banned, and when the foreign prisoners started asking to see somebody from their Embassy, they were told the ban included consular visits. I couldn't believe it. How was this allowed? When we asked how long this might go on for, we were told it was indefinite. I really started to worry. It was quite feasible that they could leave us here to rot in this cramped and putrid cell. We were also told not to expect any contact with the outside world; no letters or postcards were going to come in or go out. I have heard that even now, years later, visits are still restricted. The family of an inmate have to sit in front of a camcorder in a hut by the front gate and speak to their kin over a microphone. Physical contact is still not allowed, and nothing is allowed to be brought into the prison. This includes food.

***

It was inevitable that being cooped up in this room was going to get to the 30 men sitting around, and after a while tempers began to fray. Once again, I started to worry about my safety. I didn't want to think about what could happen if a serious fight broke out in here. Dada, for one, was beginning to get out of order. He wasn't taking the medication they were giving him, and like many nutters would store up his pills and then take them all at once, or sell them off for extra food. He was getting aggressive towards me, as I was the only white boy in the cell and he thought he might be able to get away with it. He was encouraged in these actions by the malicious Tanty and his consort Cat. Tanty was grovelling to get himself a better position in the system, and managed to get the job of giving out the food. This gave him the freedom to move about on the corridor, and the opportunity to nick some extra food for himself, but it was kind of unwritten that he would be expected to do a bit of grassing in return. This didn't seem to bother him. He was allowed to keep his job even when he caught chicken pox, mainly because of the grassing he was doing for the police in the investigation into the fire. He was a real bitch, and would walk around with an American flag wrapped around his head as a headscarf, talking about his former partner-in-crime Shampoo, another stinking Bullerman.

Cat was just a bit simple, though not a bad lad. He only had another year to do, having done about ten already for a robbery. He was one of those lads that had pumped himself up a bit since coming into the prison, and was now able to walk around with a set of biceps on each arm. Each morning he would call down to the cell beneath, making the sound of a phone ringing. It was annoying, waking up every fucking morning to hear that shit. He was a boy who had never had a cuff from his dad; had never known his dad, come to think of it. As a result he thought he was really hard. I didn't say anything, though, about the early morning wake-ups. I didn't want a bad vibe.

Dada was getting to me, especially when he started talking about Jesus being a black man, and getting killed by the white Roman soldiers. Mary had become a black woman by now, and the entire crucifixion scene had become a scene straight out of Alabama, or Mississippi Burning. This was highly inflammatory racist material, and was making me worried, especially as things looked as if they could easily get out of hand here in this cell. Nobody here really went in for the racist hate shit Dada was coming on with, but they were bored. At the least it would be nice for them to see if I could go a couple of rounds with Dada. I didn't really mind that, either, but I had a feeling that this bastard would fight with his big fangs and his long fingernails. It wasn't that the boys were especially malicious towards me as a white man; it's just that in jail men get bored, and occasionally like to see some blood spilled, regardless of whose it is.

'I am right behind you!' Dada told me, one day. He was pushing it, seeing how far he could go before I belted him. I was just getting ready to, when *Pete* managed to calm him down.

Meanwhile, unbelievably, they tried to put more men into the cell. A young Jamaican lad had moved in, and was parked alongside me. His trip was to sit there all day long, humming some of the crazy tunes he was busy making up. It was driving me nuts, especially as he continued even when I was trying to get to sleep. At one point it got too much. On the 999th time that day I had heard his tune, 'Sting her every time, sting her every time,' I just snapped, and told him that I was trying to sleep. He shut up, but then Dada had a go at him.

Apparently Dada didn't want to hear any more of his tune either, and to emphasise his point, he started waving his long, talon-like fingernails right underneath the guy's face. The guy shut up, but ended up looking like a right pussy in front of everyone for backing down so easily.

'I just don't want any trouble,' he said.

Dada took the piss out of him: 'Don't want any trouble,' he repeated his words, mocking him. Some of the other fellas in the cell laughed, but I had a sense of what was coming next.

'Just don't come around me, Dada, as you do with those two fools,' said *Pete*, referring to me as well as the Jamaican guy in the same breath. *Pete*, the one guy I knew in here, had lumped me and the Jamaican guy in the same category together. *Shit*. You could tell that tensions were rising.

Dada got up, furious, and started waving his long fingernails underneath *Pete*'s eyes. But not for long. Like a flash, *Pete* lashed out and delivered a couple of solid punches right in his face, then a couple more to his lower chest. There was suddenly blood leaking from Dada's mouth, running down the side of his throat and onto the floor. He turned his body round, to shield his front from *Pete*'s devastating punches. But *Pete* gave him a couple more, right in the kidneys. After that Dada was quiet, and didn't say boo to a goose.

He did keep asking for trouble though. He was caught masturbating over *Pete*'s face while he slept. It was Cappell, one of the Guyanese inmates, who saw this, and confronted him with it the following morning. I sat back, thinking I was now going to witness *Pete* totally demolish this guy. This was going to be a real treat. This arsehole had got up my nose, and had caused me a lot of tension for nothing. Now, hopefully, he was going to get a heavier beating. But it was not to be. *Pete* just looked at him, and said, 'So, you fucked me anyway, did you?'

Cappell went on to describe how Dada had put his prick right under *Pete*'s nose as he had slept, and when he came had pulled back and sprayed it over his own bed. *Pete* looked over at Tanty, and saw him give a slight shake of his head. This was *Pete*'s cue not to give out any further beating. Dada was being tutored by Tanty, and *Pete* was being asked to leave him alone.

It was a happy day when Dada left, and as I looked down from my window, I saw him go jauntily along the path that led to the gate. Rumour had it that the authorities would let you go directly from here, and you could make your way to wherever you were going by local ZR minibus. Another rumour was that the screws would take you back to the old Glendairy building in St Michael, and there you would sign your papers and get the bit of money the prison handed out to you on your release date. If it hadn't mysteriously disappeared.

***

For a short while it looked as though the pressure in the room was going to ease off. Surely, they weren't going to bring any more men into this cell? Couldn't they see for themselves that it was already far too overcrowded? But that is precisely what they did. They brought Horse in from somewhere. Horse was my favourite madman. He was totally crazy, and in Bridgetown the whores put him on crack and used him in a sex show for tourists. In Glendairy he was staying with the Professor, who would come up to the Mess Hall in the morning and regale anyone who would listen as to how he had tricked his way into Horse's arse the night before by telling him, in a very romantic tone of voice, that he loved him.

The Professor made it sound almost convincing, but either way it was his chance to degrade someone. Horse would always swagger up from the Farm walking like John Wayne and would never bathe—something else that gave us in the Mess Hall endless hours of satisfaction. The stench from his clothes and unwashed body was rank, and people would start throwing stones at him, and chasing him away just for fun. Horse would take any number of beatings rather than have a shower. On one occasion, someone even gave him a piece of soap, and when they inspected it upon his return to the cell, found that it was still dry. The next time, Horse returned with the soap wet, but still unused! All he had done was put it under the running tap. The next time, *Pete* escorted Horse to the shower and watched him to make sure he washed properly.

To wash, we were taken out two by two, down the corridor to the showers. There were toilets and sinks in here, too, and we made the most out of being able to wash our clothes as best we could. It wasn't easy with ordinary soap, but this at least was now in plentiful supply, as was toilet paper and toothpaste. Unfortunately, some prisoners took to sharpening their brushes into finely chiselled points, so toothbrushes became strictly controlled, and as the searches started up again, many of these and jukas made from other materials, were uncovered.

***

It was around this time that the chicken pox first appeared. It started with Mario, who caught it outside and had brought it in. He was the first one to break out in the blemishes. He tried to hide them. This is the normal reaction for someone who catches an infection like this. But as soon as the other lads saw what he had, there was pandemonium in the cell. It wasn't hard to spot the signs. He was itching and scratching non-stop. Nobody wanted to be anywhere near him but in a cell with more than 30 other men there really wasn't anywhere we could go, or put him. We made him stand apart from everyone, as far as was possible. The best we could do was put him by the shit buckets, where he remained until the screw came to take him out. Where he went, none of us knew, but someone thought they saw him over by E Block, which was a much smaller section than ours.

This was a nightmare. There were 30 of us, with nowhere to go, crammed into a cell with an outbreak of an infectious disease in our midst. The next day others started breaking out in it. Tanty had it, and like the real bastard he was he tried to cover it up, despite the fact that he was giving out the food to all the men along the top corridor of D2. He was probably the main reason why so many men caught it. Eventually hundreds in the prison came down with it.

To contain the epidemic, the screws quarantined our section of the prison. They erected a special partition, which they thought would help prevent the germs from spreading down the corridor. Instead of going down the corridor to use the bathroom and toilets there, we would now be going out through the back door, and down the steps to the outside. Down at the bottom there were open air showers. A chemical toilet was installed for shitting. We got our shower in the morning, after every other cell had been unlocked, buckets out, and showered.

Miss Amy was the portly, but pleasant officer who was attached to us at this time. I had not seen her before, but she was easy to butter up. You had to give her a nice 'Good Morning Miss Amy' as she came in, first thing, otherwise she would be in a bad mood and that meant slow openings for us. When the screws wanted to make life difficult for us, a favourite trick of theirs was to be late letting us clear out the buckets. This meant that we couldn't take any more pisses. The buckets would then be full right up to the very brim, and men would be bursting to take a piss. I heard that in some cells things became so bad with the screws playing up this way that the men revolted and began throwing piss down the corridors. When this happened, the screws would use this as their opportunity to start shooting. They loved nothing better than an easy target, and a prisoner can't fight back. Snoops was one of those shot, and badly wounded, the bullet hitting him in the leg as it ricocheted, over in E Block.

Similar troubles would break out in G and H Blocks, where the real troublemakers were. Here most of the Rastas were kept, segregated for fear that their ideas of Black Nationalism tended to spur on the other inmates to revolutionary actions. C Block also had a fair number of bad boys, particularly my old pal Sandeford, who was now holding court over there and had cemented his position with a number of other Rastas. Every now and again we on D Block would hear a massive booming sound of screams and outraged men's voices as some weird shit happened on another block. We could look from our windows and see dozens of soldiers running towards C Block with their rifles ready to fire. On one occasion, I heard that Bubba Benny had been caught giving his beloved Chucky a blow job. The men in their cell went mad when any kind of homosexual activity came to light.

Finally, one day the British Embassy came to visit. This was two months or so after the burning. It had taken them that long to get permission to come in and see us. All I knew was a couple of screws turned up and told me, through the bars of the gate, to get dressed. This took me just a couple of minutes. There wasn't much to it. I just had to slip my shirt on and my short trousers over my boxers, and that was it. Then they unlocked the door and I was handcuffed, and taken all the way down the corridor and through the gate at the end.

I was then taken down the stairs. Through a window, I saw one of the most magnificent sunsets I have ever seen. Every shade of gold was there, intermingled with mauves and deeper shades of purple, as the sun dipped beneath the sea and the deep blues and blacks of the night sky followed in its wake. Once more I was reminded of the paradise that lay outside these prison walls, and the foolish way that I had chosen to dive straight into Hell by relying on an artificial high all those years, instead of experiencing the real joys of life. I was led out along the path that runs through the warren of outbuildings that make up Harrison's Point, out past C Block to my left, past E Block to my right. Then we went through another gate up to an administration building. Inside here, I was taken, still handcuffed, to see Greita Tait, of the consular department.

She was always very sympathetic, even though she was not able to do much in the way of intervening in people's cases or immediate situations. She asked me if I had been beaten, and I said no. Apparently Jason Miller, another Brit, had been, I added. She already knew. Strangely enough, she seemed to cheer up at that. She asked me if I wanted to get a message to someone 'back home'.

'Not really,' I said. The next question was if my food was being taken from me, by other prisoners. I said no, but it occurred to me that although I was being treated alright, others might be getting shafted. I later heard that Vino was getting his food taken off him, as was *Henry*. That was it. She told me to hold tight and let this period blow over. I asked her about the possible transfer of prisoners, the exchange that had been talked about for so long, but which had never happened, at least as far as we were concerned. She thought for a moment, and then told me that from what she had seen on TV, this might be something that they could be looking at in the future. But as far as we were concerned, there were to be no easy get-outs from this piece of relatively hard nick.

I did tell her about the ridiculous overcrowding, the awful sanitation, the poor diet, and the outbreak of an infectious disease about which little was being done, and she sympathised, but I could tell fuck all was going to happen out of it. There was just nothing that could be done. There was no procedure in place to sort out the problems in the prison, especially since Glendairy had burnt. Inmates' rights were not a priority. I sat there and looked at this Barbadian national working for the British Embassy, and wondered how she felt about it all. Was she frustrated by the lack of assistance she could provide in her home country? Or was she embarrassed by the actions of those she represented? I would never know.

So, on that sour note, my little break from the cell was over, and I was taken back. As I got back all the lads were excited, asking me what was happening. In their naivety they seemed to think that a miracle was imminent. When I told them how low-key it all had been they seemed disappointed. Maybe they would have loved it if I had gone back with a cock-and-bull story about how we were all being airlifted out that night.

***

Somewhere along the line they brought the new Guyanese in. There were four; Roderick Lake being the most prominent among them. I had previously seen Lake walking around the inner fence back at the front yard in Glendairy, round and round in a circle. Although technically stuck on B corridor, he had hassled the Superintendent enough to be able to get permission to get an hour of exercise a day, and even to get a bottle of spring water brought to him. All this was for his health, apparently. Lake was a character. He and I would play chess throughout the days. I would usually beat him at chess, but when we played draughts, there was always a different outcome; at this game he was unparalleled. We played with one of our makeshift sets; the black pieces were made out of cardboard, the whites out of the polystyrene containers our food came in.

I did quite well in the chess games there. Lestor Howell gave me a few close shaves, as did Grazettes, when he reappeared. I was a bit doubtful about playing chess with someone who had raped another man, but in the end it was only a game and who was I to fight someone else's crusade? None of the other fellas seemed to give a flying fuck, anyway, so why should I?

Lake would tell me some of the stories about his home country. It seemed vast. It was a country of great natural wealth, with gold and diamond mining, bauxite, woods and waterfalls. I remembered what I had read in some of the Guyanese newspapers that had come floating round Glendairy, prior to the burning. It seemed a land full of kidnappings and murders, too, with a corrupt police force and judiciary system. Cappell, who was also from Guyana, confirmed much of what Lake said, and added that his father was the owner of a gold mine.

Bit by bit, the police started coming in and interviewing each inmate about what they had seen during the events in which the prison had been fired. They started taking prisoners out, in small groups of three or four, from each section. Eventually my turn came, and I was handcuffed and led away with a couple of others to sit in a small police bus outside G and H Blocks. Right outside these was a tent with several soldiers sitting in the shade, their rifles stacked up and ready to roll.

Eventually, I was taken inside one of the small outbuildings, where I met a couple of the huge policemen that Barbados is famous for. One of them asked me about what I knew, and I inwardly thanked the gods for having given me enough sense not to become involved in any of the destructive behaviour. For if I had, I would surely have been grassed by now! I explained to the police that my concern during the riot and prison burning was staying out of harm's way, and I didn't go back into any of the buildings when the firings started. I knew that the police would be relying mainly on their grasses for information on who had done what. In interviewing me they were merely going through the motions. The copper asked me if I saw anyone I knew doing any of the destruction, and I said that I didn't. As I was taken back into the building, some of the lads from other cells up on D2 asked me what I'd said. I replied that the only person I'd recognised was Officer Carrington, displaying that remarkable sense of bravery, in unlocking all those men up on B and C corridors, while being pelted with stones from the inmates. They laughed!

All this time, stuck in this single cell, there was fuck all for us to read, nothing for us to look at in the form of television, no radio or music, no letters from home, no writing materials. The word was that John Nurse had put us all on six months of punishment. The prospect of this continuing for six months sent a shiver down my spine. I would go mad. I had to keep telling myself it was just a rumour. Then, out of the blue, the Reverend Daniels turned up with a big stack of New Testaments, all of which were hungrily gobbled up. I began reading the Psalms. At this point I had 91 days to go before my release date. I remember this because I started reading all the psalms, every day, from Psalm 91 right down to Psalm 1. The next day I read from Psalm 90 to Psalm 1 and so on. I can still remember many of them, word for word.

It was a way to defeat the boredom, and to keep us from turning on each other, and it was very welcome.

Gambling was another device we used to get through the day, although not being a gambler, it didn't appeal to me. *Pete*, particularly, used to love putting his future meals up as the stake whenever anyone suggested a game of cards. Whenever he lost, though, I would be there to go halves with him with my food, and when he won he would always come back to me with a slice of his winnings.

It was a sad day, really, when it came for him to leave. I took the phone number of his brother in the USA, and promised to contact him. When I did phone this number, though, it turned out to be wrong, and to this day I still have no way of contacting my old mate *Pete*, even though I am in touch with many other Barbadians by post and phone.

The women from Glendairy were moved into the neighbouring F Block, which was just over the way from us. This was a great source of mystery, to actually see these exotic and mysterious creatures floating around again in their long skirts. It was a sight for sore eyes, not especially in any lustful sense, but really more aesthetically. Some of the lads would call out their declarations of undying love, and on only a couple of occasions, when it went on for too long, did the female screws over there start to complain.

Meanwhile, the chicken pox was still spreading through the prison. Some men were developing it in a really bad way. The lads were unable to get through to any doctor or dentist during all this time. If you were in pain it was too bad. Nobody cared. There was no ointment for the many men with chicken pox and no pain killers either. Even when several men went down with severe shingles they were given nothing. Men were basically left to tear at themselves in pain as their bodies gradually became covered in welts and scars, while untold damage was done to their internal organs and nervous systems. I could hear them crying out every night like babies for their mothers.

Each day we had a cleaning exercise and each day two different guys would volunteer for the duty. One would sweep up the chunks of flesh and skin that had fallen off the men's bodies during the night, while the other followed along and wiped the floor with some bleach, which we had to get from the screws. All mattresses were pulled up and placed in a pile. First one half of the cell was done, while all 30 of us stood bunched together in the bottom half of the cell. Then, when that was complete, we would all move back to the freshly-cleaned section while the two workers finished off with the second half.

Needless to say, just as we would start to clean our cell, Miss Amy or Big Papa would start taking men out for bathing. This was our chance to take a shit using the portable chemical toilet that had been brought just outside our window, if you could manage a squeeze. Many of the guys would use it at least for a wank, managing to jerk off in there without anyone watching them. Down the bottom of the set of steps was a set of pipes protruding from the wall, from which cold water could be turned on and off. During our bathing times the screws rushed us through, making us take a shit, a shower and wash our single set of boxers in the space of about four minutes.

The nurse seemed to think that what the men were suffering was all a big joke. He eventually started to turn up to give out prescribed medication but often he only had a Panadol or two to give to men who were in pain with chicken pox, shingles or toothache.

One inmate, by the name of Rudi, got a severe eye infection and this started swelling up, really badly. It went from bad to worse, and for over a week he went without any treatment. He sat there in terrible pain, constantly asking

Miss Amy to intervene, to help him get to the doctor before his eye swelled up too much and burst. Some of the more malicious lads were sitting back, secretly hoping it would fucking well burst, the evil bastards. Just in the nick of time Miss Amy got him over to the doctors, where he got treatment for it.

One day, a famous Glendairy resident turned up; a man called Murderer. He was short, stocky, and looked well tough. He said he had done time with Tupac, the famous American gangster-rapper in New York. In this he had much in common with *Pete* and Grandpa, who had travelled that same route. He would entertain us all at night with his tales of going out on robberies on Friday night, just to get a bit of lubrication going for the mayhem that was the staple diet of his weekends. His father had been one of the original Black Panthers and was doing 20 years in prison in the States for shooting a State Trooper. He himself had bullet wounds all over his legs where people had shot him but he had refused to lie down. Instead he had always got right back up and shot them back in return.

There came a day when he had a falling out with Cat. Cat got up early in the morning to play a game of cards. He was always an early riser, and even used to wake me up. Well, this time he made the mistake of waking up Murderer. Used to playing the bastard, waking people up at the crack of dawn with nobody saying anything about it, he was just about to get his arse cut. Murderer got up, and ripped the cards out of his hand, scattering them onto the floor. Cat complained, and then Murderer just picked him up, wrestled with him, and threw him back down onto the ground. There was blood all over the floor, as Cat went and curled up in a corner and began to cry. Grandpa looked over to me to see my reaction, but I just kept my face as blank as I could. I didn't want to get caught in any crossfire. Little boys who think that, by getting a set of biceps on their arms, they automatically become big men have much to learn. It is invariably guys like Murderer that teach them otherwise. Murderer was one real movie star. In the end, he took pity on this big schoolgirl and read a couple of psalms with him.

John the Baptist, an old friend of mine from D&E was brought in, also suffering from the chicken pox. I had always liked John. He was a mystic and believed in the Emperor Haile Selassie. John and I would often talk. He had some interesting ideas, even if I didn't always agree with them. But it was always interesting to listen to him. John had been given 25 years, which everyone felt was far too severe, given that what had really happened was a domestic dispute that had gone wrong. In many prisons there are many fellas who have accidentally killed their loved ones in the heat of the moment, and have bitterly regretted that one single moment of anger for the rest of their lives.

John would get up early in the morning and do some exercise, along with me and a man known as Harper. Harper was the mainstay of our exercise club, and a really strong man. Then, still before dawn, we would read our psalms by the light from the corridor. It was a really spiritual vibe that we had blowing there.

***

Not surprisingly given the state of most of the men in the cell suffering from chicken pox, and the dreadful hygiene, we started to have a particular problem with flies. For some reason, in the first hour after sunrise we would have about 50 of them in the cell. By the second hour we had 100. By 11am we had twice that. The screws had noticed it as well, and Miss Amy even went down the corridor to get a fly spray, returning with it just a few minutes later. She passed it through the grill and we began spraying in earnest. Up till now, this place had not been all that bad, insect-wise. Whereas Glendairy had been full of cockroaches, some as big as your hand, running over you all night long, and plagued with mosquitoes during the long hot summer nights, Harrison's Point, or 'The Rock', as we had started calling it, had been relatively insect-free.

Murderer was leading the fly hunt, using elastic bands. He would pull the band back between his fingers and, once he had a good aim on a particular fly, let it go. The elastic would spring forward and hit the fly, as long as it hadn't noticed his stealthy approach and made good its escape by then. Murderer was achieving a high hit rate, whereas the others' attempts were mediocre in comparison. Theories started up that the flies were attracted by the smell coming from the guys who kept masturbating on their mattresses, and one poor guy, Horse, was singled out and told to stop.

The following day though, it was the same old story, and the flies were back on top of us again. There were now clouds of them, so that when lunch came you had to eat your rice and piece of fish quickly before any flies could settle on the food in the container or on the spoon as you passed it to your mouth. The rumblings against the 'wankers' were getting deeper, and more angry. The next step to deter Horse's behaviour was to stop his food. This meant that all his food for the next day was taken off him, and shared out between certain others. Some were keen on this, as it meant extra food for them. When Horse's food came through the hatch, a hand flipped out and picked it out of the food server's hand. The supervising officer noticed this, and commented on it. They had to give the food back to Horse. The officer then stood at the gate and made sure that Horse was able to eat his food without interruption.

Apparently elsewhere in the prison other men had been taking food off those less strong or supported than themselves, and the news of this was hitting John Nurse's ears. If it had just been going on amongst Barbadians it would possibly have continued unabated, but when they started doing this to the foreigners the embassies got to know, and protests began arriving on John Nurse's desk. So, we had to think of some other way to punish Horse.

'Let's tie him up!' someone suggested.

Horse's arms and legs were tied up that night, so he couldn't masturbate. Doubts began to be expressed at this line of action, though. The screws could look upon this very negatively, and we had already started hearing about what was going on in the containers that Admin had been bringing into the compound. It was hard to believe that there could be something worse than being crammed into a filthy, stinking, fly-infested cell with 30 other men, most of whom have chicken pox, but these containers were said to be it.

For the slightest challenge, men were taken from their cells, handcuffed, and taken off to the containers, which had been improvised into mini punishment cells. Inside these they were beaten, had CS gas sprayed in their faces, and were handcuffed to a ring on the ceiling. They were left there day and night for up to a week at a time. As the days and nights passed, these men were left to shit and piss all over themselves. They were denied sufficient food, water and medical attention. None of us wanted to risk a trip to the containers so we untied Horse, and instead, the next morning, one of the Trinidadian Rastas had a go, cuffing him in the mouth and receiving a karate kick back in his ribs for his trouble.

'You can't beat me!' Horse shouted, defiantly, even though blood was running from his mouth. He had just had two teeth removed. The Rasta man, known to us as Jah Yut, had a graze on his knuckle from where he had connected with Horse's dental work. Knowing something about Horse's sexual history, all I could do was commiserate.

'There is a small possibility of infection,' I said to him, referring to the possible spread of HIV and Hep C through cuts and wounds, especially where blood and saliva are concerned. He looked at me shocked, and got hold of some bleach and poured it on his open wound, hoping against hope that he hadn't contracted anything. The screws were not giving out bleach as freely any more, as a number of prisoners had tried committing suicide by drinking it.

***

One day, Roderick Lake got into a conflagration with one of the newly promoted sergeants, a man brought in by John Nurse from the Defence Force. This idiot's promotion caused a serious ripple of disgust and dissatisfaction throughout all of the screws at Glendairy when it happened. When Lake insulted his mother, the sergeant lost control and stepped into the cell with his revolver in hand. He was ready to shoot, until another officer leapt out and took it off him, throwing it along the corridor and kicking it out of range with his foot. At that moment I was glad that none of the lads had the thought of storming the cell door, which was wide open during all of this, and getting hold of the gun. With that, a siege and possibly a mass escape, could easily have been effected. But with only three months left to go on my sentence, the last thing I wanted was trouble. It's every prisoner's nightmare that something like that happens right as you are getting yourself ready to go home!

The sergeant then pulled out his mace spray, and shouted at Lake to come forward. Lake, instead, retreated further down the back of the cell, trying to use us for cover. Then, he picked up a large bottle of water and threw it at the screw with all his might. It hit the screw full on, who then picked up the same bottle and tried to throw it back. Instead it hit the wrong man. This didn't go down too well. The sergeant came closer and started kicking and punching at Lake's large body. Lake had enough sense not to fight back, although I could see that he was struggling on that point. The sergeant then sprayed mace all over him, and this immediately spread throughout the entire cell. It was like a mist suddenly filling the room, stinging the eyes of every inmate and making it hard to breathe. I had enough sense to lie down and immediately cover my face with my shirt, breathing through the fabric and looking through it, too. Others, less experienced, tried using water to wash it from their faces. They were gasping in pain. Water only makes it worse. You have to wait till it clears. The sergeant then ran off, and locked the door behind him. A while later, he reappeared with Officer Sobers, and Lake was led off, with his legs in shackles, to see Nurse, and, after that, he spent a few days in the container.

When Lake was brought back a week or so later, he was still wearing the leg shackles. The sergeant who had him locked in them tried making out that he couldn't find the key so as to cause Lake a little bit of extra pain and suffering. I could see the chains were cutting into the side of his ankles and causing severe swelling and bruising.

***

Besides flaring up against the screws, patience was also running out with the sexual stuff that was simmering in the cell. One of them turned out to be sleeping in the bed next to mine, a man who had 'taken in' a newcomer to the cell, a very attractive lad known as Caesar. Caesar had never been in trouble with the police before and was only about 18, if that. Boy George let him sleep next to him, but one night I awoke to the whole cell going mad. Caesar had got fed up with Boy George rubbing up against him so had moved over to the gate in protest. He was prepared to stand there all night until the morning came and he could get a cell change. Murderer had woken up and found out what was going on, and suddenly there were six inmates all pounding the shit out of Boy George. He just sat there and took his punishment. When Caesar came over to deliver his portion of the necessary number of slaps Boy George looked up at him and said, 'Why don't you tell them the truth?' before more blows rained down on his head and the screw came to take him out.

Another nasty incident was when Simple came into the cell. He wandered about, up and down, holding his mattress in his arms, and calling everyone Bullers and murderers.

'That's no way to get accepted in here, fella,' one guy said to him. He wisely shut up at that, and someone found a space for him to squeeze into. I came back up to the cell one morning after my shower to see both Simple and this other guy getting well bashed. Apparently they had been caught 'in the act'; and the punishments were most draconian. I felt sorry for them as the blows and kicks rained down on them but couldn't say or do anything to intervene. Nor did I want to. I would sometimes be filled with fear as I watched this sort of thing go on; fear that it might escalate and I would be dragged into a melee, and fear that the next time it might be me on the end of a beating. But this was always counterbalanced by a sense of anger that was swelling up inside me as well as every other man in that cell. Many of us felt angry that we had to put up with these inhuman conditions while at the same time there were people in our midst who were getting up to all kinds of fuckery, making it worse.

I never actually joined in any of the violence though, because I still felt that it was very unfair that someone should be surrounded and set upon by a gang and have no realistic chance of defending themselves. I also felt that we as prisoners had enough on our hands and that this was a time when we all needed to stand together. Discipline would of course have to be imposed, but these were all punishment beatings, reprisals, for slights or crimes, real or imagined, that might have stretched back years. It wasn't for me to get involved. As well as that, I could have ended up becoming a target.

***

One morning I awoke and spotted a tiny spider in the corner of the window, slowly but determinedly weaving a few strands for the web it was trying to create. It immediately became symbolic for me, and each day I would make a point of looking to see how far it had got. At first, there were just a few girders strung in between the corners, but as the days went past, these became less angular and more interconnected. Other lads in with me made a point of checking in with the spider, and seeing how far he had got. That spider became an emblem, a mascot for everyone in that cell. One day the spider was not to be found in his usual spot. Someone found him in the middle of the floor, where there was a thin gangway in between the ends of the plastic mattresses the screws had brought in. Very carefully, one of the lads managed to get the spider unharmed onto a piece of cardboard and back onto his perch.

Another day we had an army of ants marching through the cell. There must have been thousands upon thousands of these ants, whose original nest had probably been disturbed when the building we were in was renovated. It was amazing to see the natural world still happening around us. For me, the spider and the ants were a sign telling me to be industrious when I got out, and that it might take time to get things up and running, but not to lose heart.

Some days I would look out to the beautiful blue sea and see ships and boats going past. It was strange that the natural world was so close and yet so unreachable. Great strands of razor wire stretched across the occupied beach, making it look like the setting for a war film. Soldiers would be dotted around, with rifles slung over their shoulders, on the alert in case any of the Blocks kicked off. From where I was, on the top floor of D Block, looking out over the yard, I could see most of what was going on at any time.

We could see John Nurse coming in, and one day a guy tried calling out to him, saying that we were being treated unfairly and we needed him to come over in person and see to us. He ignored this request, and instead sent a screw over to tell us not to call out anymore. The punishment would be a trip to the containers, we were told. This guy, though, was not to be so easily deterred and just picked a new target. A female officer had been caught stealing chocolates from prisoners' parcels as they came in. She was as tubby as a horse and moved slowly around the yard outside, but when he saw her he started calling to her, imitating her voice and her words when she had been brought before John Nurse.

'Ahhhm sorrie, surrrr ...' he began, imitating her accent so perfectly that immediately all the other lads in the cell would start falling apart with laughter.

'But it was only a chocklit,' he went on, in her voice. By now everyone in the cell was laughing uproariously. It must have been so embarrassing for the officer to have been caught doing something so petty. In all the times that she got it in the neck from this guy, though, this particular officer never once turned to look up, but instead would continue on her way. She was lucky not to have lost her job, as John Nurse was clamping down on practices such as this.

One morning I saw Miss Daniels walking along, on her way to the entrance to my block. I hadn't known it till then, but she was working on the cells below, where all the grasses were kept. I called out to her, but she didn't seem to recognise me. Only when one of the other lads shouted to her that it was Terry the white boy who called her, did a flicker of recognition cross her face and she give a small wave. Then she was gone.

These things helped to take my mind off the tension that was filling the cell, and the nervous anticipation with which I counted down my days. I was so close to getting out, unhurt, but with each passing day, as my release date came nearer, I feared more and more for my safety. I just couldn't face the prospect of being seriously hurt, or killed, with only a few days to go before my release.

I could tell that Grandpa wanted to have a go at me. At first it was subtle, but it was definitely there. The injuries he had received at Six Roads were evidently wearing off, and every now and then I got a little look that told me that that old aggression was back in town. One of the bad signs was that he wasn't interested in playing paper chess. Back in the Mess Hall, before he and I had fallen out, we would play chess for hours. I would produce a cigarette for him every now and again, seemingly out of thin air. This would always cheer him up, and he would drag hard on that smoke for all it was worth. But here in Room D 13, things were heading for a showdown. Day by day it was getting hotter as the days turned closer to the summer.

CHAPTER FOURTEEN

RELEASE

In the last month or so leading up to the Great Day of My Release I started my countdown. This is when you say to yourself how many days you have got left to go. Every now and again one of my mates from over the road in Cell 12, would ask me, 'How many, Terry?'

I tried thinking of where I was going to go, but all those concerns seemed tiny problems compared to those that I faced each day. Compressed as we were together, the tensions were breaking out into violence. Some of the guys in the cell had been able to find themselves bits of wood, or even pieces of tile pulled away from the shower wall in order to make up their makeshift jukas. Even these simple weapons could prove devastating when used in fighting, especially in such close quarters. Some lads had even taken their toothbrushes and filed these down against the wall to make sharp gouges.

Several times I saw men pull out their weapons and stand there, on their beds, ready to use them. If their opponent reacted, they would attack immediately, opening the man's face up easily with the serrated edges of their jukas. Most of the fights were over gambling debts. By now, some of the boys had founded their own casino. It was opened every day straight after morning food share, when there were plenty of white food bags going around. The makeshift cards would come out of nowhere, and although after a few hundred games the markings on them were difficult to determine, the experienced players were never discouraged. Somehow they could always see what was written on each of the fraying, dissolving cards. Those who lost were rarely discouraged when they had to hand over their food, though, although lunch was always felt more severely than the little rolls of bread which constituted our morning and evening meals. Lunch was normally two scoops of rice with a spoon of corned beef on top, or sometimes half a sardine. If you were already on the special diet list you stood to get a sliver of tomato added into your container.

After the prison burning, the Barbadian school meals service started bringing in the food for us. We would see the two white vans coming in each day with the food. These vans would drop off the food into the new kitchen areas where the food would be packaged up into these polystyrene containers. Each container was labelled with the name of the prisoner it was to go to. This was how the prison authorities now tried to cope with the problem of some prisoners stealing food. The weak would be singled out, although sometimes certain 'crimes' such as masturbation were given as reasons for a banishment from food decision. If the victim showed weakness or acquiescence, then the decision would be made to stick, but if the response was virulent opposition, very often the guys trying it on would dissolve into laughter and make out that they were only joking all along. But you had to be prepared to go to war about it, for real.

I heard through the grapevine that *Henry* had his food taken off him. I felt sorry for him, but he was a weird one. For a time the screws had put him in with two known Bullermen, one of whom I knew was Bloodstain. They had at first been 'friendly' to him, giving him a cigarette and trying to get him to open up. They had then gotten into their 'gay trip' of taking it in turns to screw each other, while *Henry* sat on his bunk. Then, they turned their attentions to him, but when he refused, they hit him with the leg of a chair, knocking him down. The word was that *Henry* got screwed, but when a man is raped the sense of shame he feels is so intense the last thing he wants is for anyone to know about it. So *Henry* went around telling everyone that after the blow to his head he dropped to the ground, unconscious. Bobby Burns, as a fellow British inmate, was the only prisoner who took an interest in bringing this incident to light, and apparently it took all of his powers of persuasion to get *Henry* to even report it. The British Embassy didn't do much, as their priority was in getting this hushed up so the flow of British tourists to Barbados could continue unabated. Bloodstain and the other assailant were, eventually, interviewed by the police and charged, but the court only gave them an extra six months on top of their already extensive seven or eight year sentences.

There was never any attempt by the prison authorities to separate the really dangerous raping and murdering inmates from those that had been brought in for less violent crimes. In fact, it was almost as if the guards had a perverse pleasure in deliberately mixing them up to see what would happen. Rumour was that they would take bets out on who was going to rape who, and even how long it would take before that happened.

The guards could easily get you murdered if they really wanted to, simply by putting you in with a really mad prisoner who they knew would be unhappy with you in the cell with him. Many a time I would see, through the bullseyes set into the cell doors, the results of the guards' maliciousness; fights would start breaking out and the weaker inmates would be carried off in stretchers afterwards. I made several complaints to the Embassy about this, but nothing was done. This may have been partly because the embassy staff responsible for the welfare of the British inmates was mainly Barbadian, and they may have been too afraid to be openly critical of their own country's regime.

In societies like Barbados those who stand against the police or authorities tend to get their homes burned down or cars sabotaged. They may not easily admit to this fear, either. This left us in the prison with very little support or back-up. In the end, we stopped even bothering to communicate our fears, even when our lives were in danger. There was no point, we were going to be lied to, to be left there, anyway, regardless of anything that we tried to do or say. So, eventually, when they came by and asked us what the conditions in the prison were like, we would invariably reply that everything was fine. One of the chief officers was usually standing right there. If we had said anything else, not only would nothing have happened to change that situation, but we might well have found ourselves transferred into a cell with a really dangerous cellmate.

I got to meet some interesting people in 13, though. Blow would tell me about his boat runs round the Caribbean, especially around St Vincent and the Grenadines. He told me about the time he escaped from Glendairy, by using Psalm 29 to cast a magic spell on the screws on duty. It worked, too, and he made his getaway over the wall using a blanket. From there, he was picked up by a friend and made his way out of the country.

As the Day of my Release approached, I had people left and right wanting to give me their addresses and phone numbers, which I not only wrote down, but tried to fix in my memory too. I had a sense that the administration might try to take away my address book, even though it was disguised in my New Testament. I used a code; with a biro I underlined certain letters and numbers to disguise my list of contacts. It worked, too; I was successful in getting my list out through the search on the way out.

Somehow I had managed to avoid getting myself killed, and hadn't even come down with chicken pox while all around me men were succumbing. Not to mention the fact that I had survived a major riot. I was playing my last few days very carefully, still looking over my shoulder, making sure nobody was about to come at me to make sure I never got out. I stayed as far away from Grandpa as I possibly could.

***

It might have been the day before my release that Fisher, the former East German border guard who had been caught with the Colombian boatmen, came up and delivered a couple of letters to me.

'Mail, fellas!' I exclaimed ecstatically, happy not just for myself, but also the fact that the mail was resuming meant good news all round. Fisher had a card for me. It had already been opened by the censor. It had on it a picture of a green dragon by Peter Pracownik. Years before, I had actually owned the original of this picture. The dragon had always been one of my 'power animals', and this was a good omen of positive times to come.

It reminded me of the times when I had been working in the tarot, writing books on the subject and designing tarot decks for Peter to paint the images of. Those days when I started smoking crack seemed a long way off, but this picture brought it all back to me.

Crack cocaine, especially when combined with heroin, has an unlimited ability to make you forget everything about yourself, stripping you of your identity, possessions, personal honour, dignity, everything, in fact. It truly is something almost beyond the normal earthly sense of evil. When you are trapped into that loop, all you can think about is the next hit, the next high. Everything else becomes a distraction, and the years pass very quickly before you realise what has happened. Luckily for me, and my family, something happened to stop me before it was too late.

***

The day of my release was traumatic for me. One of the screws came up and called out my name. I was trembling with nervousness as I donned what was left of my prison uniform and made a round, banging fists with each of the fellas there. I didn't miss anyone out. As far as I was concerned, each man there was a vital part of my magic circle, and I needed to feel the circuit complete before I stepped out into the outside world. They all wished me well, and then I was being taken through the door. Guys left and right were yelling out their farewells and best wishes as I was led down to the gate at the end.

It swung open, and Mr Shorey handcuffed me, then changed his mind and released me.

Walking down together, three years done since I had come into this place; I was now going back out again into society. What would the outside world hold for me? Would I be able to make it now that I had seen just how low I could go; now that I had received the biggest wake up call I could ever get? Down at the office area I was allowed to sit down, while one of the screws got my mail. In the four months since the fire none of us had been allowed any mail, except for that lot that had come in the day before. I received back all the letters and magazines that had accumulated for me in that time, but my thoughts went back to the dragon card.

When I had shown it around the cell, I had seen a number of very appreciative eyes cast upon it. One of my old cellmates, Kurt Moore, who I knew wanted the card as a design for a tattoo, was especially taken with it. I thought about it for a minute, and then sent it back upstairs to him, as a final parting gift from me. In a way it belonged in the cell; a symbol of something, perhaps hope, to those lads there that I was leaving behind.

I was then presented with a large wad of local money; some $1,160! This was the sum of all my wages over the preceding three years, and surprisingly it had remained untouched. Sometimes Admin would make deductions, especially if you ordered extra cigarettes or Christmas cards for your family at that time. You could also occasionally order hand cream, extra soaps, and so on, out of your earnings. I had rarely bothered, so, it seemed, I now had a nice little nest egg to take away with me.

I respected the fact that Admin was honouring its commitment, as I had heard the rumour that, because of the fire, no one was going to get their wages on their release. It turned out to be a false rumour for me anyway! I was then given some of the clothes that Greita from the Embassy had bought for me and left at the desk. It was nice to step into my own tracksuit bottoms and T-shirt, along with my own sandals. I felt like a million dollars.

I was then led out along the track, and the lads were giving me the best send-off anyone has ever got from that place, as far as I could see. There were hundreds of fellas shouting from just about every window as I was led along. It was a truly emotional moment. I was filled with relief that I was getting out, being released from this prison, but it also signalled for me my release from the life I had now left behind. I had finished paying for the life I had led, for the addiction and the selfish, immoral acts, and was now walking out of my own personal hell into a new world of promise and potential. But there was more than that; I was also filled with a sense of purpose—I vowed in my heart to let the world know what was going on inside the prison system on Barbados, to bring the spotlight of international attention to their plight, and maybe even divert a disaster waiting to happen. The riot at Glendairy was a major incident, but it would only be a matter of time before the system pushed the inmates into rising up again, and that would give the authorities licence to open fire, causing a huge loss of life. And from what I saw in my time there, there were many who could not wait for this opportunity. They were itching for it.

***

Up at the front gate I was formally released, and handed over to the Immigration officials. The senior of these two, a man called Jordan, was the one who affected the exit of literally every foreigner in Barbados. He remembered *Larry* and *Henry*, and how they had wanted to shave their heads, skinhead style before even getting on the plane. He knew Kenneth the Nigerian, who he had taken back to Nigeria. Kenneth received an additional prison sentence there, too, as punishment for 'bringing his country into shame abroad' when he had been nicked in Barbados.

I got into the back of their car, and as we drove along the country roads of Barbados it made my head spin to be suddenly travelling so fast. At one point we stopped and Jordan told me I could get out and buy some bread if I wanted. All three of us went into a bread shop and I looked up and down at what seemed to be a massive collection of different breads; sweetbreads, pies, pasties and patties. I had never even heard of most of what they had in that shop, although I had actually eaten a few of them since becoming a Glendairy resident. I bought a couple of things and we got back in the car. The next thing I knew, we were at Grantly Adams Airport, and I was amazed at how much it had changed in the three years since I had last seen it. It had undergone a major refurbishment in that time and was now an international-class airport, with a mall of shops and cafes.

I was taken into the Immigration area, had my photograph taken, and was presented with a signed letter from the Immigration Minister Joseph Attherley, stating that I was banned from Barbados. Jordan said that after five years I could appeal this, but he might have saved his breath; he could see in my eyes that there was no way I was coming back to Barbados.

While I was waiting for my plane, I met a Nigerian fella who had been waiting there for about two months, without any food or money, stuck between places for which he had no visas. How long he was doomed to wait there I had no idea; presumably until he could meet someone who might be prepared to lend him some airfare. Either that or, eventually, the Barbadian government would relent and pay for him to be flown out. He might still be there, for all I know.

The relief was coming off me in waves as I walked through the airport, looking at all the British tourists coming and going, looking forward to the holiday of a lifetime. Would they ever see the other side of Barbados? I thought to myself. It was unlikely. They would go back to England with tales of an exotic, beautiful island where everybody sits on the beach all day watching the crystal clear waters lap at the golden shore. They would know nothing of the poverty or the corruption, or the way in which people were treated by the justice system.

Jordan let me buy a few things from the chemist; a toothbrush, toothpaste and so on. Then, I was led onto the plane, and my passport was given to the air stewardess, to be handed back to me only when the plane had landed at Gatwick. It felt amazing to be in a plane again. So much luxury, so many beautiful women! It was all very exotic. My senses seemed truly alive and I was appreciating everything.

With a tremendous burst of speed our plane took into the air, and within moments we were looking down over a green island, basking in the sun, surrounded by a massive ocean of bright blue, getting smaller and more distant by the minute. I settled down to listen to the music on the headphones when, after a short while, food was served. When it came round, it was delicious. Three years of bread rolls had not prepared me for this.

The plane headed off into the darkening sky, with the sunset behind us. A movie appeared on the screen in front of me, some really raunchy thriller where all the characters seemed to be hookers, cops or robbers. On the plane everything looked very sophisticated, including the women and men who were our hosts and hostesses. I was dazzled by the massive presence of so many white people all of a sudden. On the flight I noticed everything that was around me, everything inside and outside the plane. As the plane entered into the great bank of darkness that had loomed up from the east, far down below, I could see the dark blue mass of the ocean across which wisps of cloud were drifting. Each hour that passed was packed with action, at least compared to what I had become accustomed to. Now and again someone passed along and down the aisle. I flipped through the plethora of channels of music and film that the handset gave me access to, marvelling in the sheer abundance of entertainment and diversion.

I looked out across the young mum and daughter who sat next to me, out through the portal at the scene of sky and ocean. I wondered what the future might hold for me. As the time slipped into the early morning, I could see the first rays of sunshine coming up over the rim of the curved horizon, like the harbinger of a new age opening before me.

The plane came in towards Gatwick and it made my heart jump to see the gently-rolling fields of England appear beneath us. So many different shades of green; light and dark. Everything seemed quite concentrated, too, with an abundance of houses and cars.

As I stepped off the plane onto British soil I felt a sense of relief at having successfully completed a long and hazardous journey. I felt like some mythological character who has just returned from Hell, with a real tale to tell.

***

My first task was to find somewhere to stay. I realised that I had very few contacts who I would want to stay with, even for a couple of days. I wanted no part of the life I had once lived. Apart from that, I assumed that most of the people I had once shared addictions with were no longer with us. I did manage to look up an old friend I had known from a few parties in London, and she was kind enough to give me some floor space. From here, I was able to start putting my life together again, but I knew it would be a difficult process.

CHAPTER FIFTEEN

Aftermath and Future

There is a great deal of re-learning to be done when you come out of jail. Everything is very different to how it was when you went in. Entire neighbourhoods change, different people come in, and others go. On top of that, the level of technology has gone up, with internet cafes on virtually every street corner. Now, access to a computer is nothing unusual. Before I went in, you needed to have a few hundred quid to be able to get to a computer terminal, now for £1 you can go on the internet for an hour, do your office work and contact people by Instant Messenger. Looking at the sudden proliferation of all of this when I came back, it really amazed me. Sitting inside a minicab I saw something else that looked almost unbelievable: a computer simulation of the road ahead.

One of my first tasks upon my release was familiarising myself with what had happened with the internet, since my imprisonment. Everything seemed much faster. I was amazed at how easy it was to use some of the newer search engines, such as Google. Gone are the days of typing in one word only to have a series of totally meaningless answers come back at you. The online encyclopaedias, such as

Wikipedia have also been useful. Imagine my surprise when I realised that I could actually join and become an editor. Looking through the material on Barbados, I was interested to see a number of articles about the country, much of it previously published in magazines and newspapers, such as the *Nation* and *The Advocate*. Long gone are the days in which only a select minority had access to newspaper libraries. Now, with the internet, every kind of information was easily accessible. Incredible! Furthermore, the same now applied to people living in every country throughout the world. I could hardly believe what had happened in the years since I had been away.

I was disappointed to discover that so very little was known about the problems in Barbados and the lack of human rights in its prison. I did manage to find a few articles here and there on the internet though. I came across an article entitled 'Racial harmony in Barbados—Is it a Myth?' In it, the writer challenges the idea that Barbados is a land of racial integration. He maintained that the white Barbadian community rarely came into contact with the majority black population, and that the idea of harmony was a myth. The whites rarely attended events such as Independence Day or Emancipation Day, which had meaning for the black people. When they partied they would go down to white night clubs in Hawkins Bay or Lawrence Gap. While black people are not actually excluded, there is a kind of unspoken apartheid policy in place at these and other places, and a lot of it, as with anywhere else, is down to money and what it can do for you. I couldn't help but reflect on the fact that I didn't meet a single white Barbadian in Glendairy.

I had lived, side by side with black people, who had accepted me and took me as one of their own. For three years I lived as most white men never will, sharing the same food, sleeping space, confinement, denial of rights, hopes and fears as some of the most oppressed people on the planet. I realised that most white people never really get to know about other races, and I felt privileged.

All the old faces I had known around London from before were gone. Virtually all of the drug-people I had known from the time of my relapse were now dead, I learned. One lad had thrown himself out of a high window. Others had simply disappeared.

Prison is a place where you can reflect back over your life and see where you have gone wrong. I knew I had taken many wrong turns. For some, prison is a place where new 'skills' of a criminal kind can be learned. But those who come into this category always seem destined to return, so confident are they in their own invincibility and society's stupidity. But for me it was a chance to get clean, and stay clean, while looking back over what had happened. I could re-learn and start to think differently, and develop a new approach to dealing with the problem of life.

Unless you can actually admit to yourself that you don't know it all, there is no way you are going to be able to start on your learning process. A certain amount of humility is a necessary starting point. This involves being able to put the past at a certain distance and admit you are further down the steps of the pyramid than is perhaps comfortable. Being stuck in a dungeon-like cell and having a bucket for a toilet for three years will do that. When I came out of Glendairy I breathed as deep a sigh of relief as I have ever known, not only because I survived a place I wasn't sure I would leave alive, but because I knew I was leaving as a changed person. I had been, as the saying goes, to Hell and back. In many ways I am still learning who I am and what my true potential is.

***

Getting my life back together was not easy, and I was prepared for some of the setbacks. As Mr Sealey predicted, it was 'two steps forward, one step back,' although I still have not relapsed back into any drug use. Alcohol, an equally negative and habit-forming substance, is something I am careful of. In our society, alcohol consumption is seen as socially acceptable, and is advertised everywhere. Yet it has wrought untold damage to the lives of countless millions, and as many accidents and crimes are linked with it as with drugs. Perhaps more.

At one point, I went along to an Alcoholics Anonymous meeting as I was concerned about my new-found tendency to find myself in pubs, asking for pints of Stella. The meeting was held in a church hall, and as I stepped inside I was aware of the diversity of people that constituted its membership. One woman was 'leading' the meeting. She told her story about how she had been on the game while she was an alcoholic, and how she had managed to get her daughter back out of care and get re-housed by the council now that she was sober. Well, I thought, there's one success story. Then others started chipping in. Some seemed to have pre-written pieces to read out loud. It was all like some Methodist chapel meeting, which is what, I suppose, the AA is based on. On the wall was a large, dog-eared poster listing the '12 steps', all of which seemed steeped in evangelical Protestantism.

The first step made me laugh: 'We admitted we were powerless over alcohol—that our lives had become unmanageable.' What a negative and self-limiting way to affirm your own utter worthlessness! These people certainly seemed to suffer from lack of self-esteem. It seemed to me that once you started thinking their way, you would definitely be doomed. The whole point of any recovery, surely, was for those concerned to break the cycle of negative and limiting thinking. It seemed to me that the AA is not about people actually recovering, but about people meeting up under the guise of wanting to solve a problem, but with other agendas in mind. Looking around at the group, I noticed most of the participants were middle class women. I wondered what on earth those agendas might be. The women were so uptight, too, so frustrated. One of them nearly bit my head off when I actually ventured to say a few words as it was my first visit. Such audacity! And that I should actually talk about what I had just gone through! She had such an allergic reaction to what I was saying that she was almost physically sick on the floor. Other women were walking out of the room as I spoke, making a big fuss, banging the door as they made their way out. I was definitely in the wrong place.

Afterwards, one of the male members stood up and handed back a large key that he had been holding onto for them. Apparently, he couldn't open up for them on Saturdays as he had a part-time job. Outside, he admitted to me that it had been an excuse, and that he had been so disgusted at their behaviour that he had decided then and there to leave that meeting of the AA for good.

Next on my list was Narcotics Anonymous. I went along to the crumbling ruin of a building in Finsbury Park, and as I went in the smell of human shit hit me. One of the people attending the meeting had defecated all over the rim and round the back side of one of the toilets in the men's loo. That something that gross could happen by chance seemed too remote; it was almost as if somebody had done that deliberately. Maybe they knew I was coming and wanted me to feel at home after my years in Glendairy! When I made it to the top of the stairs and mentioned it to the person who seemed to have the responsibility of chairing the meeting, he just laughed, which seemed strange to me. The seats were set out in a circle. I thought for a moment that we were all going to hold hands and try and make contact with the living. This was surely a séance I had mistakenly wandered into. In the very centre was a candlestick with sconces for several candles along its length. Candles had already been placed in them, and as I leaned forward I noticed that these were black. Around the candlestick, there were several laminated sheets, each with a slogan on it. On one, was the slogan 'Keep it simple,' on another, 'Just for today.'

Then, when everybody was there, the room was plunged into darkness and one by one the candles were lit. Everything suddenly became very spooky, as if we were conducting a magic spell of some dark and miserable kind. Each person present pulled a hood up over his or her head, and again, each person gave their life story, or a potted version of it, and it seemed as if everyone there was intimately involved in each quirk of everyone else's story, as if they knew what was coming next in the tale. Each person brought forth the usual story of how they hadn't actually enjoyed the drugs that they had been busy shovelling into their veins all those years. Looking at their faces, I found it hard to believe that they had stopped at all. They still looked like junkies to me, but junkies who were deceiving themselves. At the end of this meeting I had about half a dozen big hairy Scotsmen, each of whom seemed to suffer from personal hygiene problems, wanting to hug me. No thanks!

I stepped out of the building, realising that if my survival rested on people like this, I might as well give up now. I had a far better chance out there on my own. It was going to be down to me to use the knowledge I had acquired through the rehab program in Glendairy and my own grim determination that I would never put myself back into the position I had once found myself in; trying to smuggle drugs and not caring if I was caught or not, whether I lived or died.

After my experiences with the AA and the NA, it seems to me that, those who have had addiction problems are often tricked into thinking that these groups are going to help take away the cravings, and actually help in a recovery process. I can't see how that can happen, when those attending these meetings are constantly affirming that they are still addicts or alcoholics, and, in talking about their experiences, as well as listening to others', are constantly stimulating their cravings. These programmes do seem to work for other people, but they didn't work for me. Thinking back, I recalled the time when I had studied hypnotherapy with the London College of Clinical Hypnotherapy. I realised that, in successfully completing that training, I had already been given the keys to dealing with my problems; all that I had to do was activate them and open the doorways I needed to pass through. Three years in Glendairy was pretty effective aversion therapy to taking drugs. The experiences I had been through constituted the most powerful anti-drug experience anyone could ever have. Addicts and alcoholics are encouraged to think that there is somewhere they can go, where their problems will just roll off their shoulders. Or that there is a therapist, or holy man somewhere, who will take their crosses from them. I feel that they have been encouraged in this kind of thinking by those who are making money out of their continued misery, by ensuring they stay victims, clients or patients.

When you come off drugs, or drink for that matter, everything has to be relearned—even the smallest aspects of your responses and reactions to people. As a recovering addict you have to be alert and consciously work to change your response to setbacks, to situations where things don't necessarily work out. It takes time to learn to deal with things without the crutches of drink or drugs. Those muscles need time to get supple, and to get strong. But the recovering addict is often very impatient to get over their handicap, and to catch up with other people, especially when they realise how far behind they have fallen. And when you most need it, there will be no one there, because there can be no one there. This is why the buddy or sponsor system of AA and NA wouldn't really have worked for me. If I really felt like going back on drugs, I was hardly likely to confide in anyone. Those who are really serious about getting off drugs are already in that space; they are walking the walk, not just talking the talk.

Most of the AA and NA people I have met are doing a dog-in-the-manger trip. They want their cake and want to be able to eat it at the same time. They say they want to be free, but they go to a never-ending circle of meetings, where they reaffirm that they are still addicts. Over the months and years, I believe that this effect builds up in their subconscious and it becomes truly impossible for them to break free of this mould, because by then, they have effectively reprogrammed themselves so deeply into negative patterns of thought.

After NA I went along to DASH, the Drug Advisory Service of Haringey, a kind of rehab-type organisation funded by the local council. Here I was treated to free sachets of camomile tea, and placed on a list to experience Reiki healing. The Reiki really worked for me, and after a course of treatments, I found that some of the pains in my body, as well as in my mind, began to recede.

Most of the people in DASH were really positive and totally professional in how they dealt with problems that arose. They were able to help me get onto a counselling course with a rehab training organisation called KINESIS, based in Tottenham. Here I met a counsellor by the name of Lauren Hooper, who reminded me of a modern day lady Galadriel from *The Lord of the Rings*, such was the empathy and wisdom she seemed to give off. She was the facilitator on the course and I learned a great deal, which I have started applying into my life, and am able to see definite results. I passed Part 1 of the Counselling Course and was invited to come along for the interview for Part 2. I discovered, to my chagrin, that a necessary qualifying prerequisite is that I already have a 'placement' with a recognised organisation. I realised that there was no way I was going to make it through, but put a brave face on it anyway. At least I was getting familiar with the twists and turns of the counselling process. I explained at the interview that I hadn't realised that I had to have a placement organised, but that now that I know of it I have something to build towards for next years' intake. The lady interviewing me suggested that after some of the traumatic experiences I have had, it may be best if I defer my application to next year, so as to give myself time to 'get over' some of the things I have been through. To think in terms of starting on Part 2 will give me the opportunity to get some sense of perspective about where I am and where I want to go. It will also give me more time to link up with an official organisation. I have continued training in counselling, but over at the City and Islington College in Holloway road, north London, under the tutelage of Ian Garrard, the facilitator. I have since been in touch with the Medical Foundation for the Care of the Victims of Torture, and it may be with them that I eventually seek a placement.

The counselling course taught me how to deal with various things that are cropping up in my life, such as losses and setbacks. I realised that a great deal of my former drug and alcohol abuse was initially based around feelings of intense disappointment, but which then became habit-forming and difficult to change. I was unable to deal intelligently with disappointments in love, in expectations, in my career, and instead I resorted to blotting out the feelings of failure and hopelessness that I was going through.

But these setbacks occur constantly in life. I did feel like a failure when I was unable to get onto Part 2 of the course, but instead of heading off to the pub top sink a few pints of lager, I went and ate a double egg and chips in a local greasy spoon. So, although I 'failed' the interview, I felt good because I had actually passed the real test of the experience, that of successfully and intelligently managing my feelings of rejection and failure. On the top of the bus back from Tottenham Green, I felt on top of the world. I had turned a corner in my own self-development, and had finally learned to deal with the downs as well as the ups of life.

Getting back in touch with people I knew inside was a big step for me. One of the issues we touched upon in the rehab group back in Glendairy was that of resuming criminal associations. For some it can be high risk, leading them to resume the kind of activities that led up to their last bout of imprisonment, especially if they are still using. I was unsure about getting in contact with some of the lads, both British and Barbadian. Prior to the prison burning, I had committed to memory the addresses and phone numbers of several lads. I wrote to *Charlie*, my old cellmate and friend and, sent John the Baptist the two volumes that make up the autobiography of Haile Selassie. I was pleased to get a response from my old chess playing friend, Lestor Bullen, who wrote to me after an interview I did for one of the local Barbadian newspapers came out. One of his plays was awarded first prize by the Barbadian National Institute for Fine and Creative Arts, and he is working on submitting something to the Royal Court. Vino got in touch when he came out and stayed with *Bobby Burns* over at Hornsey, and I am still in touch with him. He is working in construction, getting into his bodybuilding and buying a car. *Henry* and *Larry* are floating around in the Croydon area.

***

As for the boys still in prison in Barbados, my thoughts go out to them every day. They sit inside their tiny cells, like captives in slave-ships. I think about how they are suffering from the lack of any sort of proper diet or exercise and the ever-present threat of violence from the guards who now have a free reign to do what they want, when they want. Conditions in the prison are now so hard that I fear that the next time there is an uprising, the inmates are not going to stop, and the gunmen are going to fight it out, instead of meekly surrendering their weapons, and themselves.

While I was in Glendairy, most of the inmates had stories of being tortured by the police while in custody, in order to make them confess to outstanding crimes. People told of having their legs and arms twisted out of joint, or having plastic bags sprayed with insecticide put over their heads. The bag would only come off when they were ready to confess to whatever crime the police wanted to have cleared up. I heard stories of the police 'discovering' a gun under the bed of someone they wanted to frame. In Barbados, it seems that the courts automatically take the side of the police and prosecution. Rarely does a defence lawyer get a result for his client, although I did hear that if sufficient money was available, amazing results could be achieved. I heard a story about one white boy who was arrested at the airport with three kilos in his possession. Because he had rich parents, who were able to come up with about £30,000 to pay a fine plus £20,000 for the lawyer, he was able to get out after only three weeks inside. The rest of us felt gutted, to be honest. We were sitting through sentences of several years in duration for doing the same crime. Still, that's the power of money for you!

Barbados reintroduced the death penalty; a negative step if ever there was one. I got to know each and every man sitting in those godforsaken cages when I worked the shit buckets on H&I. I heard that Josephs and Boyce were involved in the drawn-out ping-pong between the various courts in Barbados when I left the island. Most recently, I heard that their death sentence had been commuted to life, but the government of Owen Arthur, the Barbadian Prime Minister has appealed against this to the Caribbean Court of Appeal, based in Trinidad. The justice department there now faces a serious backlog, and if they decide to go ahead with all of the due executions, the little paradise island is going to be making the news a lot more than it wants to.

Following the fire, some 60 people have been charged with arson. These are extremely serious criminal charges, which could easily result in sentences of up to 30 years being handed down to those the Barbados government wants to have found guilty. It needs a certain number of people to crucify, in order to save face. Not being one to hang around inside burning buildings, I don't know who did and did not set the fires, but one thing I can say is that it is going to be impossible to truly assign guilt in a case like this. Monkey Man and Roland Yarde, who was shot in the leg by the Guyanese solider, are among those charged. Apparently, the 'star witnesses' are the four main Bullermen who Carrington always liked to have hanging around: Arling James, chief electrician and murderer of his wife and two children; Patrick Graves, murderer of his mother; Chuckie, serial sex offender and molester of young boys; and Frank Carter, the Chief Carpenter from the Farm, who was caught shagging a male prostitute. All four are notorious Bullermen and male rapists. All four are stuck there until the day they die. So they each have a vested interest in saying whatever the administration wants them to say, and involving and implicating whoever

Admin wants them to. But what did they see? The minute the riot kicked off, James, Graves and Carter were taken out of the range of the ordinary prisoners and kept in safety. So I can't imagine that they actually saw anything that could truly be relied upon as evidence. But that is beside the point. I believe that the government of Barbados wants to restore its lost pride by victimising a certain number of inmates who may have been more vocal in wanting change or in protesting against certain human rights violations in the past. A trial such as this cannot fairly take place in Barbados. This much is recognised by the government there, and it is making plans for the trial to take place elsewhere in the Caribbean. It will be interesting to see if the proceedings are going to be open to the public, or, as it has already been hinted at, will be closed off to the world's press. The old adage that 'justice needs to be seen to be done' certainly applies.

***

On the internet, I found a US State Department Country Report on Human Rights Practices in Barbados, for the year March 2005–March 2006, in which the problems in the prison are recognised. In particular, the report listed unsanitary cells, inedible food, unclean drinking water and the denial of visiting rights as problems in Glendairy. The report also noted that the prison failed to inform families quickly when prisoners had serious health problems, that lawyers were unable to see their clients and that the police routinely used excessive violence in their investigations. The report also catalogued various prisoners who had died at Harrison's Point. They only knew the half of it, but at least some of the issues were being highlighted.

One of the first websites I came across upon my return to the UK was www.foreignprisoners.com. The site is run by a team of people presided over by an amazing lady called

Kay Danes, who was herself imprisoned with her husband in Laos for a year on trumped-up charges. Upon her release she wrote a book, called Nightmare in Laos, also published by Maverick House, which describes what happened to her. Looking through her site, I was struck by the similarities between Camp X-ray in Guantanamo Bay and Harrison's Point. They are both very similar in style, and how they are run. The difference is that at Harrison's Point the men know when they are getting out.

I am trying to get someone with a history in human rights abuses involved in the cases of the men I have left behind back in Barbados; men like *Charlie*, serving an indeterminate sentence for the manslaughter of his girlfriend; men like John the Baptist, serving 25 years for the same crime; men like Jeffrey Josephs and Lennox Boyce, waiting to get hanged, not knowing whether they are going to get their necks popped or not; men like Toffee, having to shit in a bucket every day for the last 17 years while waiting to go to the gallows. I have been in touch with organisations that were involved in the Bloody Sunday enquiry to see if they can help. I have contacted Amnesty International many times but have yet to get a response from them. When I look at their website, I see the prominence they are giving to better reported, higher-profile campaigns, such as Guantanamo Bay. I contacted the human rights office of Harvard Law School; they have a department that looks at international human rights abuses by Third World governments. One of their success stories was getting Trinidad to ban the use of flogging as a punishment in its prisons, a practice that is still in the official rule book for Glendairy Prison. I am going to continue to do whatever I can for my boys back in Glendairy. I may not have the resources of an organisation, but I can at least set up internet groups on Google, MSN and Yahoo about the Glendairy Prison Uprising.

Another thing I have been able to do since being back, is get my writing back on track. I have joined the National Union of Journalists. I attended one of their conferences on the freedom of the press at their national headquarters in London. An important part of developing my writing craft, as I see it, involves going along to writers groups and listening to the work of others. I am doing this in Crouch End, in north London, where I live. I am finding that my relationships are changing. Increasingly I am meeting people on the basis of their interest in the arts. I am discovering a dearth of previously unrealised talent and ability in some of my friends, in particular Diana Defries and Suzanna Clancy, who are both brilliant as artists and writers, and both of whom I greatly admire.

***

There are a number of problems for me to solve. Around the time when my daughter was born, there was a computer game came on the market called Myst, in which you had to make your way through a mysterious set of worlds and work out, from the clues given, what had happened and what you next had to do. The real world is similar, in a way, in that there are real challenges and contradictions for me to resolve, but somehow I have the feeling that as long as I stay on course I'm going to get there.

On my return from Barbados, I found that Evelyne and my daughter's lives had moved on. When I was released it was one of my priorities to find them both. It took some time but eventually I found them through the publishers we had worked with when writing our tarot books. Evelyne was wary initially, and still is. They know that there is always the possibility that I will relapse and I have a long way to go to build up the trust I once had. In the meantime I am going down to visit as much as I can, to get to know my daughter, who is fast becoming a young woman. I feel that I can have a very positive part to play in her upbringing.

It has been important for me to try to make amends where possible, because I know I have harmed people with my actions. Realistically though, I know that much of my life has become totally occluded to me, and all I can do is realise that I am still learning. What I hope I can do by training as a counsellor is to help others in their life situations. Hopefully they won't have to go through the things I have.

In reading how I passed through some of the experiences I have described in this story, I would rather make the point that there is little I haven't been through in my journey to Hell. I hope that my future counselling work will only be enhanced by this. I have tried to be as candid as I can be with the reader; not out of any desire to glorify my misdeeds— quite the opposite actually; there was nothing glorious in what I did—but basically to clear them away from my past. Writing about them is the most cathartic experience imaginable. I know that many of the things I have written about I have been very lucky to come out of alive, and if anybody was to feel a compulsion to repeat what I have done, then this book would be in vain.

***

The writing of this book has been strange. Each time I think I have finished and put it away, I find myself coming back to it with other ideas, with other things that need to be said. Is there a cure for drug or alcohol addiction? It's the question my mind keeps coming back to. I think there is. If you are an addict, ultimately there is a severe limit on how much help you can expect from any of the 'professionals' in the field. They cannot ever really know what has happened to you. They have read their books, they may even think they actually understand you, but at the end of the day it is going to be about you yourself committing to your own process. Consistency of purpose is the most important prerequisite for anyone seeking 'a cure'. You can't 'get high' if you truly want to 'get free'. The two do not go together.

One analogy that often comes back to me came from one of the Seventh Day Adventist church meetings at Glendairy. The speaker described creating a new response in terms of making a new path through a field. To turn that new path into a more established road, you had to walk over it many, many times. Similarly it would take time for any old pathway to become disused and overgrown. This is how it is with our behaviour patterns. Repetition is the key to learning new ways of dealing with things like frustration, disappointments and personality traits we cannot accept in ourselves. To really give up drink and drugs requires tremendous courage and sacrifice. For each addict there will be an individual road to freedom. What works for one person may not work for another. Fear, especially, is something that is extremely deeply rooted in a lot of people's bodies; fear and helplessness. It may be that counselling and the more psychologically-based therapies can only take a person so far along the road to freedom, and that something else, homeopathy in my case, is needed to get right down into the person's soul and free them.

For me a big step was getting back in touch with my ex-wife and daughter, and also my son in New Zealand. It was difficult to decide how much to say and how much to leave out. In my case I went for the honest approach, and perhaps overdid it slightly. In any event, at least I am back in my right mind now and can think rationally.

***

There are dark places in the world; some where you would not expect to find them. Nobody ever wants to walk into

Hell, but they don't realise until it is too late that that is exactly what they are doing. When people start out taking drugs, all they see are pretty rainbows and a drug-induced Garden of Eden. But with each step they take they get closer to some sort of Hellish reality from which there is no return. Barbados was the end of the line for me. It was there that I went through it all and realised I had to start backing out of the path I had taken and choose a new life. I feel like I have been really blessed—to be able to have gone through some of these things, to reach the very depths and stare into the abyss, and be able to come back to the surface and tell my story—I only hope to high heaven that my experiences can help others avoid getting trapped in some of these dark places.

I look back at some of the crazy, drug-induced stuff I have done and recognise that all I can do now is progress along the route I have worked out for myself and try to fulfil my potential, and thereby my destiny. There is only so much satisfaction to be gained in looking back. Now I want to look towards the future.